INSIDE STALIN'S KREMLIN

OTHER BOOKS BY PETER S. DERIABIN

The Secret World (with Frank Gibney)

The Penkovskiy Papers (Translator)

Watchdogs of Terror: Russian Bodyguards from the Tsars to the Commissars

The KGB: Masters of the Soviet Union (with T. H. Bagley)

The Spy Who Saved the World: How a Soviet Colonel Changed the Course of the Cold War (with Jerrold Schecter)

КРЕМЛЬ
INSIDE STALIN'S KREMLIN:

An Eyewitness Account of Brutality, Duplicity, and Intrigue

Peter S. Deriabin

with

Joseph Culver Evans

Brassey's

Editorial Offices:	Order Department:
22883 Quicksilver Drive	P.O. Box 960
Dulles, VA 20166	Herndon, VA 20172

Brassey's books are available at special discounts for bulk purchases for sales promotions, premiums, fund-raising, or educational use.

Library of Congress Cataloging-in-Publication Data

Deriabin, Peter, 1921–
    Inside Stalin's Kremlin : an eyewitness account of brutality, duplicity, and intrigue / by Peter S. Deriabin, with Joseph Culver Evans.
        p.   cm.
    Includes bibliographical references and index.

    1. Deriabin, Peter, 1921–   . 2. Defectors—Soviet Union—Biography. 3. Communists—Soviet Union—Biography. 4. Soviet Union—Politics and government—1936–1953. 5. Soviet Union. Ministerstvo gosudarstvennoĭ bezopasnosti. I. Evans, Joseph Culver. II. Title.
    DK268.D47A3   1998
    947.084'092—dc21
    [B]   98-16578
                                                                        CIP

ISBN 1-57488-235-x

Designed by Pen & Palette Unlimited

First paperback edition 2000

10 9 8 7 6 5 4 3 2 1

Printed in Canada

CONTENTS

Publisher's Note

Peter Deriabin delayed writing *Inside Stalin's Kremlin* until the passage of time had lowered the risk of retribution by the Soviet Union. Mr. Deriabin also wanted to protect former colleagues who would face punishment had he disclosed what he had learned from them any earlier. Later, other book projects and his important work with the CIA delayed his coming back to this book until, with the writing contributions of Joseph Culver Evans, a draft manuscript was completed in 1989. When Mr. Deriabin died in 1992, his son, Peter Deriabin, Jr., edited the manuscript, added material from his father's notes, and sought publication. The result is the book you see here, a remarkable record of a critical time in world history.

Note On Russian Names

Russian names consist of three parts: the first name, the patronymic, and the last name or family name. A combination of the first name and the patronymic is a commonly used form of address. The patronymic is derived from the father's first name. For example, Peter Sergeyevich is Peter, son of Sergey. The same is done in the feminine form also, using the father's first name—Larisa Petrovna is Larisa, daughter of Peter.

A diminutive of the first name, such as Petya for Peter, is used between friends and relatives or in addressing children and young people.

Preface

Among the countless number of crimes they committed, no single outrage by Josef Stalin or his chiefs and successors made me switch loyalties. No shock of suddenly seeing through their shams turned my ideology upside down. My faith in the Soviet system eroded under the cumulative effect of observing, day after day for a decade, our leaders' crimes and hypocrisy. Eventually I rebelled. I had had a surfeit of distortions of the ideals of Communism, the leaders placing power ahead of principle and subjugating my compatriots by force and deceit.

I, one of the most privileged, had watched from a ringside seat inside the Kremlin. I spent my first 33 years within the Soviet system. In my teens I began my career as an activist in the Communist Party of the Soviet Union (CPSU), and in my early 20s I commenced ten years' service in the State Security apparatus later known as the KGB (*Komitet Gosudarstvennoy Bezopasnosti*, or Committee for State Security). Colleagues elected me secretary (chief executive) of two State Security cells within the CPSU. The level of that position provided a separate entree to secrets, in this instance the Party's explanations to us privileged few concerning policy and personnel actions. I learned from them even more about the faults of the leaders. Duty made us protectors of their safety, defenders of their rule, witnesses to their private lives, and sometimes participants in their behind-the-scenes maneuvering for power. As their bodyguards, we saw the leaders unvarnished, exactly as they were in character and deed beneath the exalting propaganda ladled out to our countrymen.

Inside Stalin's Kremlin describes the influences that compelled me to shift allegiance. I discuss my personal situation and frame of mind as I moved from defender of the Soviet system to silent dissident within it to defector. I disclose details of events—many witnessed firsthand, the rest known from past associates—that affected more than my attitude; some of the incidents and episodes altered, where they did not end, the lives of others. Some have had an everlasting impact on history.

Western media, objective though it tries to be, betrays a general lack of understanding about the emotional crises that precede and follow defections by the elite of Soviet society. Many of us did not fully comprehend our motivations at the time we defected. (The correctness of my motivations has been constantly confirmed by living all these years in the United States.) No two defectors act on an identical set of motivations, of course, but in describing my experience I hope to help the American public's evaluation of us. We paid a great price, most of all emotionally, to be here.

Americans ask us defectors, quite rightly, why we did not see through the fraud of Kremlin-style Communism sooner, and when we did, why we did not try to make improvements while still inside the Soviet system. An auditor has trouble detecting fraud if he examines books that contain cooked, crooked figures and has nothing to compare them against. He may be loathe to delve deeper if the bank or company has a spotless reputation. Well, in the Union of Soviet Socialist Republics (USSR), the leaders master the news and cultural media, which is to say all the outlets of propaganda. They make sure that the people see only the fraudulent set of books and—as long as they are in office—spotless reputations of incumbents. Russians rarely have a basis for comparison.

For example, when Stalin died, my mother-in-law ran around Moscow weeping in grief, wringing her hands, and exclaiming, "What shall we do? What shall we do?" She was a well-educated woman, a reader of Communist Party propaganda, including the newspaper *Pravda (Truth)*. She was representative of the millions of my country-

men who mourned the loss of a man portrayed to them as our benev-
olent "Great Leader."

People in the West and we in the MGB (*Ministerstvo Gosudarstvennoy
Bezopasnosti*, or Ministry of State Security) Guards Directorate knew the
true Stalin, the vicious and vindictive Stalin. Rough estimates of the
deaths he caused outside of combat—deaths in the 1928–38 famines
and in the purges of the 1930s and 1940s—range from 29 million to
65 million. The higher figure matches the population of New York State
and New England in the 1980 U.S. census. It is about six times the
number of noncombat deaths attributed to Hitler. The millions of
mourners in March 1953 had only the faintest notion, or none at all, of
Stalin's crimes. Defectors are among the few exceptions, for we have
managed to glimpse the truth. I was the rarity who perceived the truth
in Moscow before being given the opportunity to live in the West.

Perfect as the system was portrayed to the Soviet people, there cannot
be room for improvement in the ways the Party governs the country and
the leaders rule the Party. Any small fry who suggests that an improvement might be made here and there, such as free speech or free elections or free enterprise, automatically becomes "an enemy of the people." Nearly perfect as the means of repression are in the USSR, an
enemy of the people, and often his close relatives and friends, undergoes
standard treatment by State Security. Investigation, harassment, arrest,
interrogation, and torture precede sentences to death, jail, prison camp,
or, nowadays, psychiatric wards. While within the Soviet system, we
defectors—regardless of our status, small fry in comparison with the
leaders—had been powerless to improve it and fearful of the consequences of raising our voices. Outside, many of us try to atone for our
past sins of omission by illuminating the system for Westerners. I do in
Inside Stalin's Kremlin.

The truth about Stalin's death still lies hidden after nearly half a century. The Soviet people have been told only what the medical bulletins
said at the time; only a few of Stalin's close associates know more than
the barest facts; the principal witnesses have disappeared; and the West
has been given contradictory and unlikely stories.

They began the deception the moment Stalin was stricken and they continue the deception to the present day. Stalin's inheritors first began to issue official communiques only four days after he was stricken and just before he died, and then the doctors and medical administrators responsible for these communiques dropped from sight (and some perhaps from life). Khrushchev gave a new and different version in his Secret Speech in 1956. His regime then floated other stories to the West via the Soviet writer Ilya Ehrenburg (in a talk with Jean-Paul Sartre, widely published in the fall of 1956) and via P. K. Ponomarenko, ambassador and former party leader.[1] Khrushchev gave yet another variant in his postretirement "memoirs."[2] Immediately after that, Roy Medvedev, carrying on Khrushchev's revelations of Stalin's crimes, transmitted a modest hearsay report that generally fitted what Khrushchev had said.[3] In 1972 I published some of the facts known to me,[4] and in 1976 A. Avtorkhanov, interpreting these and other data, concluded that there had been a plot and that Stalin had probably been murdered.[5] Moscow's reply was contained in a short book by Roy Medvedev in 1979 that spent no less than nine pages rebuffing us and others.

> A few months after he died the story that Stalin had been murdered began to spread among some of the most devoted worshippers in Georgia. Some of the rumors were started by people who had only recently been in Stalin's guard[6] or 'service'; other accounts were circulated by his son Vasiliy.[7]. . . On the whole these rumors were rather fanciful or totally outlandish.[8]

I have told some of what I know in two books, but not in detail. I submit here what I personally learned (and how I learned it), limiting my deductions to what seems necessary to put these facts into focus.[9]

Until recently, two personal considerations stopped me from publishing the full story. Both stemmed from my certainty that, after I defected, Soviet investigations produced reports minimizing the extent of my access to secret information. I thought it safest to let the sleeping bear lie, to let Soviet authorities underestimate their losses: I must not incite punitive actions before the passage of time lowered the stakes. By now, enough time has passed for me to proceed.

The first consideration that delayed publication of the full story was that the revelations at last made here could incite Soviet authorities to carry out the death sentence imposed on me in retribution for defecting. My name has long been on the "watch list" of Soviet citizens against whom State Security—the present-day KGB—should take "active measures," a euphemism that in my case means kidnapping and killing. I renounced my Soviet citizenship to become a naturalized American, knowing that this new status makes no difference to the government of the USSR. The KGB will, if it can, carry out my sentence to death regardless of protections guaranteed by the U.S. Constitution. Now that I approach the end of my life, it is less important to me that my public disclosures might renew efforts to spirit me away from America or to assassinate me here.

The second consideration was that it was from my associates in the CPSU and State Security, by word of mouth and in classified documents that I read but did not sign, that I learned the guarded secrets that here are being disclosed publicly for the first time. My revelations will surprise and embarrass the Soviet leadership, which I presume has rested only a little uneasily with the investigative reports of the damage caused by my defection. These reports took at face value the statements by my past associates about the extent of my knowledge. Understandably, to save themselves from punishment for exceeding the bounds of security, they would have claimed to the investigators that I knew no more than was necessary for me to know in order to fulfill my official duties. They would have falsely attested that I did not know much that was damaging to the security interests of the USSR and the self-interests of its leaders. Until now I have had an obligation to protect my old comrades and former sponsors, my friends who lied about the secrets they gave me. Today, however, they are dead, dying, or insulated by their high ranks from punishment for indiscretions.

In 1944–45, after serving five years in the Soviet Army and being wounded four times in battle, I was assigned to Moscow with the military counterintelligence organization SMERSH. This was the acronym for Stalin's slogan *"Smert Shpionam"* ("Death to Spies"). From 1946 to

1954 I belonged to the MGB, specifically to the Guards Directorate. From February 1947 to May 1952 I was responsible, inter alia, for protecting the leadership—as personnel officer and party secretary—in Stalin's bodyguard organization. I continued to have access to the bodyguards' secrets until September 1953.[10] Then in 1952 I belonged to the First Chief Directorate (or Foreign Operations Directorate).

For an officer at my mid-level position in the Soviet system during the years 1947 to 1952, the Personnel-Security Department of the MGB Guards Directorate provided the broadest possible access to restricted, sensitive information about the leaders and how they operated.

Only the Guards Directorate penetrated the Kremlin wall of secrecy with regularity. It supplied Stalin and his senior subordinates with their domestic servants and chauffeurs as well as the squads of personal bodyguards that surrounded them around the clock. It also managed the Moscow housing, country dachas, resort areas, and Westernized clothing and food stores reserved exclusively for the leaders. It had a separate unit to staff the Kremlin hospital, treat routine ailments, and call in the country's top medical specialists, as necessary. While performing these duties, Guards officers learned about their charges' private lives—the family quarrels and temper tantrums, the philandering and alcoholism that were prevalent, the illnesses and abortions. Our officers observed the leaders' profligate spending on luxuries. They watched the behind-the-scenes maneuvers for power—Stalin to maintain his, subordinates to protect theirs or to undermine and grasp the power of others, including Stalin. Additional secrets came the way of the directorate through its fulfillment of certain clandestine missions assigned by Stalin orally (never in writing) via Minister of State Security Victor Abakumov.[11]

Mine was the only department to deal daily with all echelons of all the Guards Directorate, where the suicide rate averaged two a month. We met on personnel matters—security problems, background investigations, staff vacancies, questionnaires, and so on. It was unavoidable that we knew plenty of what the rest of the departments knew.

Soviet authorities recognized that every Guards officer possessed intimate knowledge of a kind that potentially could jeopardize his loyalty to Stalin and to the system. Special security precautions therefore were taken. More rigorously than elsewhere in the MGB the test of political reliability was applied to candidates and, periodically after they were hired, to employees. I devoted most of my working hours to the security function, which was to examine candidates' and employees' political reliability; I myself underwent the same scrutiny and, obviously, always passed the test. Lest they bolt and reveal their knowledge, former Guards officers were denied permanent assignments abroad except in allied Communist countries. In the confusion at the Center in 1953 I slipped through the net and went to the legal residency in Vienna, Austria.

Throughout our tours in the directorate we received reminders of the MGB regulation against spreading false rumors—anything derogatory said against the leaders must be false, of course—and engaging in loose talk about our work. Violations carried sentences of five years in a labor camp. This rule and punishment did not stop us from gossiping. Friendships developed, naturally, from the working relationships among the more than 100 personnel-security officers in our department and between us and directorate officers in general. Friends, naturally, exchanged confidences. I had no cause to doubt the accuracy of stories recounted by my Guards Directorate sources. The MGB had trained us to observe and report objectively, and friends do not mislead friends. The stories I heard were consistent internally, consistent when repeated, consistent with other information, and sometimes confirmed in proclamations by the government and Party.

The turning point of my disaffection with the system came during my first years in the Guards Directorate, where, better than any place else, an observer learns the fallacies of Soviet-style Communism and discerns flaws of character in the leaders. (To my knowledge, I am the only former Guards Directorate officer ever to have received a permanent posting outside the Soviet Union.) The turning point of considering defection as an option occurred sometime before I managed to transfer to the Foreign Operations Directorate in April 1952. Posted to Vienna in September 1953, I reached the decision to defect in November of that year, but I was not quickly able to arrange the circumstances for placing myself securely in American hands. Within three months, nevertheless, new developments were forcing me to make my move. The breaking point came on February 15, 1954.

On that date I created the opportunity to be out on the streets by myself. It seemed that I had a fair chance of avoiding Soviet acquaintances on my way to the American sector of Vienna. I encountered none en route. I crossed the boundary line, walked through the gates of the nearest U.S. installation, and asked for political asylum.

The antecedents of the MGB were the Cheka (the VChK, or the *Vserossiyskaya Chrezvychaynaya Komissiya po borbe s kontrrevolutsiyey, sabotazhem i spekulyatsiyey,* the All-Russian Extraordinary Commission for Combating Counterrevolution, Sabotage, and Speculation) at the time of the 1917 revolution. This was followed by the GPU (*Gosudarstvennoye Politicheskoye Upravleniye,* State Political Administration), the OGPU (*Obyedinennoye Gosudarstvennoye Politicheskoye Upravleniye,* United State Political Administration), the NKVD (*Narodnyy Kommissariat Vnutrennikh del,* People's Commissariat of Internal Affairs), and the NKGB (*Narodnyy Kommissariat Gosudarstvennoy Bezopasnosti,* People's Commissariat for State Security), in that order. Renamed the MGB in 1946, it temporarily merged with and shared the title of the Ministry of Internal Affairs (*Ministerstvo Vnutrennikh del,* MVD) in 1953. A year later the MGB separated from the MVD and became the KGB. To avoid confusion I usually refer to it here as either the MGB or State Security.

Regardless of the nomenclature, this is the primary and commanding organization of State Security, which engages abroad in espionage, counterintelligence, and such clandestine operations as political warfare, sabotage, and assassination. Its main activities are directed internally, toward suppression of resistance to the current regime and toward preservation of the power and well-being of the leaders.

The other intelligence-gathering component of the Soviet Government is the GRU (*Glavnoye Razvedyvatelnoye Upravleniye,* Chief Intelligence Directorate) of the General Staff, Ministry of Defense. It does not encroach upon State Security's preserve inside the USSR or upon the counterintelligence function abroad.

State Security and the GRU each have a "legal residency" in every foreign country where representatives of Soviet government and quasi-official institutions are permanently stationed. Members of a legal residency, under the charge of a chief known as the "resident," operate under the guise of working for these institutions. In Vienna, while ostensibly employed as an assistant chief of administration in the Soviet High Commission, I reported to the MGB resident. He was Colonel Yevgeniy Kravtsov, there under the alias Kovalev, which he had previously used in Switzerland and Turkey, and under cover as a counsellor of the embassy. Although he was no less vigilant than the next MGB officer, public records show that Kravtsov, no favorite of mine, took the blame for my defection. He was demoted and transferred to the MVD.

Colonel General Victor Abakumov remains little known to the world, but from 1946 to 1951 he was, after Stalin, one of the three most powerful persons in the Soviet Union. (The others were Politburo member Georgiy Malenkov, chief of Party cadres, and the virtually anonymous personal aide to Stalin, Aleksandr Poskrebyshev.) In return for his complete loyalty, coupled with the requisites of a keen mind and utter mercilessness, Stalin delegated that power to Abakumov by retaining him as minister of State Security during those five years. Simultaneous with Abakumov's appointment to the position in 1946, Stalin downgraded Abakumov's most prominent predecessor as the head of State Security, Lavrentiy Beria. Beria eased his way back. He reached his zenith a few months after Stalin died in 1953 by taking control of the State Security apparatus while challenging the power of the rest of Stalin's successors. Between 1951 and 1953 two men with far less influence headed the MGB. This was a time when Stalin played an even more direct part in the use of State Security to maintain his position as the final arbiter of policies and personal fortunes. The imprints of Stalin, Abakumov, and Beria—and to a lesser extent those of Malenkov and Poskrebyshev—were left on my professional career and private life. They appear in every aspect of this account.

Peter Deriabin, 1989

Prologue

Josef Stalin and his lieutenant, Lavrentiy Beria, kept up a sometimes amicable, sometimes hostile relationship for the last 15 years of Stalin's life. It is essentially the story of their relationship that I will tell, not from the outset but from the time when they secretly embarked on separate courses that ended in a showdown and in bloodshed. Along the way the story has as many dark turns as the novels of the celebrated 19th century Russian novelist Dostoyevskiy.

The time frame for my account begins soon after the USSR defeated Hitler's Germany in what Soviet citizens call the Great Patriotic War. It concludes following the death of Stalin in 1953. This period approximately coincides with my service in Moscow with the Ministry of State Security. In focusing on that period I am able to set the record straight on the Kremlin power struggles that occurred then, the most obscure period since the 1917 revolution. The acronym for that organization is MGB. It was the forerunner of the KGB, the Committee *(Komitet)* for State Security. Both major characters in the story, Stalin and Beria, had personal interests, influences, and stakes in the MGB.

Credit for the details goes to well-informed MGB colleagues who took me into their confidence, principally my very good friend Volodya Petrochenkov and my boss, Colonel Serafim Goryshev. They showed me how Stalin and Beria dominated the battlefields of Kremlin internal

1

politics. The rest of our leaders were, by comparison, lambs awaiting slaughter by the lions.

The more I learned about Stalin and Beria, the more I feared them both. My MGB comrades feared them, senior Communist Party officials and government ministers feared them, every reasonable citizen with any knowledge beyond the propaganda in the Party newspaper *Pravda* feared them. We feared others, but less so because they were less powerful, less ruthless, less vindictive than Stalin and Beria were. And Beria feared Stalin just as Stalin feared Beria.

What a strain and drain for a person—a nation—to carry constantly this weight of fear, distrust, and anger. My closest analogy for Americans is the atmosphere in a community where an unidentified serial killer is on the loose. Which of us will the killer strike next, and when, and why?

But in those days, through the vast area that is the Soviet Union, the names of the serial killers were known. They were widely known in the MGB and at the top Communist Party and ministerial levels; yet no one prevented Stalin and Beria from roaming free, virtually unfettered.

Stalin's appointment of Beria in August 1945 to head my homeland's development of atomic weapons sets the stage for the story I will tell.

> We have evidence that within recent weeks an atomic explosion occurred in the USSR.
> — Harry S. Truman, September 23, 1949

Stalin and Beria must have been gratified by that single, flat sentence in President Truman's brief written statement. The president was announcing to the world what his administration had learned many months before: The American monopoly on atomic weapons was finished. The Soviet Union had achieved military parity (or near-parity) with the United States, and the USSR's position in world affairs would strengthen. Stalin, thanks partly to Beria, owned an A-bomb three years earlier than Western experts had predicted.

At the super-secret Manhattan Project in World War II Los Alamos, New Mexico, an international consortium devised A-bomb technology while spies stole that technology for the Soviets. Only after Hiroshima and Nagasaki were devastated in August 1945, only after the Soviet Union detonated its first A-bomb in July 1949, were A-bomb spies rounded up. The naturalized British scientist Klaus Fuchs was the first arrested, in 1950, soon followed by the Americans Harry Gold, David Greenglass, and Julius and Ethel Rosenberg. The Italian-born scientist Bruno Pontecorvo disappeared from England that same year, resurfaced in Moscow, and for his services received the highest honor awarded by my native country, the Order of Lenin. Espionage by itself, however, did not cause the United States to lose a portion of its latest military advantage over the USSR.

Ever dubious of intelligence information from spies, Stalin waited for American A-bomb technology to be proven in wartime conditions. Radioactive fallout was still settling on Hiroshima when he created the equivalent of the Manhattan Project and designated it Directorate Number One of the Council of Ministers. No Directorate Number Two or any other directorate came under the Council. That alone signified the uppermost priority given by Stalin to pulling even with the United States.[1]

Directorate Number One drafted scientists and technicians to apply the stolen secrets toward developing Stalin's A-bomb. Besides the spy ring in the United States, Soviet intelligence services furnished countless unwilling participants. These included German engineers, mathematicians, and physicists who had been captured in wartime and spirited to the USSR, as well as slave laborers who mined uranium in Siberia. Reluctant help also came from uranium miners in East Germany, prodded by the presence of 450,000 Soviet occupation troops and thousands from State Security.

Who better to manage the A-bomb program for Stalin than Lavrentiy Pavlovich Beria? Beria, like Stalin, was a native of the Republic of Georgia, younger than Stalin by almost 20 years. Beria, the State Security careerist, became head of the service at age 39. Beria, the Communist Party functionary, had risen in 1939 to candidate (nonvoting) member of the ruling Politburo (Political Bureau) headed by First Secretary Stalin. Beria, who since 1941 had been a deputy chairman of the Council of Ministers under Chairman Stalin. Beria, who was indebted to the supreme leader Stalin, tsar of personnel throughout the Soviet system.

When he ascended to power in March 1985, Mikhail Gorbachev announced the policy of *glasnost,* commonly translated as openness but also meaning publicity. I applauded this concession to truth and stood by for the results. Subsequently, Soviet media denigrated Stalin and Beria, revealing information about their prewar crimes. Although the details portray them as the villains that they were, Soviet media reports show that Stalin—not Beria—today retains a substantial body of defenders. Many Soviet citizens remain spellbound by the false image of Stalin that he created in propaganda, and many overlook the terrible costs of his modernization of my homeland.

Soviet leaders who succeeded Stalin passed verdict on Beria in December 1953, but fundamental facts were divulged neither then nor, in spite of *glasnost,* the policy of openness, later. Similarly, published reports on other aspects of the postwar years fall well short of giving the complete history of Stalin's and Beria's machinations against each other. Neither they nor other Politburo members have been called to account, postmortem, for all their crimes.

Numerous crucial facts about the internal political battles in the Kremlin have not been previously told. Some facts that I present are definitely not on official record in Moscow. Perhaps some are still lost or hidden in the archives of the KGB and the Party. Probably certain facts linger only in the memories of aging men like me.

Peter Deriabin, 1989

PART ONE

INSIDE THE KREMLIN

1

Back and Forth

February in Moscow is not recommended for tourists. Snow reaches the peak of its annual accumulation, and the mercury hovers around 10 degrees below zero. Muscovites learn to adjust their lives, slog on till spring, and down more vodka. Vodka warms cold bellies. At times it thaws inhibitions.

I had had my share of vodka on the Trans-Siberian Railroad, five days of riding in chilly carriages from the town of Barnaul, beyond the Ural Mountains, which divide the Eurasian continent, and 2,500 miles of tracks to Moscow's Yaroslavskiy Station. It was exciting to be back after almost a year, back to the variety and vitality of the capital, back to flocks of attractive girls, back with colleagues and friends, especially Volodya. Altogether an improvement over Siberia, and a little warmer.

In a few days I would celebrate my 26th birthday. Moscow and I seemed ready for each other that February day in 1947.

Of those who tried to argue me out of quitting State Security the year before and returning to Siberia for the rest of my life, Volodya Petrochenkov had put the case most succinctly.

"I'm a specialist in personnel work," he said, "and any personnel specialist would say you're making a big mistake. You've got a history that guarantees a good career in our service. You certainly are a model of the Soviet man."

7

"Well, what if I am?"

"Look at your record, Petya."

Volodya knew every detail in my personnel jacket.

NAME: Petr Sergeyevich Deriabin.

MGB RANK: Captain.

NATIONALITY: Pure Russian. (That is, my parents weren't Ukrainians or Jews or from any of the other Soviet minorities.)

BACKGROUND: "Poor peasant," as the entry on my birth certificate noted.

PERSONAL: Born on February 13, 1921; raised in villages of Altay Kray, Siberia; parents deceased; brother killed in wartime combat; only close relative a younger sister.

POLITICAL RELIABILITY: Communist Party member; the elected secretary of several Party cells; family apolitical.

EDUCATION: High school diploma; certificate from a two-year institute for teachers.

MILITARY SERVICE: Conscripted in 1939 and entered the Red Army as a private; discharged in 1944 with the rank of first lieutenant; fought in the defense of Moscow in 1941; one of the 151 men in the regiment (out of the original 2,800) to live through the Battle of Stalingrad; participated in the campaign to retake the Ukraine; temporarily disabled three of the four times wounded in action; received 11 decorations for bravery.

The State Security organization for counterintelligence in the Armed Forces recruited me out of the Red Army, and in April 1944 I entered the SMERSH Higher Counterintelligence School on Stansislavskiy Street in Moscow. SMERSH was the contraction for the name which, as the faculty liked to remind us students, Stalin had given us—*Smert Shpionam*, meaning "Death to Spies."

During the school year of 1944–45 I received training in techniques for surveillance, investigations, and interrogations. The emphasis was on rooting out enemies of the people. Time out was taken every so often to give us target practice on a firing range and lessons by professional teachers in—this tickled Volodya—ballroom dancing.

While the rest of the graduating class dispersed to military units in the front lines, the ten of us with the best grades stayed in Moscow. My assignment was to the headquarters of Naval SMERSH, but the job that I had there bored me. I was a full-time Komsomol (Young Communist League) secretary (the only position I would ever hold where the Party paid my wages). At my youthful age and with five years of armed combat under my belt, I couldn't generate great enthusiasm for collecting Party dues and maintaining files on Party members, or leading Party meetings and parroting Party propaganda.

Volodya and I met during my first week in Naval SMERSH, and our friendship thrived from that day onward. I made friends with others as well, including bartenders and barflies, a Jewish actor, some of the women I dated, and quite a few SMERSH officers. Socializing and taking in Moscow got me through those 11 months.

"Are you sure about trading your career for—well, for what, Petya? You don't know the kind of work you'll get in Siberia," Volodya said.

"I'll do what I did before the Red Army pulled me in, teach in a high school."

"Maybe. The pay won't be as high as it is here."

"No, but. . . ."

"I'll put in a word with the chief of Naval SMERSH to try to get you into something more interesting," he said.

"Yes, but. . . ."

I didn't tell Volodya my additional personal reasons for wanting to leave Moscow. In the first place, I had not seen my kid sister Valya in a long time, and from her letters, which were few and far between, I could not be sure that she was content to live with our aunt and uncle. An older brother ought to assume responsibility for the upbringing of a teenager like Valya.

In the second place, I felt homesick for the Altay Kray. I missed hiking through the foothills of the snowcapped Altay Mountains, fishing the rivers, and having moments to reflect in quietude, without city sounds in the background. I missed the farmers and tradesmen who paid almost no attention to fashions, politics, *Pravda,* or the goings-on in Moscow.

So, disregarding advice that soon proved to be sound, I pulled up stakes and set out to make a new life in Altay Kray.

Valya, it relieved me to find, was happy and well cared for by our relatives. Altay Kray, although as beautiful and peaceful in the rural areas
as I remembered, was something else. The towns and small cities
looked run down; food wasn't plentiful despite the rich farmlands in the
region; men, women, and children wore cheap, poorly fitted clothes;
and most of what I used to have in common with the people had dissi-
pated. They were tired from years of overwork, tired and pessimistic.

Although welcome to resume teaching high school, on a teacher's
income I could not earn enough to support the wife and children I
wanted. State Security, under its new initials MGB, took me back at a
salary that made a family affordable. Colonel Vladimir Ruzin appointed
me to his secretariat in the MGB office in the Altay Kray city of Barnaul.

Reading Ruzin's correspondence, I was unable to take any satisfaction from MGB activities in his district. The Center in Moscow insisted
on our uncovering enemies of the people; yet if fair judgments were
made of those whom the MGB investigated, we had but a slim number
of cases. Fair judgments were not made. Ruzin had a quota of arrests,
and, unless the quota was met, he would be fired. The Barnaul MGB
therefore mounted provocation operations to ensnare, convict, and sentence innocent victims.

Tanya Zakharova made my life in Altay Kray bearable, Tanya with her
common sense and calm disposition, pretty Tanya with reddish blond
hair and deep-set eyes. We picked up where we had left off when I had
gone into the Red Army six years earlier. We fell in love, and she came
to Barnaul to live with me out of wedlock.

The Barnaul MGB was none the wiser when I passed Tanya off as my
wife. In fact, she knew that marriage to her spelled the end to an MGB
officer's career. Tanya's father was an enemy of the people who had
been arrested in the 1930s campaign to eliminate kulaks (the class that
hired field workers and thus stood in the way of collectivization). The
elder Zakharov was exiled to a distant part of Siberia and died there.
Making matters worse for us, in mid-1946 the Barnaul MGB happened to
open an investigation of her brother for criticizing economic conditions.

MGB procedures called for reviews of files on its employees' new in-
laws. Had Tanya and I married, the file review would have prompted my
immediate dismissal because of her father and brother. If that happened,

the best job I could hope for was to teach school for a pittance—and still no marriage.

Always of fragile health, Tanya contracted pleurisy in the autumn of 1946, and a cyst developed on one lung. Her prognosis was good, but she died in January 1947.

After that I had no need or desire to stay in Altay Kray. By this time Volodya had become deputy chief of the MGB personnel department that handled cadres at the Center, and I asked him to arrange my transfer from Barnaul to Moscow, anywhere at all in Moscow. He wrote the telegram that arrived in Barnaul within a couple of weeks of my request: "Captain Petr Sergeyevich Deriabin is ordered to report at once for work in the Central Apparatus of the MGB."

"Comrade Petrochenkov is speaking on the other line," the operator said.

"Please, I'll wait. Tell him Deriabin is right here in Moscow, calling from Yaroslavskiy Station."

"Hold on, Comrade."

Even at the noon hour the station had transients of all sorts milling about. The average person here wore better clothing than did residents of Barnaul, yet not noticeably better than the way Muscovites dressed during the Great Patriotic War. The station was as shabby as ever, as run down as all the other train stations in the capital. Money for maintaining public transportation facilities went into the Moscow Metro, of marble halls and brilliant chandeliers. Our underground showplace was worthy of Comrade Stalin, the Party, and my glorious country.

The station telephones had no sound shielding. The din of people and baggage moving, coupled with the screech of steel wheels on steel tracks, made hearing difficult.

"Is this Deriabin by last name, Petr Sergeyevich by first name and patronymic, Captain by rank?" The voice at the other end was deep, hoarse, authoritative. I did not recognize it.

"Yes, sir."

"Is this the Deriabin who had gotten red leather boots from the Americans, then lost them during combat with the Germans?"

"Er, yes, sir."

"Is this Deriabin, the Casanova, who broke the hearts of a thousand women?"

"Volodya! It's you, you son of a bitch!"

For several seconds my pal laughed too hard to speak. Finally, "Welcome to Moscow, you son of a bitch yourself. Are you sober enough to come to the Center before the weekend?"

"Do dogs scratch fleas? Of course I am. When? Now?"

"Is five o'clock satisfactory, Petya? That gives us an hour to gab in private before the end of the three hours we get off every afternoon here in the Center. Then it's 6:00 P.M. to midnight for all except the chiefs. They have to hang around till four or five or six every morning in case they're needed by the Big Chief. Comrade Stalin doesn't go to bed any earlier. And then everybody from our minister on down checks in again at 11 to begin another day. I can't think why I'm telling you this—you'll find out when you check in officially."

"Maybe we should postpone to the weekend," I suggested.

"No, no. I want to see you right away. In fact, I must see you right away, before anybody else does. For your own good. If you don't show up till five, I'll have time to snatch a nap."

"I can guess why you're worn out, you rascal."

Volodya the philanderer wasn't so much wedded to his wife Natasha as to her apartment. Since housing in Moscow was at a premium, rarely did MGB officers and other government workers receive coveted assignments in the capital unless they personally arranged for accommodations. A single woman who had rights to an apartment in Moscow thus drew career-minded suitors like flies to a sausage factory. Witness Volodya pursuing Natasha's dowry.

In my case, by oversight the MGB had not invoked the housing requirement when summoning me to Moscow. Until I took a Muscovite as my wife, I fended for myself—beds in the apartments of girlfriends and of colleagues away on travel or postings. Sergey Bannikov, who had been a friend of mine since we were together in Naval SMERSH, loaned me his apartment when he was sent on assignments to outlying MGB offices.[1]

"No," Volodya said, "Natasha manages to keep me penned in, or likes to think she does. Ha! You and I will have a chance to play the field like we did before you scampered to Siberia."

He reminded me to pick up an MGB pass to enter the buildings at the Center and gave me directions to his office.

In wintertime, darkness descends on Moscow by five o'clock. That afternoon I walked the streets, seeing familiar sights, saving until last the Kremlin and the Lenin Mausoleum on Red Square. I looked up toward the low clouds already aglow from the lights of the city.

Up there, high among spires on the onion domes of the fairy-tale edifice called St. Basil's Cathedral, and over there, on the roof of the State Historical Museum, I had guarded Comrade Stalin against assassination. Through binoculars I could make out the Big Chief on the reviewing stand for the parades. I got better sightings of him later, when stationed at ground level for other Red Square parades on May Day, on anniversaries of the Great October Revolution, for the Victory Day celebration in 1945.

Stalin always led the small procession into Red Square at precisely 9:58 A.M. by the clock in the Spasskiy Gate Tower of the Kremlin. He climbed two flights of outside steps to the top of the mausoleum, which lies below the Senate Tower. At the stroke of ten he was in position for the parade to begin. At the stroke of noon the last in the parade passed him.

The Big Chief made himself seem equal in stature to the tallest of his lieutenants on the platform by wearing lifts in his shoes and by standing on a 6-inch stool. The lifts caused a peculiar walk. His head and shoulders hunched forward, his tiny strides like those of women in old-fashioned hobble skirts. The stool was out of parade spectators' and marchers' line of sight.

Physical security for Stalin was tightest at the parades. Beforehand, ammunition was removed from the military marchers' weapons and from the Air Force planes overhead. (Civilians, of course, weren't allowed to bear weapons.) At these spectacles I was a member of the honor guard that protected the Big Chief's life. Usually I carried a 9-mm automatic pistol (a Tupolev-Tokarev).[2] Twice I manned machine guns in observation posts high above Red Square. With sidearms showing when in uniform, or with gun concealed when in civilian clothes, when stationed on ground level I circulated among the spectators, keeping one eye on them and the other on the pageantry.

Many others had small arms too. They were Guards officers, in and out of uniform, complemented by a sprinkling of officers chosen by other directorates for the honor of protecting the Khozyain (Russian for the Big Chief). Still, that was not sufficient. Backing up these 10,000 MGB officers were over 4,500 uniformed MGB soldiers, who would rush or fire from their concealed positions beneath the Kremlin if a disturbance arose. These included a battalion of machine gunners from the First Dzerzhinskiy Division, a battalion of officers from the Kremlin Kommandatura, and a Kommandatura regiment equipped with machine guns and light artillery. Still, that was not sufficient. Hundreds manned positions overlooking the square. The equation at Red Square parades worked out to roughly two on the special detail guarding Stalin for every one of the 10,000 invited guests, each having been investigated beforehand. State Security could never be overly vigilant against enemies of the people. I enjoyed the colorful displays and the marchers' precision. I took pride in the might of our military, but I tittered with the rest one May Day when a tank broke down, spewed smoke, and was towed away.

All Politburo members rode in bulletproof cars, almost all of them ZIS models (later ZIL), which had Packard engines. A special section of the Guards Directorate oversaw their assembly at the plant.[3]

Sightseers mobbed Red Square in summertime, but in this bleak February weather their number had dwindled to a handful. I turned away and in five minutes arrived at the square named for Felix Dzerzhinskiy, the Pole whom Lenin appointed to be the first chief of State Security. Dzerzhinskiy was memorialized for obliterating counter-revolutionaries and other opponents of Lenin.

Clustered near the square were the main MGB buildings.

Following Volodya's directions, I went down Dzerzhinskiy Street past House Two on the corner. First came the new nine-story section of House Two, or Dom Dva, as State Security personnel called it. The new section was a memorial of a different kind—to the several hundred German prisoners of war who performed manual labor at the construction site, only to be shot by State Security for their hard work. Further along I passed the old, dark brick section of Dom Dva. Its wing, known as the Lubyanka Prison, held enemies of the people undergoing interrogation, awaiting execution, or being held pending transfer.

Volodya had said that his office was down Dzerzhinskiy Street from Dom Dva, at Number 12. I would backtrack there after the formalities at the MGB pass office, provided that I could make my way through the storm that had commenced. Snow fell fast, the density of the flakes dimming the street lights. My eyes watered from gusts of wind almost as cold as Siberia's.

Another man might have excused himself, but Volodya wanted to see me, to tell me something important. I, of course, looked forward to the fun of being with Volodya again.

2

Reunion

"Come in and shut the door behind you," Volodya called out when he heard my voice.

We laughed and hugged and clapped each other on the back, and I meant it when I said how well he looked. Volodya was six years older and a little taller than I. He hadn't lost his slim figure or any of his dark, wavy hair. Women said he was handsome. If I pointed out that his nose was disproportionately large, the women replied that it did not matter to them.

"I was sorry to hear about your wife, Petya."

"Thanks, but she wasn't really my wife, you know. I took a shortcut and introduced her in Barnaul as my wife." This wasn't the time to let Volodya in on why I did not marry Tanya Zakharova.

"Knowing you, I'm sure she was attractive," he said.

"I've spoken to Natasha, who sends her love, and you are hereby invited to eat this evening at the Petrochenkov apartment. I'll quit work a couple of hours early."

"Perfect. Can I sleep overnight on the your couch?"

"Only if you bring a bottle or two of vodka."

"Sure."

I asked why Volodya needed to see me so urgently. "For your own good," he had said. My friend shook his head and put a forefinger to his lips. Even offices in MGB headquarters, it seemed, were not immune to microphones and eavesdroppers.

"Oh, I just want to bring you up to date on your old girlfriends—which ones you should stay away from because they're married now and have jealous husbands. Certain news can wait till we're alone in my apartment tonight." To make sure that I comprehended his message, Volodya stressed "alone."

"How's Bannikov?" I asked in reference to another of the hell-raisers when we were together in Naval SMERSH.

"Seryozha? Still not up to his old tricks, still faithful to his bride of a year or so ago. You were best man at their wedding, Petya. Can you explain why he chose to marry the woman who cut his hair in the head-quarters barber shop?"

"I can't. Bannikov knew when they married that she lost her virginity to the hundredth man before him."

"That whore hasn't changed the habit of dropping her pants for who-ever is handy," Volodya said. "At a party over the New Year's holiday last month, she came at me. Out of respect for Seryozha, I, of course, turned her down."

He started talking about my next job. Senior officers on the MGB panels that reviewed personnel nominations had approved my posting to the "elite outfit of our entire ministry." I would serve in the Guards Directorate.[1]

I was to be one of the counterintelligence officers who staffed the directorate's Personnel-Security Department. The boss there—my new boss—would be Colonel Serafim Goryshev, a deputy chief of the direc-torate. Volodya knew Goryshev well because he had been in charge of Volodya's department until being transferred recently.

"You set me up for this," I accused.

"Yes, I did, if you mean that I stuck your personnel jacket under Goryshev's nose. He liked what he read. The fact that you've been a Communist Party activist off and on since before the war is prima facie evidence of your trustworthiness. Nobody, including the Big Chief—Comrade Stalin keeps the directorate under a microscope, they say—nobody, including him, could fault Goryshev for choosing you."[2]

"But, Volodya, if you'll excuse the aspersion regarding your specialty as a personnel officer, the work in Goryshev's department sounds pretty dull."

"You idiot, that department offers more excitement than you think. According to Goryshev, his counterintelligence officers work with the people who protect the Big Chief and the rest of our leaders. Bodyguards live with Politburo members day in, day out, year in, year out, so you'll come to know about things that go on inside the Kremlin—secrets that aren't known anywhere else in the Center. What an opportunity to be on the inside!"

"I can live without opportunities like that," I said. "Knowledge could be a bomb waiting to explode in my face. What other drawbacks are there?"

"Well, Comrade Stalin doesn't tolerate mistakes, especially in the Guards Directorate. Goryshev says he's busy, not just because the directorate is expanding. He has to scour Moscow for men to take the place of bodyguards who screwed up. Depending on the mistake, offending Guards officers who don't get fired go to prison, or labor camps, or some miserable MGB outpost beyond the Urals."

"Punishment isn't the action I'm looking for," I said.

"You want action, Petya? Well, now you can actually afford our Moscow night life—the pay scale in the Guards Directorate is the highest in the Center. Goryshev says that's to reward bodyguards for their loyalty to the Big Chief and for keeping their mouths shut. And they do keep them shut. None of the rumors that fly around the Center originate there."

"You can convince anyone of just about anything, Volodya. Remember the girl you had believing that you're a descendent of Catherine the Great? She was entranced by the notion of toying with male equipage that you inherited through royal bloodlines."

"Liar," he said, smiling. "Anyway, I've convinced you."

"Not quite." I stood up and walked to the window, which gave onto a view of a courtyard below and Malaya Lubyanka Street with the French Catholic Church of St. Louis.

Legally arrested or illegally kidnapped, MGB prisoners were driven past that church. They rode between high steel gates, the padlocks removed momentarily, at the entrance to the courtyard. They then dis-

appeared into the Lubyanka Prison. There were no graveside cere-
monies or cemeteries for executed prisoners or those who died during
interrogation. Corpses left the Lubyanka after midnight, carted away in
vans disguised as delivery trucks for the MGB cafeteria in Dom Dva. The
bodies were cremated.

"Do you ever see them, Volodya?"

"See them? Oh, you mean enemies of the people going to and from
the Lubyanka. Once or twice a week, standing where you are. . . ." He
went on to say, " 'Not quite convinced,' I believe."

"Well, I'd like to look at other options."

"Other options!" Volodya's hot temper was showing. "You have only
one other option. When I tell Goryshev and Goryshev tells the panels
that you may not care to work in the Guards Directorate, the chiefs will
say, 'Who would have the impertinence to question our decision? We'll
fix Deriabin.'

"They'll send you to help run a labor camp beyond the Urals. You
should know how quickly a man's balls freeze in Siberia. You'll spend
half your time trying to keep warm. The rest of the time you'll juggle figures to conceal production shortages. Production norms for labor
camps are as unrealistic as they are in factories. More unrealistic, considering that the poor bastards in the camps are sick or starving or
both."

I remembered hearing about an acquaintance in State Security who
committed suicide while he was on the staff of a labor camp. After a
year there he shot himself, and his relatives contended that he no
longer could bear to watch the inmates suffering.

"Okay, okay, I'm convinced," I said. "You win."

"I didn't win." Volodya grinned. "It's simply that you didn't lose. . . .
Let me stop prattling for a few minutes, and I'll get these personnel
papers ready for the chiefs to sign. Do you want to look over my shoulder to see how it's done?"

"Thanks all the same. I don't want to slow you down when you're up
against a deadline."

"This won't take long." Volodya flipped through and arranged a stack
of documents, then took them to the outer office for a courier to pick
up. "There, that's finished. Now I'll pass along official information

about the Guards Directorate. Official, Petya, because nobody gets in trouble for telling you."

Comrade Stalin himself had interviewed Goryshev, showing the importance of Goryshev's new position. This was a standard practice of his before letting certain nominees enter the Guards Directorate, including department chiefs, his personal bodyguards, and his house-keeping staff. The directorate answered to our minister of State Security, Volodya said, but it was the Big Chief who made policy and issued operational orders.

It was he who on the first day of that very month, February 1947, instructed all MGB units to put top priority on Guards Directorate requests for immediate action. "Goryshev believes, and I agree, that this *instantsiya* makes your directorate first among equals. Units throughout our service are at its disposal,"said Volodya.

In our jargon, an *instantsiya* was an unsigned and unannounced order issued by the highest authority in the Party or the government. Always, of course, that authority was Stalin.

The directorate chief was General Nikolay Vlasik, an old comrade of the Big Chief's from the 1919 Civil War who doubled as his personal photographer. Volodya said that Vlasik bordered on being illiterate and that he prided himself in this deficiency. Vlasik insisted on subordinates having no higher than a grade school education, lest they take it into their heads to think for themselves. "Therefore, Petya, hide from Vlasik that you finished high school and two years at a teachers' institute."

Volodya was willing to bet a ruble that no more than five other Guards officers would have as much formal education as I had had. I was distinctive in the Guards Directorate not only as one of its few com-bat veterans but also as one of three or four officers with graduate schooling.

"What's your opinion of Goryshev?" I asked.

"You shouldn't have any problems. A friendly guy, as long as mistakes by his people don't get him in hot water. Plays favorites, but gives every-body a fair deal. A hard worker—16 hours a day and all that, though he doesn't demand overtime from his people except in emergencies. We got along well. We still do. He keeps in touch, as I've indicated."

"Then you two fraternize during off-duty hours."

"No, we don't fraternize in bars or chase women together," said Volodya. "Goryshev doesn't take heavily to drink, and he's strictly a family man. His two youngsters go to a private school in Sokolniki Park. We play chess sometimes during the afternoon breaks, but he's a terrible player. Not athletic, either. Goryshev is overweight and is forever talking about dieting, which he does one meal out of 50."

"Always a State Security officer?"

"Always. Served on one of the battlefronts during the war and won promotions and decorations. Goryshev has a solid reputation. He's relatively young to be a colonel—a bit older than I, in his mid-30s, I'd judge."

"Who's his second-in-command, Volodya?"

"An officer who's been with the bodyguards for a long, long time. I guess Colonel Strekachev's greatest value to Goryshev is knowing about skeletons in the Kremlin closets. Funny story: Strekachev's wife got wind of the affair he's been having with a typist for the CPSU Central Committee and bitched to some muckety-muck in the Party apparatus. Result: a Party reprimand that prevents Strekachev from ever being promoted to general."

The clock on the wall of Volodya's office showed that the afternoon break had ended. "I should leave," I said. "I'll be at your apartment around ten tonight." We shook hands. "Thanks again for getting me out of Barnaul and back to the Center."[3]

"That's what friends are for," he said.

After supper, after Natasha admonished us about consuming too much vodka and retired for the night, Volodya spoke of the "important news that affects all of us in the MGB."

"You recall my telling you," he said, "that the Big Chief in effect has taken personal charge of the directorate. He has put in as the token chief someone unquestionably loyal to him, his old sidekick General Vlasik. Though trusting Vlasik's loyalty, he must realize that Vlasik rates low on brains. That's why Comrade Stalin himself gives final approval on Vlasik's deputies, like Goryshev. In addition, the Big Chief is beefing up the bodyguards with lots more men. Finally, there's the *instantsiya* that he issued not long ago. The order moves the directorate to the top of the heap in State Security.

"These things I've just gone over relate to what happened earlier. They relate to Beria." Volodya was whispering, in case his normal voice could be overheard, and we continued to whisper while talking about this matter. "Last year the Big Chief suddenly discovered that he was surrounded by bodyguards from Georgia. On the surface, that might seem acceptable because Comrade Stalin is from Georgia . . ."

"And so is Beria," I broke in to remind Volodya.

"Exactly, and Beria has built up a bloc of loyalists in Georgia, sort of easing out the Big Chief's people. Well, these Georgian bodyguards were brought in by the guy whom Beria handpicked to succeed him at the head of State Security. Comrade Stalin became suspicious of all these Georgians. He decided that the Guards Directorate couldn't be trusted to protect him while it employed Georgians, so he fired every last one of them.

"As you know, the Big Chief reorganized State Security, got rid of the Beriaite who was the commissar, made us into a ministry, and brought in our new minister. His purpose, I tell you now, was to cut off Beria's ties to our service, where Beria and his gang ran the show."

Volodya, with his contacts in MGB headquarters, surely was better informed than someone who just arrived from Barnaul; yet during the past year I had seen a sign that Beria remained in Stalin's favor. I raised this reservation.

"But the Big Chief," I said, "promoted Beria to full member of the Politburo less than a year ago. I think that argues against Beria having lost any power."

"Yes, the Big Chief did promote him, but that's sheer window dressing, just like his elevating Beria to the rank of marshal two years ago. Nobody's vote counts in the Politburo, or in the Council of Ministers, except Comrade Stalin's. The promotions might have been intended to salve Beria's feelings, put him off his guard. Perhaps it will work."

"You have a pretty fair notion of developments that aren't being printed in *Pravda*. What's ahead for us, Volodya?"

"How should I know? How does anyone know? I do know that regardless of his exalted titles, Beria lacks the power he once had because Comrade Stalin fired his followers in State Security. I do know that Beria isn't the kind to submit meekly and fade into the landscape.

He's every bit as vengeful as Comrade Stalin. He's smart and patient and slippery."

"Your conclusions, then," I requested.

"I think the Big Chief is cautious about taking stronger actions against Beria in case Beria has the means to retaliate. Assassination by Beria or by a Beriaite, for example. That's why there are more body-guards hired to protect Comrade Stalin."

"Well, if you're right—and I don't disagree with you, Volodya—we ought to avoid the cross fire that's certain to come eventually. The problem is, we don't know from which direction the guns will shoot."

"The real problem," Volodya said, "is not knowing which side to be on, or what might land us in hot water, or whom to trust."

We moved on to less troubling subjects. When the second bottle of vodka was empty, we went to bed.

3

Two Georgians and Soviet Jewry

Stalin and Beria were born of the Georgian minority, one of the smaller ethnic groups in the USSR and much smaller than the Slavic majority. Georgians constituted less than 5 percent of the total Soviet population. The Republic of Georgia's 27,000 square miles, half the size of America's state of Georgia, lies in the southernmost region of the country. The capital of the republic, Tbilisi, and Moscow are separated by over 1,000 miles.

Stalin might be called a mainstream Georgian. His place of birth (on December 21, 1879) was the town of Gori in the Caucasus Mountains, 50 miles from Tbilisi, and his parents had the last name Dzhugashvili. Stalin, which is the Russian word for steel, changed his name during the reign of the last of the tsars as did Vladimir Lenin (born Ulyanov), Molotov (born Scriabin), and other Communist revolutionaries.

Beria came from an ethnic minority within the Georgian minority. He was born (on March 29, 1899) in a village in the district known as Mingrelia, bordering on the Black Sea and Turkey. Not far away is the Republic of Armenia and, beyond it, Iran. In Beria's youth this area was in turmoil, a land of shifting alliances among the natives, Mingrelians included.

Like Stalin, Beria became another scourge of Georgia by killing off competitors. He joined State Security at the age of 20 while the civil war of 1919–20 was in progress, when victory by Lenin's presiding Bolsheviks over the White Russians was uncertain. Beria amassed power, assembled a coterie of loyalists, and purged his enemies— labeled enemies of the people—in Georgia and neighboring Trans-caucasus republics. He moved to Moscow in 1938. Before year's end Stalin appointed him Commissar of State Security. From then until 1946 either Beria or a Beriaite held that position. Probably another of Beria's qualifications was his height, barely 5 feet tall, like Stalin. (Nearly all of Stalin's deputies were men of short stature.)

An aspect of Beria's native Mingrelia became increasingly important to his relationship with Stalin: The Jews of Georgia concentrated in Mingrelia. Georgians called Beria "the Mingrelian Jew," and his mother was rumored to be Jewish. Beria chose Jews for jobs in State Security and in a major government agency that he later headed, Directorate Number One (atomic weapons). In defense of these selections he said, "No matter that they are Jewish. They have good heads." These facts assuredly registered with Stalin, an anti-Semite. They were also to register with me in the context of the unfolding of the Mikhoels affair.

Married or single, many MGB officers devoted their three-hour afternoon breaks to affairs with girlfriends. Still a bachelor, I had that intention when I went to the apartment of Yuliya Kuznetsova during an afternoon break in January 1948. Yuliya, an operetta performer, lived with her mother, the property manager in a theatre. The elder Kuznetsova was at home when I arrived, and both women were in tears. I swallowed expressions of frustration and asked what was wrong.

"Our friend Mikhoels is dead," I was told. "He died in Minsk. A truck ran over him in the street and killed him. It wasn't an accident. The truck driver struck Solomon Mikhailovich intentionally."

"When? Who killed him?"

"Yesterday or last night. Word of it is racing through theatrical circles today. You ought to know who the murderers are, Comrade Deriabin."

The accusation and the formal "Comrade Deriabin" said everything. The Kuznetsova women, who knew me to be an MGB officer, thought the MGB guilty in the death of Mikhoels, a famous Jew. He had been the leading actor and director in Jewish theatres. When I protested, truthfully declaring total ignorance of the matter, they embellished the accusation: I should have told them to warn Mikhoels, I didn't trust them, I had as much blood on my hands as the truck driver, and so on.

On the basis of that unwarranted suspicion, my romance with Yuliya Kuznetsova had come to an end. Ah well, there were other pretty girls to be found in Moscow. Yet, if the Kuznetsovas happened to be correct about MGB responsibility for the slaying, the likeliest culprits worked in my own Guards Directorate.

Nicknamed Operod (short for *Operativniyy Otdel'*, Operations Department) this component of the directorate had a mission to kill enemies of the people. The killings were carried out on the personal orders of Stalin, whether or not a court had imposed the death sentence. Stalin's purposes should be served without any neat legal distinction being drawn between execution and murder. Victims were shot in the basement of the Lubyanka Prison, but I had not heard of Operod taking lives anywhere else.[1] Besides, capital punishment had been outlawed in May 1947, seven months before Mikhoels died.

Against the possibility that the department had taken up the sideline of street assassinations, I visited Operod the day after my imbroglio with the Kuznetsova women. I got the chance to ask, "Have you heard the rumor that Mikhoels is dead?"

"It's not a rumor," the Operod officer said. "Mikhoels is as dead as the flowers in a funeral wreath."

"You seem damned sure of yourself."

"I am, Captain Deriabin. We ourselves took care of him exactly the way that the Big Chief wanted it done."

He repeated Stalin's orders: Mikhoels should be eliminated in a manner that would make his death appear to be the clumsy work of MGB amateurs. The Operod officer did not volunteer the rationale for killing Mikhoels, and it would have been imprudent for me to probe further. I obtained the answer in a few months.

Stalin made a big show of having Mikhoels's killers apprehended. He assigned to the investigation in Minsk a Moscow police detective famed in the USSR as the "Russian Sherlock Holmes." On orders from the MGB that originated with Stalin, the local police in Minsk pretended to cooperate with the detective but obstructed him. They could not (would not) trace the license number of the truck that struck Mikhoels, and the license number was the only solid clue. Consequently, no arrests were made.

My boss in the Guards Directorate, Colonel Goryshev, chief of the Personnel-Security Department and one of the deputies to Lieutenant General Vlasik (chief of the Kremlin's Guard Directorate), told me why Stalin ordered the murder of Mikhoels and why the murder was committed in such an unusual manner. As his trust in my discretion increased, Goryshev had taken me more and more into his confidence about Kremlin secrets. I was, I suppose, Goryshev's favorite among the 110 counterintelligence officers who were subordinate to him.

Goryshev was in a talkative mood, puffing on one of Stalin's cigarettes after a repast from the Kremlin restaurant. We commiserated with each other over the recent rejection of an applicant whom both of us recommended for employment. The MGB deputy minister for Personnel had returned the man's file minus an endorsement. To show us why the man was turned down, the deputy minister circled in red the entry "Jew" (for nationality).

"I don't understand this bias against Jews," I said. "They're not enemies of the people in my book."

"Nor in mine," said Goryshev. "Nevertheless, our books aren't being read by the Big Chief. He's reading his own."

"I'm sure you've heard about the Mikhoels case." If that statement were interpreted by Goryshev as provocative, I had my line of retreat prepared.

"Yes, run over by a truck in Minsk, I was sorry to hear."

My boss's response was encouraging, so I asked why it had been necessary for Mikhoels to die in this way. Goryshev motioned me closer to him, and in an undertone gave me the answer. "The Big Chief told Operod to make it obvious that Mikhoels was murdered. The death was to be a warning to Jews."

"A warning against what?"

"Against persisting in their attempts to form a Jewish autonomous republic. Mikhoels was one of the ringleaders. The wife of Comrade Molotov was another."

"I read *Pravda* religiously, Serafim Vasilyevich, and *Pravda* hasn't reported anything on a Jewish autonomous republic."

"It hasn't and it won't," Goryshev said. "These Jews wanted to set up a republic in the south by the Black Sea, in the Crimea, and have Sevastopol as the capital. They pointed out to Comrade Stalin that the farmlands and orchards down there are going to waste—the Tatars who had lived there had been deported during the war. They also pointed out that Ukrainian and Byelorussian Jews whom Hitler had displaced could now be resettled in the Crimea."

"The proposal sounds reasonable to me," I said.

"It didn't to the Big Chief. Definitely not. He called it a 'Trotskyist idea,' and you know that the Jew Trotsky used to be the Big Chief's main enemy of the people.[2] He said Zionists and Americans were behind the proposal because an autonomous republic for Jews would help toward creating an independent Jewish state on Soviet territory.

"That wasn't all. Comrade Stalin said the Americans would use the autonomous republic as the beachhead to take over the Baku oil fields. What do you think of that, Petr Sergeyevich?"

"With all respect to the Big Chief, I wonder where he got this information about the Americans' plan."

"Probably there isn't any information or any such plan," Goryshev said. "In my opinion, the Big Chief is worried about the United States and has a personal disliking for Jews. The proposal by Mikhoels and the others gave him a chance to weave the two together into a fabric of conspiracy. The whole affair, that is to say, is a fabrication."

Goryshev added that Beria tried to dissuade Stalin from implementing this purge of Jews.

Although Stalin went forward with the purge, he allowed Beria to retain Jews in the organization that he was then supervising, Directorate Number One. Stalin needed them and he needed Beria. He wanted atomic weapons. Under Beria, Directorate Number One detonated its first A-bomb in July 1949.

Soon after the Great Patriotic War, Stalin began an anti-Semitism campaign in the media. The frequency of criticism of people with Jewish names clearly indicated that the Jewish minority at large was under attack, but the word "Jew" did not appear, or at least not often. The media used the phrase "rootless cosmopolitans" to mean Jews. This campaign dovetailed with the postwar deterioration of relations with the West, and it was salted with accusations of a dangerous conspiracy involving Americans, Mideast Jews, and Soviet Jews.

A Government *instantisya* subsequently indicated that an official policy of anti-Semitism was now in effect. It required the dismissal of Jews from ministries engaged in secret work. Jews, the order said, must not be allowed to have access to classified information—information that, according to Stalin, the American and Israeli conspirators valued.

Operod executed Molotov's deputy foreign minister and about 30 other Jews, all alleged by Stalin to have been active in the conspiracy. A number of Jewish conspirators were jailed during this purge of 1948–49. One was Molotov's wife,[3] attended in a labor camp by servants whom the Guards Directorate supplied. She went by her maiden name Polina Zhemchuzhina. She stayed in a labor camp for almost five years until, after Stalin's death in March 1953, Beria (then in charge of the MGB) honored Molotov's appeal to release his wife.

The purge resulting from the *instantsiya* forced about 10,000 Jews out of jobs in the MGB, although our minister did protect a few from dismissal. It also forced the Jew Kaganovich into idleness and caused his brother to commit suicide. For the sake of appearances, however, Stalin allowed Kaganovich to retain the titles of Politburo member and deputy premier.[4]

Goryshev and I hit it off well from the first interview I had with him, a day or two after my reunion with Volodya in February 1947. Early on, my new boss invited me to address him less formally, by his first name and patronymic Serafim Vasilyevich, rather than by rank and last name. Colleagues speculated that we were related. Certainly my high standing with Goryshev contributed to their taking the course with me that he himself followed—he divulged sensitive information that otherwise I would not have obtained.[5]

His rank and position gave Goryshev space in the main MGB headquarters building. After uniformed sentries checked identification badges in the entry hall on the first floor, visitors climbed a short flight of stairs leading to the second floor, to Goryshev's Room 209. A secretary-typist sat in the anteroom, which had double doors opening into my boss's office. Inside it looked like other chiefs' offices in Dom Dva—a safe, mismatched bulky furniture, a conference table with ten chairs trimmed with leather, a bare floor, telephones, a decanter and glasses, totally drab. The personal touch was a photograph of Stalin and Defense Minister Voroshilov taken by Directorate Chief Vlasik, an accomplished photographer.

Goryshev would call me in for off-the-record chats once or twice a month. Our conversations lasted as long as two hours. They covered the Personnel-Security Department, the Guards Directorate, the MGB, the leadership, whatever seemed to cross his mind.

"Relax, Peter Sergeyevich, and have one of the Big Chief's cigarettes," he would say. Stalin smoked the Severnaya Palmyra and Gerzogvina Flor brands, taking one or two from a new pack and then discarding the pack. His bodyguards retrieved the partial packs for the chiefs of our directorate.

Or Goryshev would say, "This is more food than I should eat. Help yourself to the tray from the Kremlin restaurant." (It served Politburo members.) Dozens of times I heard his litany that "the Big Chief put me here" in the Guards Directorate. Remarks like these were Goryshev's reminders to listeners that he had influence and good connections. I forgave his bragging.

Over our five years together I grew to regard with affection this stocky man of medium height with receding brown hair, a round face, a flat nose, and tiny ears. He sympathized with my problems and helped me in any way that he could. Goryshev, I gathered, admired a person who had traded fire with the Germans during the Great Patriotic War, although, unlike me, Goryshev had not seen battle service. His brother worked as an agronomist in Altay Kray, wrote letters lauding the beauty of my native province, and enjoyed living there. This, too, brought us closer together. Goryshev sympathized with the losses of my father when I was very young, my brother killed during the war, and my mother while I was fighting Germans near Moscow. I, in turn, showed interest in his children's activities and their progress at the school in Sokolniki Park. He appreciated that for him I broke the rules that pro-hibited the disclosure of discussions at meetings of MGB Party activists.

4

Zhdanov vs. Malenkov

Volodya and I returned to the Petrochenkov apartment late on a Saturday afternoon in the autumn of 1947. His wife had gone out shopping for several hours, to stand in long lines at state-run food stores, and we were free to celebrate the victory by the team we rooted for. Moscow Dynamo Football Club had won again. These "amateurs" should always win. They did nothing to earn their keep as MGB employees but practice and play soccer.

On the second or third foray into our supply of vodka, Volodya hopped from evaluating Dynamo players to lamenting the plight of Jews. "Most Muscovites are prejudiced against Jews," he said. "They envy Jews for their intellect and good jobs."

"That bias is prevalent in the Guards Directorate," I said. "There wasn't any such thing in Siberia. I doubt whether there was any in your neck of the woods either."

"None," said Volodya. "But, handling personnel matters here in the Center, I see hardly a day pass without our chiefs turning down Jews for assignments. Under the rules, a man being Jewish shouldn't hinder him, but it does."

"Lately, from what *Pravda* and other newspapers are printing, our chiefs appear to have support in the highest places, in the Kremlin." I was referring to the anti-Semitic propaganda campaign that had been flourishing for some time. "Zhdanov is the official spokesman."

To all citizens the charismatic Andrey Zhdanov was many things. He was with Stalin on the policy-making Politburo of the Communist Party of the Soviet Union, with Stalin on the policy-implementing Secretariat of the CPSU, a hero of the thousand-day Siege of Leningrad. In defense of the largest USSR city after Moscow, the residents of Leningrad stood with the ill-equipped, undermanned Red Army and fought Hitler's troops to a standstill. The city was saved thanks partly to Zhdanov organizing supply lines across the wintertime "road of ice" on frozen Lake Lagoda.

Zhdanov headed the Leningrad Party Organization from 1934 until Stalin brought him to Moscow in 1945. Currently his job was to update Party dogma on the basis of the writings of Lenin, Karl Marx, and other Communist theoreticians.

"Yes, Petya, he's the official spokesman for the Party when the Big Chief isn't. It's like watching a horse race, following where the Big Chief positions certain leaders in relation to each other. First one goes ahead, then another, then another."

"Right now Zhdanov has the inside track, but Beria isn't out of the running. Even though he no longer calls the tune for the MGB, he has Malenkov. You could say Beria is paired with Malenkov as a double entry in the race."

"By appearance," I said, "they look as if they were bred in different stables. Still, you're probably right about them being paired. Beria's bodyguards and Malenkov's tell the same story, that they're often in each other's company."

Beria was short, swarthy, balding, smooth-shaven, and had a paunch; he wore a pince-nez for effect and tailor-made suits. Malenkov also was short and smooth-shaven. He had thick black hair, was pudgy, wore unstylish clothes, and needed glasses to read.

Their friendship dated back to 1938, when Beria moved from Georgia to a senior position in State Security headquarters and Malenkov worked on the staff of the CPSU Central Committee. Both became deputy premiers, and in 1946 Stalin promoted both to the Politburo. But a little later both suffered setbacks.

Besides removing Beriaites from the MGB in mid-1946, Stalin suspended Malenkov from the CPSU Secretariat and exiled him to faraway Tashkent. The demotion stripped Malenkov of his responsibility for Party oversight of all "organs of State Security," which included the MGB, the police (the MVD), the public prosecutors, and the judiciary. In Tashkent he handled the comparatively unimportant task of managing agriculture in four southern central Asian Republics. Malenkov was allowed to return to Moscow shortly before I returned in February 1947.

Zhdanov gained the power that Malenkov lost. At the time Stalin removed Malenkov as a CPSU secretary, he named two Zhdanov protégés to serve in the Secretariat with him, Zhdanov, and his own adopted son. One of the two newly appointed Zhdanovites was Aleksey Kuznetsov, and the organs of State Security were advised that henceforth Kuznetsov, in place of Malenkov, would be their point of contact in the Secretariat.

Kuznetsov had been promoted the year before to succeed Zhdanov as local leader of the Leningrad Party Organization. His rapid rise in the Party apparatus was taken as an especially strong sign of Zhdanov moving up to second place in the hierarchy, ahead of Malenkov and Beria.

About Kuznetsov, Volodya said, "He can't keep track of us in State Security the way Malenkov did when he was our overseer in the Secretariat. Malenkov used to receive reports concerning MGB administration and MGB operations, and on behalf of the Party he approved certain appointments...."

"All appointments down to department chief and section chief in the Guards Directorate."

"Yes, well, you people in the bodyguards are an exception. The rest of our service approvals by the Secretariat go only as far as directorate chief."

"Anyway," Volodya continued, "Kuznetsov isn't on the distribution for any of these reports from us. Insofar as the organs of State Security are concerned, the Big Boss is filling Malenkov's shoes in the Secretariat, so he has given Kuznetsov an empty responsibility. And I do mean meaningless."

"It will be interesting," Volodya said, "to see how long Zhdanov will have the lead in this horse race."

"That might depend on whether he keeps his thirst quenched."

"Oh?"

"Yeah. His bodyguards tell me that Zhdanov is an alcoholic. He's drunk a lot of the time—misses important meetings and shows up at others staggering and incoherent."

"Just like you and me," Volodya joked. "Let's have one more vodka to toast our Dynamo team. Our wet blanket Natasha will soon come back from shopping."

Alcoholism may have clouded Zhdanov's judgment, leading to two mistakes made by *apparatchiki* (full-time employees) of the Party and by government officials belonging to his faction. In both cases they crossed Stalin.

Zhdanovites antagonized Stalin on an internal political matter involving their home base of Leningrad. Among themselves they put together a plan to reorganize the Russian Soviet Federated Socialist Republic (RSFSR), by far the largest of the USSR's 15 republics. This drastic reorganization would not only bring the structures of the RSFSR Party and government in line with those of the other 14 republics, it would shift the RSFSR capital from Moscow to Leningrad, take from Stalin certain duties associated with managing the RSFSR, and turn over to Zhdanov's protégés the day-to-day management of the republic.

To justify their proposal when submitting it to Stalin, the Zhdanovites said the reorganization would relieve him of burdens too heavy for a man in his 60s. Less than convinced, Stalin was by nature suspicious, and first of all suspicious of Leningraders. He accepted the opinion held by MGB officers in the Center that Leningrad harbored the highest concentration of enemies of the people—a riffraff of artists and members of the intelligentsia.

Zhdanov and Zhdanovites, Stalin said, were trying to usurp his authority. That interpretation of motives demonstrated their serious miscalculation about his willingness to surrender power. The reorganization plan went into the Kremlin trash heap, and the Zhdanov faction went down in Stalin's estimation.

Another costly mistake by Zhdanovites was their positive attitude toward Marshal Tito of Yugoslavia immediately before he broke with Stalin in 1948.

Russians took Tito prisoner during the First World War. He converted to Communism, chose to remain in the USSR, and was recruited as an agent for State Security. His record of cooperation during the 1920s and 1930s persuaded Stalin to let him leave the Soviet Union in the 1940s and to lead partisans against German occupation forces in Yugoslavia during the Great Patriotic War. With the defeat of the Germans in 1945, Tito formed the Communist government that ruled that country.

Tito's cooperation with State Security continued during the postwar period, although on a diminished scale. Tito did not necessarily follow the wishes of Stalin and the Center, and the MGB suspected him of collaborating with imperialist powers. On the other hand, the MGB and the Yugoslav service exchanged secret reports such as details on wartime Nazis and Nazi collaborators in Yugoslavia; Tito made MGB headquarters his first stop on visits to Moscow; and a Guards Directorate general led a group of advisors sent to Belgrade to train Tito's personal bodyguards.

Zhdanov took the lead for the USSR to sponsor the formation of the Cominform (short for Communist Information Bureau) in October 1947, with headquarters in Belgrade. Eight European Communist parties joined the CPSU in organizing this propaganda arm of the international Communist movement.

Almost immediately a dispute broke out over the direction to be taken by the Cominform. It either would be a tool for Stalin and the CPSU Central Committee to manipulate at will, or it would be as Tito wanted, a forum where European Communist parties voiced opinions that might run contrary to the CPSU's. Tito went a step further. He and the Bulgarian Communist Party chief laid out a plan to form an East European federation. Stalin considered their plan a trick designed to set Eastern Europe on a path of independence from the USSR.

While the Cominform pot was boiling, an emissary from Tito traveled to the Soviet Union in January 1948. In Moscow Stalin and the CPSU Central Committee gave him the cold shoulder. Afterward, in Leningrad, however, Zhdanovites feted the emissary and indicated sympathy with Tito's position.

Out of these events developed the split between Stalin and Tito that never healed. In June 1948 the Cominform formally denounced Tito for holding "anti-Soviet opinions incompatible with Marxism-Leninism" and for leaning toward the West. Unless he admitted his errors, the proclamation said, Yugoslavia would be expelled from the Cominform. The Yugoslav Communist Party shot back the next day with a vote of confidence in Tito. That reply compelled Stalin to dissolve the Cominform.

Stalin issued a standing order for the MGB to assassinate Tito, and organization of the operation to assassinate him was placed in the hands of a committee of senior MGB officers chaired by a brother-in-law of Malenkov. Their efforts could not get past the planning stage, however, due to the tight security practices of the Yugoslav bodyguards whom the Guards Directorate had trained. For lack of a better way to vent his frustration, Stalin fired the MGB general who had supervised their training.[1]

In July 1948, one month after the contretemps with Tito in the Cominform, Stalin signaled his anger with the renegade Zhdanovites. He restored Zhdanov's rival, Malenkov, to the CPSU Secretariat. Zhdanov was allowed to remain in the Secretariat and the Politburo, at least for the present, but Stalin limited his authority in Party affairs.

Another month passed, and Zhdanov was dead. He died on a boar-hunting expedition at his dacha in the Valday region, between Moscow and Leningrad. Beria, Malenkov, and others signed the obituary in *Pravda*. Stalin did not, a clear sign of his low esteem for Zhdanov.

According to the obituary, doctors ascribed the death to "an infarct of the myocardium," in layman's terms a type of heart condition. The doctors who certified the cause of Zhdanov's death in August 1948 would get caught up in a hurricane of accusations and investigations that brought the Soviet Union to the brink of a sweeping purge by Stalin in January 1953. Meanwhile, the Zhdanov faction underwent a bloody purge in which Malenkov and the minister of State Security took a personal part.

Stalin had picked Colonel General Viktor Abakumov for this ministry in 1946, just before the expulsions of Beriaites from the Guards Directorate and from other State Security jobs. The appointment was not announced, and after it did become public knowledge seven years later, the official Soviet position had been that Abakumov and Beria were in league throughout Abakumov's tenure as our minister. That position enabled the Soviet system to allot Beria a share of guilt for certain crimes during the 1946–51 period, but it is a position taken contrary to facts.

In truth, Stalin picked Abakumov in the conviction that his new minister would keep Beria out of State Security activities. The expulsion of Beriaites in 1946 was merely the first action by Abakumov to show me and my colleagues that he was following Stalin's orders to dampen the influence of Beria in the MGB. Abakumov did so whenever possible, with relentless determination. MGB officers considered the minister of State Security to be the linchpin of Stalin's defense against Beria.

Abakumov circulated instructions that, when the MGB forwarded reports to the Politburo, Beria was the one Politburo member who should never be a recipient. He deceived Beria by telling him that the MGB had—when, in fact, it had not—removed hidden microphones that intercepted conversations of senior officials. After a half-year as minister, Abakumov issued a proclamation that criticized his predecessor, Vsevolod Merkulov,[2] for "serious failures in the important work of locating counterrevolutionaries." Since Merkulov was a Beria protégé, the proclamation was a not-so-subtle attack on Beria.

A native of Taganrog in southern USSR, Abakumov came from the Great Russian ethnic majority. He was almost six feet in height and athletically built, the trimmest State Security general I ever saw. His taste for things foreign was reflected in his Western-style clothes, all made from Russian, East German, or Hungarian fabrics. English fabric was chosen for his military uniform (presents from the British queen to Soviet soldiers and officers during World War II). My bosses judged him to be more sharp-witted than introspective, quick to grasp a complicated operational plan and quick to make operational decisions.

Abakumov joined State Security in 1917 and spent his career in the service. During the Great Patriotic War, while directly subordinate to Stalin, he was in charge of the Red Army counterpart of Naval SMERSH. Red Army soldiers and Soviet civilians feared Abakumov's organization more than they feared the German invaders.

SMERSH arrested soldiers on the slightest suspicion of disloyalty or defeatism. It arrested most civilians in territories liberated from the

German Army and accused them of collaborating with the enemy. By the tens of thousands, these innocent citizens went before SMERSH firing squads or to labor camps in Siberia.

When Stalin purged the Jews from government ministries in 1947–49, Abakumov did retain a few he regarded as essential. He was, nevertheless, a party to the murder of the Jewish theatrical personage Mikhoels, to the execution of some 30 Jews, and to the imprisonment of others. Under Abakumov, too, the MGB committed countless additional atrocities—killing, incarcerating, or torturing alleged enemies of the people.

One such group was the Zhdanov faction in 1949–50, victims of the purge that was revealed to the Soviet public in December 1953 as the so-called "Leningrad Affair."

The circumstances of Zhdanov's death in August 1948 intrigued his followers, and one of his two legatees in the CPSU Secretariat, Kuznetsov, took the initiative to conduct an investigation. He began making private inquiries in his capacity as the Party secretary with (nominal) oversight of the organs of State Security. Kuznetsov was unaware that Stalin received MGB reports about him that were based on clandestine eavesdropping and on details from his personal bodyguards.

This information infuriated Stalin; Kuznetsov had recklessly exceeded his authority. Looking into the cause of Zhdanov's death was not the business of Kuznetsov. If anyone were to conduct an investigation, it should be Stalin, and at that time Stalin would rather not have the case investigated.

Kuznetsov was in hot water with Stalin anyway. Word had reached the Kremlin that on the walls of the Party organization building in Leningrad, Kuznetsov's photograph was larger than Stalin's. Added to this insult was the injury of misrepresentation in election returns. A letter to the CPSU Central Committee, simply signed "an old Bolshevik," had complained about the Leningrad elections to the USSR Supreme Soviet in 1946. "Although I did not cast my ballot for Comrade Kuznetsov," the letter read, "he won by a unanimous vote. How is this possible?"

More MGB reports indicated to Stalin that Kuznetsov was spearheading a conspiracy to seize power. Zhdanovites had revived the plan to reorganize the RSFSR and transfer the capital of the Republic to Leningrad. Kuznetsov was dismissed from the CPSU Secretariat in February 1949.[3]

Stalin pretended to give him a Party position that would require his transfer to the Soviet Far East, but Kuznetsov never left Moscow. He went to the CPSU Central Committee building on Staraya Ploshchad' for an appointment with Malenkov. Waiting for him in Malenkov's office were Abakumov and officers from Operod. They handcuffed and blindfolded Kuznetsov, led him to an MGB sedan with drawn shades, and took him to the basement of the Lubyanka for immediate execution. Kuznetsov's death certificate—completed by an MGB doctor, signed by Abakumov, and witnessed by the executioner—was forwarded to Stalin without comment. The press did not announce his death or print an obituary.

At this time a Soviet law banning capital punishment had been in effect since May 1947 and was not rescinded until June 1950. The killing of Kuznetsov in February 1949 violated that law; yet Soviet encyclopedias, in acknowledging his death, at first falsified the date. They recorded it as September 30, 1950, i.e., when executions were legal, and only started to give the correct date partway through Khrushchev's regime.

Two contingents took trains from Moscow to Leningrad later in February 1949. The first contingent of 500 MGB officers and other ranks included the chiefs of Operod. The second contingent filled two sleeping cars on the "Arrow" express, one car containing bodyguards and miscellaneous MGB personnel. The other car carried Malenkov, Abakumov and 20 representatives of Sled-Chast', short for Sledstvennaya Chast', the MGB Unit to Investigate Especially Important Cases.

This wave from Moscow brought about the execution of up to 100 people in the Zhdanov faction, the imprisonment of as many as 300, and the dismissal of about 2,000 in Leningrad and elsewhere. There were no trials, and Stalin ordered a media blackout. The purge was so extensive that news about it passed by word of mouth through many cities in the Soviet Union.

A macabre sideshow of the Leningrad Affair occurred in the spring of

1949, while Stalin was having Zhdanovites shot, jailed, or fired. He gave his blessing to the marriage of his only daughter, Svetlana, to Zhdanov's son Yuriy. The ceremony over, the bride and groom took up residence in the Kremlin apartment occupied by the widows of Zhdanov and Zhdanov's brother-in-law.

The CPSU Central Committee formally acknowledged the purge almost two years afterward. The Leningrad Party Organization, it said in a secret letter read aloud at a meeting of us MGB Party activists, "failed to maintain vigilance." Kuznetsov had been guilty of "self-promotion and Trotskyism," putting himself above the Politburo in MGB matters.

Malenkov, once again the CPSU Secretary with oversight of the organs of State Security, had also regained his job on the Central Committee staff as head of Party cadres. He had outlasted his rival Zhdanov and defeated the Zhdanov faction. He was now second in command to Stalin in the Party, with no strong challengers on the horizon.

5

Vigilance

Maintaining vigilance against enemies of the people was everyone's civic duty, but the backbone of vigilance was the Guards Directorate. After all, it fell mainly to us to protect Stalin's life and partly to us to defend his power. On the grounds that assassination is not defensible, I was able to rationalize our protection of Stalin's life. I drew the line, however, at flaunting the laws in defense of his power—the clandestine intrusion into private lives, the illegal arrests, the torture, the killings. That sickened me. So did those who followed Stalin down this path.

In the forefront were Guards officers of Operod who engaged in terrorism for Stalin and spied on his rivals. Operod officers were stationed not only in Moscow but also in outlying MGB offices. They worked closely in these respects with two components outside our directorate, Sled-Chast' and the Special Technical Department. For its espionage operations Operod could bring into play a large network of unpaid informants and 3,000 to 3,500 surveillants.

I'll mention in passing that Operod had additional functions— security clearances for civilians employed in the Kremlin, the CPSU Central Committee, and the Council of Ministers; periodic investigations of the leaders' personal bodyguards; security checks along the routes of travel most frequently used by the leaders; and investigations of everyone who wrote letters to Stalin, favorable or unfavorable, on the theory that any letter writer had assassination in mind.[1] The department was a major contributor of anti-Stalin, antiregime jokes to the collections of General Vlasik and Poskrebyshev, Stalin's chief of staff and personal aide. Examples:

During his 70th birthday celebration in 1949 Stalin said,

> "I'm ready to give every drop of my blood for the cause of the working class." Soon he received a note which read, "Comrade Stalin, why give your blood by drops when you can give it all at once?"

> Citizen A: Do you want to see our dear leaders?
> Citizen B: Very much.
> Citizen C: Who first?
> Citizen D: Beria's widow during Stalin's funeral.

Such jokes aside, I can't think of anything humorous to say about Operod or the Guards Directorate.

Lieutenant Colonel Okunev's section of three or four Guards officers worked out of an office that was down the hall from my boss's on the second floor of Dom Dva. Seldom did I observe others in the office except Okunev, who went there to draw from and replenish his stock of vodka. He could be seen elsewhere around the Center, staggering drunkenly through the halls and drooling. We thought Okunev's appearance and public drunkenness a disgrace to the service, and an appeal was made to retire him from the MGB. Minister Abakumov replied: "Anybody in Okunev's specialty ought to drink as much vodka as he needs, but I'll entertain your suggestions about a replacement." No one wanted his job.

The "specialty" of Okunev's section was killing, killing on oral (never written) orders from Stalin to murder outside prison walls or execute within. Stalin himself, Minister Abakumov, and General Vlasik's deputy for operations, Lynko, formulated the plans for Okunev and provided the detailed guidance.[2] (Vlasik and a succession of colonels who commanded Operod usually did not participate.) Enemies of the people were killed during, as well as before and after, the period when Soviet law banned capital punishment, from May 1947 to June 1950.³ Okunev staged his murders to look like accidents. When acting as Stalin's executioner, he escorted prisoners to the basement of the Lubyanka Prison, shot them through the head, and mopped up the blood. Then his trucks and men, under the guise of delivering provisions to the MGB officers' restaurant next door, carted the corpses to the Moscow crematorium. They dumped the ashes in the Moscow River.

Operod routinely debriefed the chiefs of each of the squads of personal bodyguards assigned to Party and government leaders, all of whom Stalin suspected might challenge his authority. Coming off duty, the bodyguards registered with their chiefs everything that had transpired on their shifts. The squad chiefs were questioned by Operod on three subjects: A) every reference to Stalin in conversations that had been overheard; B) meetings of the leaders that took place out of Stalin's sight; and C) family quarrels. Some squad chiefs skipped reporting as many details as they could—Malenkov's chief bodyguard, for example, because they were brothers-in-law.

When Abakumov became minister in 1946, he forbade the MGB from retaining derogatory information on Politburo members and CPSU Central Committee secretaries. Excepted from the order were Operod and the Special Political Directorate, which was likewise on the lookout for counterrevolutionaries and terrorists. Operod therefore prepared its reports on the leaders in one copy only, for the personal attention of Stalin. The reports were routed via Poskrebyshev, who stored them in his safe.

The Guards Directorate recruited, assigned, and paid the household servants of the leaders, but servants were off-limits as Operod sources. Stalin rejected Abakumov's proposal to use them in this manner. An Operod officer quoted Stalin as asking Abakumov, "Why bother? Operod would merely be debriefing them for information that by and large I already receive. And what if some wretched cook let slip to a

Politburo member's wife that she secretly reports to an MGB officer? No, that's too risky. I forbid it. And incidentally, Abakumov, don't let Operod use relatives of Politburo members as informants, either."

Operod supported the work of the Special Technical Department, which was eavesdropping.[4] It had the chiefs of bodyguards report when the coast was clear so that technicians could install, remove, and repair microphones in the homes and offices of Stalin's rivals. Stalin formed that department during World War II. In taking command in 1946, Minister Abakumov replaced Major General Kuzmichev with Lieutenant Colonel Karasev as the department chief and expanded the program. By 1951 more than 100 transcribers and technicians occupied two floors in one of the MGB headquarters buildings where I was located, 12 Dzerzhinskiy Street. Others manned the dozen listening posts around Moscow. The reports of this department also were prepared in one copy only, for Stalin.

One of my girlfriends, the redheaded Nina Makarova, told me that transcripts of conversations had not always been reliable. She had been in the department since its inception, she said, and "for years I monitored conversations 'live,' without having a way to check for accuracy. But as soon as Karasev got the equipment from Germany after the war, we began taping what we heard. Now I can correct errors that would formerly have slipped by." I tried to make light of her remarks. "Your mistakes must have saved some people from the Khozyain," I said, not adding that other mistakes might have resulted in punishment without cause. Nina didn't think my comment worth a smile—she was too sober-minded anyway, and that is why I stopped dating her.

Offices and a restaurant for MGB officers lined three sides of the courtyard of the main MGB Headquarters building at Dom Dva. On the fourth side was the six-story Lubyanka Prison. Here the prisoner was incarcerated in one of the 200 or so cells on the upper five floors. His view of everything but the sky was blocked by a cover over the window of the cell. He would stay in the Lubyanka for as long as it took the MGB to "prove" his guilt. He would be interrogated during irregular trips to a room on the ground floor. He might be tortured to get a confession or to implicate others.[5] He might be murdered in the basement by Okunev. If he survived the Lubyanka, he would finish his servitude in a labor camp in Siberia or in the Butyrskaya Prison, a mile and a half to the north. (Besides Lubyanka and Butyrskaya, the MGB had the Lefortovo Prison near Taganka along the Moscow River.)

Interrogations were conducted by Sled-Chast' on referrals by Stalin, based upon his whims or the reporting of Operod, the Special Technical Department, and the Special Political Directorate. Sled-Chast' assembled evidence for the airtight cases that prosecutors presented in court. Investigators on its staff of about 150 had received judicial training; yet they predicated investigations on the assumption that the accused were guilty as charged. "State Security never arrests anyone who isn't guilty," according to a bromide that the MGB chiefs reiterated. Stalin expected Sled-Chast' to obtain confessions, however outlandish the charges, by whatever means necessary.

Investigators weren't supposed to torture prisoners unless they had the approval of Abakumov, and they concealed their use of torture from prosecuting attorneys. A Sled-Chast' investigator, a neighbor of mine, told me of a prosecutor who suspected that torture had brought about a confession. He insisted on verifying the confession by questioning the accused personally. The three men gathered in an interrogation room at the Lubyanka, the prosecutor on one side of the table. On the other side, out of the prosecutor's sight, my neighbor held the switch for an electric wire connected to the prisoner's testicles. The prisoner, prompted by an occasional electrical charge, followed the script of the confession to a T. The prosecutor was satisfied. My neighbor was commended.

6

A Doctor Cries Murder

In September 1948, a few weeks after Zhdanov died, a colleague in the Guards Directorate contradicted the cause of death given in the obituary. My colleague had been the Personnel-Security Department officer for the detail of Zhdanov's personal bodyguards. He claimed to be speaking to me on the basis of authoritative information.

"The bodyguards found Comrade Zhdanov unconscious," this officer said. "He was dying from a bullet taken in the head."

"What was it—suicide?"

"I don't know, Petr Sergeyevich. It could have been a suicide, or an accident, or a murder. There wasn't an investigation. The doctors who examined the body wrote down what they did, something about Comrade Zhdanov having a heart problem, and the case was closed."

"Why was it hushed up like that?" I asked.

"I'm not sure. Maybe the chiefs of our directorate wanted Comrade Stalin to believe the death was due to natural causes. You see, if the Big Chief were told about the bullet wound, he'd blame the bodyguards for not doing their job. Our chiefs—let alone the bodyguards and me and others—would be punished."

I heard no more about the attribution of Zhdanov's death to a bullet wound. These unknown waters seemed too deep and dangerous for my

MGB friends to tread. As far as I am concerned, the question of the cause of this death is still open.

Central to the Zhdanov matter and to many events during the 1948–53 period was the Medical-Sanitary Directorate of the Kremlin (*Luchebno-Sanitarnoye Upravleniye Kremlya*, abbreviated to LSUK). Although funding for LSUK came from the Ministry of Health, then headed by Dr. Yefim Smirnov, that ministry had no control over LSUK activities. It was the Guards Directorate that hired the medical staff and told LSUK whom it could treat.

My directorate monitored the patients' care and issued security clearances for the outside medical consultants LSUK called upon to attend our leaders. Five LSUK consultants signed the Zhdanov death certificate. One of them was Stalin's personal physician, Dr. Vladimir Vinogradov, relatively unknown but an important minor figure in Soviet history.

All 600 full-time employees of LSUK, including 90 to 100 staff doctors, belonged to the MGB, specifically to the Guards Directorate. One employee was Dr. Lydiya Timashuk, a middle-aged radiologist who worked at the central LSUK facility on Kalinin Street. She had a support role in treating the ailments of the alcoholic hypochondriac Zhdanov.

I first heard about Timashuk in 1950, from the former chief of Zhdanov's bodyguards, General Boris Sakharov, a likeable man though stupid and poorly educated. The only Guards Directorate position for which he could qualify after the death of Zhdanov was Duty Officer, answering routine phone calls for our chiefs and dealing with couriers. We became acquainted late in 1948.

During a discussion in 1950 I complained to Sakharov about the extra investigative work created for us by wild accusations.

"You needn't look farther than LSUK to find false accusers," he said. "You know about Timashuk, don't you?"

I told him that I did not.

"Well, Timashuk gave us headaches with her wild accusations. I'm not alone in thinking that she's nutty. Minister Abakumov thinks she is. Still, he lets her stay in LSUK. Maybe it's safer keeping an eye on her there than turning her loose to cause trouble somewhere else."

"What did Timashuk do, Comrade General?"

"She wrote a couple of crazy letters to the Big Chief. The first letter, in November or December 1947, made the ridiculous claim that doctors were trying to kill Comrade Zhdanov. They were deliberately prescribing wrong medicines for him, she said. Then damned if Comrade Zhdanov didn't die the following year, and damned if Timashuk didn't write a second letter. That was in September or October of 1948, and she said the doctors had succeeded in their attempts at murder."

"The charges were wild, but presumably they were investigated," I said.

"Sure. The day the first letter landed on Abakumov's desk he called me into his office. 'What sort of woman is this Dr. Timashuk?' he asked. I already had the answer in my head because bodyguards observed her with Comrade Zhdanov when he visited the LSUK hospital. Before I answered the question, I wanted to double-check with my men and talk to my contacts in LSUK.

"Everybody I spoke to said they thought part of Timashuk's brain is missing. She lives in dreamland and makes up fantasies. That's how I advised our minister."

Sakharov was a handsome fellow, always in uniform despite the fact that MGB officers normally wore mufti except on ceremonial days. Now he was preening himself in front of a mirror and humming a military march. His expression indicated thoughts far removed from our discussion.

"A person like Timashuk is a threat to everybody," I said, getting the conversation back on track. "Did our minister let her accusation rest there?"

"No, Petr Sergeyevich. With the first letter, Abakumov took the precaution of directing Sled-Chast' to examine the files on all the doctors who prescribed medicine for Comrade Zhdanov. There were a slew of them. He ran from one to the next for remedies.

"Sled-Chast' pulled in a few doctors for questioning, discrete questioning to avoid a possible uproar. Of course, nothing against them was uncovered because nothing substantial was in Timashuk's accusations to begin with. Abakumov decided that somebody had 'inspired' Timashuk for the purpose of getting him in hot water with the Big Chief."

"That's how it stood after the first letter," I prompted.

"Yes, but then she wrote the second letter. There was hell to pay considering that Comrade Zhdanov had just died. Abakumov told Sled-Chast' to reopen the investigation and put more oomph into it. This time they threw three doctors in the Lubyanka and gave them a tough going over—you know how Sled-Chast' usually interrogates, Petr Sergeyevich. It was not the toughest going over that can be dished out, but one of the doctors died in jail, they said from pneumonia. Who'd believe that?"

"I don't know anyone who would. Did the doctors confess?"

"No confessions. Nothing. I told you Timashuk is nutty. Regardless, our minister didn't want to take any chances, so he revoked the security clearances for the two doctors who lived through a hard spell in the Lubyanka."

Sakharov also told me what Abakumov had done, or rather had not done, about his hypothesis that an unknown person or persons "inspired" Timashuk to write to Stalin. He did not inform Stalin about the first letter. Perhaps Abakumov suspected that if he were its target, Stalin himself had been the "architect."

Timashuk's second letter worsened the problem for Abakumov. He could hardly tell Stalin about it without admitting the existence of the first letter and trying to explain why Stalin had not been informed. No explanation would satisfy Stalin. He would blame Abakumov and the Guards Directorate, anybody and everybody, for failure to prevent the "murder" of Zhdanov.

And as Abakumov also knew, Stalin so distrusted subordinates that he insisted on being informed about any fact or allegation that smacked of conspiracy. Stalin believed that conspiracies abounded, that conspirators meant to kill him or, at minimum, to dilute his power; no one was above suspicion. Thus the doctors who murdered Zhdanov might just as well be preparing to murder Stalin, and Abakumov was failing to fulfill his obligation of protecting Stalin's life.

Colonel Goryshev confirmed that these worries inhibited our minister from disclosing the first two Timashuk letters to Stalin. My boss mentioned Abakumov's concerns later in 1950 when he told me that Timashuk had resumed writing accusatory letters. In her third she reiterated the charge about doctors misprescribing for Zhdanov and added a new claim: they used the same method to kill Zhdanov's brother-in-law, Aleksandr Shcherbakov.

When Shcherbakov had died in May 1945, doctors affiliated with LSUK had listed a heart condition as the cause. He was an obvious candidate for this kind of fatal illness—grossly overweight, a heavy smoker with asthmatic wheezes, a drinker in gigantic quantities, always on the go. While not as influential as Zhdanov, Shcherbakov was also a CPSU secretary. He simultaneously held the positions of senior political officer in the Soviet Armed Forces and chief of Sovinformburo (Soviet Information Bureau, a propaganda organization of the Party).

"How did Abakumov handle the third letter?" I asked Goryshev.

"Gingerly. He took it to the Kremlin, to Poskrebyshev."

More than anyone else, Aleksandr Poskrebyshev had Stalin's confidence and shared his secrets. He arrived in Moscow in the early 1920s to work under Lenin. After Stalin succeeded Lenin, Poskrebyshev became Stalin's chief of staff in the mid-1930s—private secretary, guardian of appointments, ghostwriter, screener of reports, accomplice in actions against enemies of the people. Poskrebyshev collaborated with Stalin in daily, direct supervision of the MGB and the Party, and Stalin consulted him on the composition of the Politburo and the CPSU Secretariat.

"It was logical for Abakumov to go to Poskrebyshev with the letter," I said. "I've heard that they get along well."

"Oh, they do, Petr Sergeyevich, and I venture to say that Abakumov wanted to trade on Poskrebyshev's friendship with General Vlasik. Needless to say, LSUK comes under Vlasik as the chief of our directorate, and I'm sure you know too that Vlasik and Poskrebyshev enjoy... er, they get together socially."

The sex-and-drinking orgies staged monthly by Vlasik, Poskrebyshev, and Stalin's son Vasiliy were as well known in the Guards Directorate as they were well concealed from Stalin. Held by Stalin on the same high level of trust with Poskrebyshev, Vlasik had helped to raise the motherless boy Vasiliy.

"So did Poskrebyshev show the letter to the Big Chief?"

"Far from that," Goryshev said. "They agreed that the only thing to do was to suppress all three letters from her and henceforth ignore Timashuk's accusations. Abakumov returned from the Kremlin with a warning to Sled-Chast'."

"A warning?"

"Our Minister told Sled-Chast', 'If the investigation of the doctors is reopened again, we'll all lose our heads.'"

Stalin would see to that.

7

The Fourth Letter

More than six months went by before Goryshev, in the summer of 1951, spoke to me again about Lydiya Timashuk's letters charging murder in the deaths of Zhdanov and Shcherbakov.

"I thought that after her third letter, Abakumov and Poskrebyshev buried those allegations," I said.

"They didn't reckon with Ryumin of Sled-Chast'."

"You mean that insignificant 'little Mishka'?"

"The same," said Goryshev.

"Little Mishka" and I had a nodding acquaintance from passing each other in the corridors of Dom Dva. Guards officers told me that Lieutenant Colonel Ryumin held a law degree and was reputed to be a good interrogator but nevertheless stood on a low rung in the ladder of command. His title was investigator, one notch below senior investigator, and he held a subordinate job in a section within one of the Sled-Chast' departments. I asked how Ryumin and Timashuk were connected.

"You remember that Abakumov gave the Timashuk letters to Sled-Chast', and Sled-Chast' ran investigations in 1947–49. Well, down in the depths of Sled-Chast' Ryumin came into possession of the file on Timashuk. Recently, he sent the third of the Timashuk letters to the Big Chief with a cover letter that he himself wrote. That makes four letters, altogether."

"It's mighty strange his bosses in Sled-Chast' and Abakumov let Ryumin do that," I said.

"They didn't even know about it, Petr Sergeyevich. Poskrebyshev didn't know about it either. Someone personally handed Ryumin's letter and the last letter from Timashuk to Comrade Stalin.... Hmm, I think Malenkov is a likely candidate. He's the CPSU secretary who has the organs of State Security under his wing. Or Beria could have been the channel from Ryumin to the Big Chief. There's no love lost between Beria and our minister, as we know."

Goryshev took an incoming phone call from Vlasik. They discussed a personal bodyguard who had reported for duty with the smell of alcohol on his breath. After agreeing to fire the officer, Goryshev resumed our talk.

"Our comrade general pays attention to the really important things," he said sarcastically. "Now, where were we?"

"The Big Chief has one letter from Timashuk and a cover letter from Ryumin," I said. "What did 'little Mishka' write?"

"That Minister Abakumov ordered Sled-Chast' to close the investigation, and that getting to the bottom of Timashuk's story would be difficult. Ryumin, I suppose, considers himself up to the task and a candidate for it."

"Difficult?" I said. "Why, all Comrade Stalin need do is ask the question Abakumov did: What kind of woman is Timashuk? Everyone knows she's a trifle crazy."

"Not crazy according to Ryumin, Petr Sergeyevich. He made her out to be a true heroine. He explained to the Big Chief why the investigation would be difficult: because one of the doctors died in prison during interrogation, as you know. Ryumin said that this doctor should have been considered a prime suspect in a big conspiracy against the Soviet leadership."

Poskrebyshev warned Abakumov about Ryumin's stunt and also told Vlasik, Goryshev said. He could not predict what Stalin would do next, but to him the outlook for Abakumov looked bleak.

Between the times when Timashuk wrote her second and third letters to Stalin, I began to date Marina Makeyeva. She was a good-looking young woman—red cheeks in an oval face, brown eyes that sparkled, dark blond hair, a good figure. Marina had been employed for several years as a stenographer-typist in the Secretariat of Politburo Member Kaganovich.

The courtship turned more serious under my bosses' increasing pressure on me to marry, pressure from as high as a deputy minister. To the MGB, bachelorhood wasn't a natural state for a man past 25 years of age. I made sure that the files in the Center contained no derogatory information on Marina and her family—no enemies of the people in her background—unlike the obstruction to taking Tanya Zakharova as my wife in 1946. I married in June 1949 in the standard civil ceremony, the only kind that the Soviet state would recognize.

For the first half-year after our wedding Marina and I resided with her parents and grandmother in an apartment typical for Muscovites: one room 20 by 30 feet for the five of us, food cooked on an electric burner, no bathtub, a washbasin shared with two other families, an outside privy. When Marina became pregnant, I told Goryshev I would quit unless he found us better quarters in one of the Guards Directorate's dozen apartment buildings.

Within two weeks I was assigned an apartment with a balcony at 48/A Chkalov Street. This L-shaped, dark grey, nine-floor structure in central Moscow held some 450 Guards families, living in single rooms. Two families and my wife Marina and I shared a common entrance hall, kitchen, and bathroom, and we split the utility bills three ways.

Marina and our baby daughter Larisa stayed behind at a dacha we rented in the summer of 1951, and I returned alone to 48/A Chkalov Street on a Sunday evening in August. Walking through the five-story archway from Chkalov Street, I entered the courtyard. It was brimming with Guards officers. They sat on benches around wooden tables, paced around in twos and threes, and clustered near the entrances to the apartment building. They spoke in undertones and took swigs from bottles passed from hand to hand. No one smiled. The somber scene seemed like a party after the funeral of a friend. I hesitated at the archway.

"Welcome back, Petr Sergeyevich," several greeted me.

"Join us as soon as you get your luggage inside," one said.

"We've got something to tell you," said another.

"Bring vodka," demanded Vasya, a captain too outspoken to go any higher in the MGB. "We're running short at this table."

A bottle of vodka in hand, I hurried to rejoin them. "What's this all about?" I asked.

Minister Abakumov was under arrest. Abakumov of all people!

He had gone from his office in Dom Dva to meet Stalin in the Kremlin and straight from there to a cell in the Lubyanka Prison. None of us knew the reason, and all of us were too stunned and too frightened to hazard guesses. From the perspective of Guards officers, our minister was a Stalin loyalist if ever there was one. But then, were not we all?

We rehashed the points in Abakumov's favor. Morale in the MGB was high. Old-timers said that Abakumov had raised State Security effectiveness to an all-time high. He had been faithful to Stalin's orders in purging the Zhdanovites and, within limits, in ridding the MGB of Jewish personnel. He had gone the extra mile to keep Beria out of State Security affairs, in accordance with the wishes of Stalin. He gave first priority to the protection of the Big Chief's life—frequent meetings with the chiefs of the Guards Directorate, personal supervision of security at the Red Square parades, on and on in that vein.

"What more could the Big Chief want of our minister?" Vasya asked. No one answered.

"Maybe the arrest was a mistake, and the Big Chief will release Abakumov," someone suggested. The rest of us rejected the thought without saying why. Not even Vasya was so foolhardy as to blurt out that Stalin never admitted his errors.

"Maybe Abakumov will eventually come back to the MGB," said someone who must have known that he was whistling past the graveyard. Stalin hadn't spared the lives of two of Abakumov's six predecessors, and there were rumors of his having killed two others. Of the former chiefs of State Security, only Beria and a protégé of his (Vsevolod Merkulov) were still alive and free.

My colleagues reported that Abakumov was not the only one in the MGB front office who had been arrested while I was on holiday. Seven of his nine or ten deputy ministers were with him in the Lubyanka. The first deputy minister had escaped, however, and for the interim he was in nominal charge of the MGB.

We stayed in the courtyard long after darkness fell. We cast about for positive signs, and at last Oleg remembered that, according to people who had seen him on the previous Friday, our chief hadn't appeared to be perturbed.

"What crap!" Vasya disagreed. "General Vlasik doesn't get ruffled unless the Big Chief kicks his behind."

The group at our table laughed. It was the only time anyone in the courtyard did that night.

I encountered the wife of Colonel Ivan Chernov, Chief of Abakumov's Secretariat, early in the following week. We had been friends since our days together in Naval SMERSH. Leaving her office in the Center, she caught sight of me in Dom Dva and pulled me aside. In tears Chernova said that her husband expected to be arrested in the near future.

Similarly, Lieutenant Colonel Kuznetsov (not to be confused with the Kuznetsov executed in February 1949), who headed the detail of Abakumov's personal bodyguards, awaited imminent arrest, his wife told me in September. I did my best to comfort her, but Kuznetsova was inconsolable.

"They questioned him yesterday, Petr Sergeyevich. They're questioning him today. They'll question him tomorrow." Her voice rose. "Soon they'll take him to the Lubyanka, and they'll beat him till he tells them everything he knows about Abakumov. Then they'll beat him till he tells them the lies they want to hear." She began to sob. "Oh God, he never did anything to harm the Big Chief. Can't you think of anything that can be done for him, Petr Sergeyevich?"

I murmured something unintelligible and patted her shoulder. If Kuznetsova hadn't been so distraught, she would not have asked such a pointless question. An officer with her years in State Security ought to know that nothing tempered Stalin's rampages.

The toll from Stalin's purge of the MGB went higher that autumn of 1951. Just as their wives had feared, Colonel Chernov of the minister's

Secretariat and Lieutenant Colonel Kuznetsov of the Guards Directorate were arrested. So was Yakov Broverman, a Jewish colonel who drafted Abakumov's correspondence and orders, and the chief and the two deputy chiefs of Sled-Chast'.

By the spring of 1952 dozens of other Sled-Chast' officers had been jailed. Lieutenant Colonel Kuznetsov received a 15-year term for failure to report misconduct by the minister. MGB tribunals also doled out labor camp sentences to the subordinate officers in Sled-Chast', up to 25 years for some.

One deputy minister later returned to work in the Center, another was reassigned away from Moscow, and the remaining five disappeared. Stalin held in abeyance disposition of the cases of Abakumov, Chernov, Broverman, and the three top men from Sled-Chast'. They were kept in the Lubyanka but were not interrogated.

The fate of Abakumov's wife touched me personally. During my previous tour of duty in Moscow, while she was a fellow officer in Naval SMERSH, Tonya Smirnova and I had dated. Then just as Tonya started encouraging me to go beyond hand-holding, I got wind of her relationship with Abakumov. She was his mistress—or "mattress," as one officer put it. Hardly one to vie for a lady's hand when an adverse outcome was a foregone conclusion, hardly one to alienate a man so powerful, I backed off.

Abakumov divorced his first wife to marry Tonya. Later our paths crossed in the vicinity of Dom Dva, and she always greeted me with a smile. Each time we chatted briefly about trivial things before I excused myself and hurried away. Far be it from midlevel officer Deriabin to arouse Abakumov's jealousy.

On the day when Abakumov went to the Lubyanka, Tonya and their newborn baby were staying at an MGB rest home in the North Caucasus spa of Mineral'nyye Vody. The MGB flew mother and child to Moscow. There Tonya underwent interrogation in a safehouse located a few blocks from her husband's cell.

The confession by Tonya included an admission that Abakumov had spent 70,000 rubles of MGB money on a gift during her pregnancy. He had arranged for our representatives in Vienna to purchase a Western-made baby carriage. After ten days' questioning, Tonya was released.

The MGB dispatched her and the child to Siberia for resettlement under an assumed last name. I heard no more about them.

At Goryshev's insistence, I accepted election in 1949 to be acting secretary of the Party organization in the Personnel-Security Department. The current secretary, Major Shesteryakov, had become ill with terminal cancer. I remained in that unwanted, unpaid, part-time job for three years while continuing my counterintelligence work. A special advantage of the position was the opportunity it gave me to learn classified information that the CPSU Central Committee disseminated to us Party activists but not beyond.

Stalin had appointed Politburo Member Nikita Khrushchev as secretary of the Moscow Party Organization in 1949. Two years later Khrushchev chose to come to the MGB Officers' Club and address several hundred of us Party activists from State Security in the windowless auditorium. Such a visit was without precedent.

Not by chance, Khrushchev's subject was our responsibility to the Party. His underlying purpose apparently was to invigorate CPSU discipline—for which read "loyalty to Stalin"—in the aftermath of the arrests of the MGB chiefs in August 1951, the month before Khrushchev spoke. He mentioned our former minister only once during his 45 minutes on the podium. He said that Abakumov had failed to detect "the nationalistic-Trotskyite tendencies" of the Leningrad Party Organization. (In other words, Abakumov had been remiss before he and Malenkov led the purge of the Zhdanov faction in 1949–50.) Khrushchev thus implied that, for this reason, Abakumov, his deputies, and many other MGB officers were being sent to prison.

Later the CPSU Central Committee repeated the charge about Abakumov's "lack of vigilance" regarding the Leningrad Party Organization. This and additional accusations appeared in a secret Central Committee letter that was read aloud to us MGB Party activists a month or two after Khrushchev's speech. Among the misdeeds of Abakumov were

- Failure to take "active measures" against Zionists and failure to heed the Central Committee about removing Broverman from the minister's Secretariat. (True, for Abakumov evaded Stalin's order to dismiss all Jews, and Broverman was one whom he protected.)
- Misappropriation of government funds. (True, according to the confession of Abakumov's wife, Tonya.)
- Ignoring "Communist moral principles" by participation in extramarital affairs and misusing government property by entertaining these women in bedrooms of our officers' club and of MGB safehouses. (True, from what I heard in the Guards Directorate.)

Abakumov had a very serious personal weakness that eventually became part of the pretext for arresting him. The weakness was women. Abakumov went to extremes, not in aberrations like the rapist Beria, but in frequency. He compounded the problem by taking his women to apartments that were supposed to be reserved for quite another type of clandestine meeting, between MGB officers and their agents. Time after time Abakumov compromised these safehouses, which thereupon lost their operational utility, by exposing them to outsiders—actresses, cheating wives, secretaries, foreign visitors, God knows who. Abakumov also took girlfriends to a special room in the MGB club where he stored expensive gifts for them. (Many other State Security generals were similarly guilty.)

One such girlfriend was Olga Chekhova, a German movie star. Abakumov had dispatched a plane to Berlin for her. She was flown to Moscow and taken to the best MGB safehouse for a 72-hour rendezvous. I have seen her photograph in MGB files. Then in her late 40s, she was singularly attractive. Olga was a distant relative of the Russian writer Anton Chekov. She was the descendent of an uncle of his who moved to Germany in the late 18th or early 19th century. She had circulated among the highest levels of the Nazi leadership, and she had been a Soviet agent since before the war. MGB files contained photographs of her with Hitler, Goering, and Goebbels together; with Martin Bormann; and with the last Gestapo Chief, Mueller—all taken before and during World War II. State Security recruited Olga before World War II but lost contact with her during the war, resuming the contact toward the end of 1945. As of 1952 the MGB had determined

Olga resided in West Germany, was considering her for operational use, and for the stated reason of tracking down a rumor that she made a trip to Moscow just after World War II (the one sponsored by Abakumov, presumably) asked the Berlin/Karlshorst residency to find out more about her.

Abakumov, furthermore, had been inattentive to complaints that the chief of his Secretariat, Chernov, was rude toward and uncooperative with elements of the MGB. Finally, our former minister had "evaded Party discipline," a catch-all phrase that could mean whatever the prosecution wanted.

I confided in Goryshev the basic reason indicated by Khrushchev and the CPSU Central Committee for the purge in the MGB. He expressed skepticism that Stalin jailed Abakumov for poor coverage of the Leningrad Party Organization. Goryshev said that he had an idea about the true reason but would not share it until checking further.

He phoned me in a few days. "About our last discussion. Interesting news. Come to my office during the afternoon break when nobody's around."

"I've confirmed my suspicions," Goryshev said as soon as I had closed the door. "We lost Abakumov and the others due to that damned Ryumin from Sled-Chast'."

"Did 'little Mishka' write another letter?"

"He didn't have to. His original letter and the third one from Timashuk caused all the trouble. The Big Chief summoned Abakumov. 'I understand you've been investigating Dr. So-and-So,' Comrade Stalin said. Abakumov admitted this, and then Comrade Stalin sprang the trap. 'I'd like to question the doctor myself,' he said. Abakumov had to say that the doctor died in prison while undergoing interrogation."

Goryshev interrupted his account, unlocked a desk drawer, and set out a bottle of the best Armenian brandy. I handed him glasses from the tray holding the water carafe, and my boss poured three fingers of brandy in each glass. We lifted our drinks to each other and drank the brandy in a single draught.

"You're more accustomed than I am to resorting to alcohol in crises, Petr Sergeyevich, but we both know why that was needed."

"Yes, Serafim Vasilyevich," I said in a low voice. Never before had we drunk together, nor would we ever again.

"Well, Abakumov's meeting with the Big Chief went from bad to worse. Comrade Stalin dragged out confirmation of everything Ryumin had written. And the existence of the previous two Timashuk letters. And her contention that LSUK doctors killed Comrade Zhdanov and Comrade Shcherbakov. And, of course, the fact that an investigation was conducted off and on for several years without the Big Chief being told.

"When he finished extracting the facts from Abakumov, the Big Chief pressed an emergency button, and, by prearrangement, his bodyguards came running. He ordered them to handcuff their minister—our minister—and have him taken to solitary confinement in the Lubyanka."

"Why arrest the deputy ministers?"

"Comrade Stalin thinks they took part in Abakumov's conspiracy to keep him from knowing about the investigation. Likewise the others, including the chiefs of Sled-Chast'."

"From the standpoint of Comrade Stalin," I said, "a conspiracy did exist."

"Oh, yes, but keep in mind that two conspirators haven't been arrested," Goryshev said, "and they haven't because the Big Chief is unaware of their involvement."

Goryshev meant the conspirators Poskrebyshev and Vlasik. Perhaps in the hope that they would intervene to save him, Abakumov had managed to hold back their involvement from Stalin.

Unanswered was the question of why Ryumin—and why Timashuk, for that matter—wrote to Stalin? No one with whom I spoke knew their motives. The least sinister explanation is this: Ryumin was driven by ambition, Timashuk by zeal, and both by righteousness. But conceivably a person wanting to depose Abakumov "inspired" the four letters. Abakumov suspected this, and if he was right, I think that person could have been Beria.

8

A Dread Disease

Relations between Stalin and Beria deteriorated during the years 1946 through 1948. The earliest sign of Stalin's distrust was his dismissal of Beriaites from the MGB and, on suspicion of misplaced loyalty, Georgians from the Guards Directorate. Stalin then went out of his way to slight Beria. He promoted the chiefs of bodyguard details for all Politburo members except Beria's chief, who remained a colonel as the rest moved up in rank to general. Stalin would agree to meeting Malenkov but then cancel the appointment if Malenkov said that Beria planned to join them.

At the beginning of 1949, Directorate Number One, under the Council of Ministers, was on the verge of success. The imminent addition of atomic weapons to the USSR's arsenal reflected well on Directorate Chief Beria, bringing about a reversal in Stalin's treatment of him. This was shown initially in the Republic of Georgia, where local events often foreshadowed developments on the national scene. In January 1949, a half-year before the first test explosion of a Soviet A-bomb, the Communist Party Organization in Georgia elected Beria to become an honorary member of its Central Committee, like Stalin. Soon the Georgian Party newspaper commented that the republic had two "fathers," in the persons of Stalin and Beria.

Stalin rewarded Beria's achievements at Directorate Number One with another Order of Lenin in March 1949. The front page of *Pravda* displayed a two-column photograph of Beria and a joint message to him from the CPSU Central Committee and the Council of Ministers. It began, "We warmly congratulate you, the true pupil of Lenin and colleague of Stalin, on your 50th birthday. . . ." The unwritten message was that Stalin held Beria in high esteem.

Annually Stalin took long working vacations at southern spas, away from Moscow's winter weather. A retinue of nearly 1,000 bodyguards, plainclothesmen, servants, and others from the Guards Directorate accompanied him, 300 to 400 plainclothesmen for whom I was the personnel-security officer.[1] Colleagues told me about the air of conviviality whenever the Georgians Stalin and Beria got together at the Black Sea resort of Sochi in 1949 and 1950. They laughed at each other's jokes, told in the Georgian dialect. They drank Georgian wine. They prepared shashlik Georgian-style over open fires, and Beria, otherwise a vegetarian, ate the lamb.

The charm Beria exuded for Stalin and, when he wanted, for others was not his only commendable trait. He was intelligent, fast on his feet, humorous, and moderate with alcohol. He had endless energy and an enormous capacity for work. His vision of our country and the world, I believe, was broader and more objective than Stalin's and the rest of our leaders'. But the character defects of Beria—sly, overly ambitious, cruel, and ruthless—outweighed whatever good could be said about him.

Also, he was addicted to sex. Beria did not rein in his lust for females, and this was a subject of everyday gossip in the MGB and among Muscovites in general. Stalin apparently shrugged off mutterings about Beria's sexual deeds. One complaint went all the way to the Politburo during the Great Patriotic War. On train trips to battlefronts, it was reported, Beria took along two railway carriages filled with "secretaries who in reality are whores." Stalin's reply suspended discussion. "Comrade Beria is tired and overworked," he said.

Stalin, with his appetite for gossip, must have listened to some of the accounts that I heard in the Guards Directorate, but he did nothing to stop Beria. One set of these Beria-on-the-prowl stories by my fellow officers matched in all major respects. Whenever Beria's plump but attractive wife Nina and their son were away from Moscow—and Beria sent them away often—he cruised by car through Moscow with his chauffeur and the colonel in charge of his bodyguard detail. They searched for teenage girls to kidnap.

When they found a teenager who fit Beria's specifications, the two aides forced her into the car. They drove to the Beria residence, a house isolated behind a high wall off Aleksey Tolstoy Street. Unless the young girl acquiesced to having intercourse with Beria, she was either over-powered or drugged, then raped. After Beria had finished with the girl, the chauffeur and the Guards colonel drove her back to where the escapade had begun.[2]

One teenager happened to be the daughter of a fairly high-ranking government official. The mother threatened to name Beria to the CPSU Central Committee as the rapist of her daughter if he did not provide a comfortable life for the girl. Beria paid the blackmail, in tens of thousands of rubles.

A passage in the memoirs of Svetlana Alliluyeva suggests the possibility that her father, Stalin, knew about Beria's rapes of teenage girls. Ms. Alliluyeva wrote of an incident in 1941, when she was a 13- or 14-year-old visiting her friend, Beria's wife:

"I was talked into staying the night. Next morning my father suddenly called in a fury. Using unprintable words, he shouted, 'Come back at once! I don't trust Beria!' I left completely baffled."[3]

It is not easy for me to understand why Ms. Alliluyeva was baffled at the time she wrote her memoirs. Rumors of Beria's rapes became common coinage among women in the Soviet elite.

In connection with my work for the Personnel-Security Department of the Guards Directorate, I learned still more and still worse about Beria during the winter of 1949–50. A Guards lieutenant phoned me then for an urgent, private meeting.

While he was on the way to my office, I looked through his file for clues as to the problem he might present. I did not know him well—the lieutenant was quite new to the bodyguards and to the detail of several hundred plainclothesmen who patrolled the Arbat, a main Moscow thoroughfare that combines features of New York City's 42d Street and Washington's Pennsylvania Avenue. The file was spotless. It showed, moreover, that my directorate had hired his wife to be a servant in Beria's home.

"Yes, Lieutenant?"

"Comrade Major, I come to you in confidence."

"Of course. You see that we have the room to ourselves, and the door is closed."

"Oh, yes, Comrade Major, but I . . ."

The lad flushed, then paled and seemed on the verge of fainting. I told him to be seated and poured a glass of water for him.

"Thank you, Comrade Major. I—I come to you because of Zhenya— she's my wife, Yevgeniya Ivanovna. She is faithful to me," he said defiantly. "She's not at fault."

"Who is?"

From the back of his throat, the lieutenant spoke the full name very, very slowly. "Lavrentiy Pavlovich Beria."

"Did I hear you say 'Comrade Beria'?"

"Yes, Comrade Major," and in the same manner, eyes downcast, he repeated Beria's full name.

"And why is Comrade Beria at fault?" I was sounding like an interrogator, softly though I put my questions.

"Zhenya's not to blame." Again defiance. "Lavrentiy Pavlovich Beria raped her... right there where she works, in his house. Lavrentiy Pavlovich Beria paid her off with coupons to buy a dress. Some payment for what he did!"[4]

"Just a moment, Lieutenant. Consider what you're saying."

"I am—I do, sir."

"All right, your wife tells you that she's been raped."

"Lavrentiy Pavlovich Beria has syphilis, Comrade Major, and he gave his syphilis to Zhenya."

"And I'm supposed to believe you."

"Please believe me, sir," he said.

"Well, don't expect any sympathy or help from me with your outlandish statements about Comrade Beria."

Yet the young man spoke the truth, I was sure, except about Beria's syphilis. Venereal disease had not been hinted at in the sex stories about Beria that went around the Guards Directorate.

For the better part of an hour I questioned the lieutenant, who stuck to his story. He said that for confirmation I should check with the LSUK doctors who had diagnosed Zhenya's case of syphilis the day before. Gradually I eased up on the unfortunate fellow, and I sent him away with my promise to follow through as soon as possible. I hastened to my boss.

"You've done well," Goryshev said, "especially by reinforcing to the lieutenant that nobody should be told of the allegation about Comrade Beria's syphilis.

"Now," he sighed, "the case is in my hands. Leave the man's file with me for the time being, Petr Sergeyevich. When it's returned to you, don't enter anything about the ... er, report. Be sure to destroy your notes from the interview."

I didn't see either the file or the lieutenant again. Goryshev notified me the next day to fill the man's vacant slot in the plainclothes detail for the Arbat. Subsequently he told me that the Guards Directorate gave Beria a false reason for transferring the lieutenant's wife from his household staff. Goryshev added, "She's responding well to treatment, I'm told."

My wife Marina worked in the Kremlin building where Beria's Secretariat was located, and she harped on how envious she was of the 20 women Beria employed there, all blonds like herself. They did not work as hard as Marina, they came and went as they pleased, they spent office hours in shops and beauty parlors, and they dressed better than Marina, better than some of the wives of our leaders. I got tired of hearing about it.

I saved my information about Beria's syphilis until she next mentioned the "ideal conditions" in his Secretariat.

"Maybe you ought to apply for a job there," I teased.

"You haven't suggested that before, Petya—you and your innuendos about the 'off-duty assistance' by Comrade Beria's secretaries. What changed your mind?"

"Oh, something that came up in the Center the other day."

"It would be wonderful if you would help me get work with Comrade Beria."

"Up to a point I would help you, Marochka."

"Up to what point?"

"I'd help you dye your hair a lighter blond," I laughed.

"Go on—laugh some more." My wife was nettled. "I can take care of myself."

"Can you take care of syphilis?"

"What? Syphilis?"

"Not so loud, Marochka. I merely asked whether you think you can take care of syphilis."

"I don't know what you're rambling on about or why. What does syphilis have to do with Comrade Beria?"

"Your Comrade Beria has it."

Marina knew that Guards officers learned things about our leaders that never became generally known in Moscow, much less a topic in *Pravda*. Although I did not hear any more about the ideal conditions in Beria's Secretariat, I thought she was unconvinced of his having syphilis. Unconvinced, that is, until the following summer.

Very few Muscovites enjoyed the privilege of owning dachas, but most Guards officers earned the income to rent rooms in dachas for summer vacations. Marina and I did each year. We invited a Guards captain and his wife to spend a weekend with us during our vacation in 1950.

Prospects for an enjoyable weekend grew even brighter when I met the childless couple at the village train station. The captain introduced me to his remarkably beautiful wife and proffered their armloads of vodka, wine, and delicacies. Marina immediately took to the captain's wife. While they chattered in the dacha and fussed over our little Larisa, we men sauntered out to walk through the fields. The attention that had been given my infant daughter led the captain to tell me his story.

Formerly his wife was one of the blonds employed in Beria's Secretariat, and his wife had been forced into having intercourse with him. As a result, she contracted syphilis. Higher-ups in the Guards

Directorate claimed that the diagnosis regarding his wife had been Beria's first knowledge of his condition. They arranged medical care for the wife at LSUK and her transfer to other work.

"But, Petr Sergeyevich, Olga can't bear children due to the disease she caught from Comrade Beria. To be honest, in bed we're like brother and sister, not husband and wife. I love her all the same. . . ." The captain's voice broke. "It's shitty. . . His curse on her lives eternally. . . ." Crying, he turned away.

We went back to the dacha and drank ourselves stupid. After our guests left on Monday morning, I told Marina. The epithets she used to describe Beria were not ladylike.

In 1948, 1949, and 1950 Stalin had gone on vacation to Sochi in southern RSFSR, some 50 miles from the border with the Georgian Republic. In 1951 he went to another resort on the Black Sea, this in Georgia. The purpose of his choosing to go to that republic at that time was to commence undermining Beria's power with an attack on Beriaites in their stronghold.

This proved to be Stalin's last trip from Moscow. He was too busy to leave the capital in the winter of 1952–53, and he died in March 1953. Beria returned to Georgia from time to time, though, mending political fences and rallying supporters.

The first report to reach Moscow that the Stalin-Beria relationship again had soured was an announcement by the Georgian Party's Central Committee in November 1951. Muscovites read that the Party accused three senior officials of protecting unnamed criminals. At MGB headquarters we recognized all three as Beriaites, which meant to us that Beria had lost his grip on affairs in his native Georgia. The Big Chief was back in the driver's seat there and back on the warpath.

Stalin's purge in Georgia later became known as the "Mingrelian Conspiracy," since Beria, the Mingrelian, was the ultimate target and many of those implicated were from that district of Georgia. The conspirators allegedly belonged to a Mingrelian nationalist organization that, with the assistance of "imperialist powers," intended to overthrow the local regime. The case against the conspirators was manufactured from false evidence, as MGB officers told me in 1952 and as

Khrushchev said publicly years afterward. Stalin masterminded the "Mingrelian Conspiracy" to dilute Beria's power.

The purge of Beriaites lasted into the winter of 1952, long after Stalin had left the Georgian resort for Moscow. According to the Georgian press, it resulted in hundreds—thousands, according to MGB officers—of dismissals from jobs in the Georgian Party and government. Some of the most senior Beriaites were arrested.

When the Guards Directorate personnel accompanying Stalin once more returned to the Center from Georgia, they told me that Beria had not visited Stalin during his vacation of 1951. The nights of the two Georgians engaging in Georgian revelries had ended.

I mentioned this to Goryshev at one of our periodic off-the-record sessions in his office.

"So? So? You've jumped to a conclusion," my boss said. "Sometimes you're too smart for your own good, Petr Sergeyevich. Out with it. What are you getting at?"

"Well, I was thinking back to the case of the lieutenant's wife, the woman with syphilis. Remember? I put that together with the Big Chief not socializing with Comrade Beria any more and with reports on the purge of Beria's men in Georgia. I wound up with the notion that someone of Comrade Stalin's noble character would be distressed to find out that a Politburo member was infecting women with syphilis."

"The Big Chief didn't hear about it from me," Goryshev said in a defensive tone. "Somebody else told him." He waved his hand in the direction of the nearby office of Guards Directorate Chief Vlasik. "Not face to face, Vlasik to Comrade Stalin. Poskrebyshev was only too pleased to convey the evidence about Beria's syphilis."

Guards officers surmised that Poskrebyshev disliked Beria.

"Comrade Stalin still doesn't know that our directorate has had this information so long—two years or more, I'd estimate," my boss said. "I needn't explain to you, Petr Sergeyevich, why we kept this secret to ourselves."

Goryshev did not have to tell me that the Guards Directorate feared retaliation by Beria if the secret were leaked to Stalin.

"In addition," he continued, "maybe Vlasik kept the syphilis a secret all this time as a way of returning a favor by Beria. Without Beria, Vlasik would have been out on his ass in 1946."

"Back when the Big Chief reorganized the bodyguards."

"Back then, yes," Goryshev said. "Comrade Stalin intended to shove Vlasik out and send him to unimportant duties away from Moscow. So Vlasik went down south to the Big Chief's dacha on Lake Ritsa to ask for a second chance. On instructions from the Big Chief, the body-guards didn't let him inside the grounds.

"While Vlasik was wandering around the lake, along came Beria who took him by the hand and led him to the Big Chief—the bodyguards, naturally, couldn't stand in the way of Beria. Whatever he told Comrade Stalin won Vlasik his present job. He could thank Beria for that."

"But why advise the Big Chief now, Serafim Vasilyevich?"

"It wasn't 'now.' It was after the arrest of Minister Abakumov when he was told the syphilis secret; that is, a month or two before he decided to go on vacation in Georgia last fall."

"All right, but why advise the Big Chief at all?"

"That takes some guesswork," Goryshev said. "My guess is that Poskrebyshev and Vlasik suspected the Big Chief was about to learn the fact independently, from an outsider. By necessity, to protect them-selves, they had to beat the outsider to the punch. The Big Chief was advised that Beria has syphilis, although not that LSUK made the diag-nosis a long time ago."

My boss withdrew two cigarettes from a pack of Stalin's Severnaya Palmyras, handed one to me, and let me light his. He took two or three deep puffs before resuming.

"Anyway, the Big Chief went into a rage. He was furious because he thought he could have contracted syphilis from Beria—not that such a thing would be possible just from their eating and drinking together, but the Big Chief must be ignorant about the way the disease is transmitted."

"Except that between two men ..."

"None of your 'except thats' today," Goryshev said stiffly. "Hmm ... To continue, the Big Chief didn't want Beria to know that he knew about the syphilis—if Beria knew that he knew, it might provoke Beria into doing something extreme, something that could threaten lives.

"The Big Chief's anger might have made him irrational. He got the idea that his own doctor had been in on the secret for some time. He accused Vinogradov, who's been the physician treating Comrade Stalin for years and years. Vinogradov pled ignorance. Better that than confessing to the unforgivable sin of withholding information from the Big Chief."

"Did Vinogradov withhold the information?" I asked.

"I don't know. He could have. The LSUK staff prescribed the medication in the cases of women contaminated by Beria, and Vinogradov is on the panel of LSUK consultants. But innocent or not, he paid a price. The Big Chief declared that he wouldn't be a patient of Vinogradov's any longer. Now the minister of health, Smirnov, is the doctor taking care of the Big Chief.[5]

"Well, that's enough on this very delicate matter," Goryshev said. "Let's finish our cigarettes and get back to work."

"Before we do, Serafim Vasilyevich, I'd like to be sure that I haven't misunderstood you. Is it correct to say that Comrade Stalin has turned against Beria?"

My boss nodded.

"And is it correct to say that Comrade Stalin's reason was the information about Beria having syphilis?"

"Absolutely," said Goryshev.

We stubbed out our cigarettes, and I left his office.

Less than a year after this conversation Stalin's hostility toward Beria was indicated on the pages of *Pravda*. Until today, however, the origin of his hostility has not been known outside State Security and the Kremlin. The shame of publicly admitting that a Politburo member contracted and spread syphilis might have been too great for successive Soviet regimes.

9

The Independent Commission

Since 1946, when his principal protégés in the MGB were fired, Beria's influence over State Security had been reduced to whatever covert support he could muster from lesser protégés who remained in place. His following at the national level in the second center of power in the Soviet system, the CPSU, was too weak to be effective, although he could count on fellow Politburo Member Georgiy Malenkov. Their close friendship of many years' standing was budding into a clandestine alliance, and Malenkov brought to the alliance two great assets. Stalin had restored him as chief of Party cadres and as the CPSU secretary having administrative oversight of the organs of State Security.

If Beria were to realize his ambitions for supreme power, it was essential for him to regain some authority over MGB affairs. Obstruction in the form of Minister Abakumov would bar Beria's way until August 1951. After that time others, such as Poskrebyshev, who headed Stalin's Secretariat, and Guards Directorate Chief Vlasik continued to stand fast to block him.

Stalin's absences from Moscow on extended vacations afforded Beria an opportunity to rebuild his power base in State Security. While Stalin was away during the winter of 1950–51 and again during the autumn of 1951, Beria exploited this opportunity. With Malenkov's help, he took steps to worm his way into MGB affairs by initiating investigations of the Guards Directorate. They had identified its Achilles' heel, which was its bloated budget. Except for them, financial data on the directorate had escaped the attention of Stalin and the rest of the Politburo.

The budget covered more than the costs of protecting Soviet leaders' lives with bodyguards, teams of surveillants, and personnel-security officers. Its expenses ranged from building, furnishing, maintaining, and staffing their residences to special schools for their children and special stores for themselves. For Stalin the directorate operated the farms, vineyards, tobacco land, distilleries, bakeries, and so on that supplied him personally with provisions safe for consumption.

The directorate assumed another type of financial burden during the late 1940s. Hidden from scrutiny by non-MGB auditors was a budget item for "pocket money"—30,000 rubles (the equivalent of over $4,000) paid under the table each month to each leader. Minister Abakumov proposed and Stalin approved this directorate outlay as a means of inducing the leaders to observe Soviet laws. The extra 30,000 rubles beyond their regular salaries might stop them from dealing in the black market and speculating in foreign currency.[1]

While Stalin vacationed in Sochi during the winter of 1950–51, Beria and Malenkov ordered the Finance minister, Arseniy Zveryev, to report to the Politburo on the directorate budget for the coming year. An outsider had never been permitted access to these figures, and the report would have no precedent. It showed that in 1951 the directorate, with under 10 percent of the MGB manpower of 850,000 people, expected to spend nearly 50 percent of the money allocated to the ministry. The figure for the bodyguards was three billion rubles. (At the official exchange rate of 1951, 3 billion rubles amounted to $415 million.)

Stalin, as a Politburo member, received his copy of the Finance minister's report while he was still in Sochi. Surprised at the sum of three billion rubles, Stalin accepted Malenkov's companion recommendation on disposition of the report. It was passed to the staff of the CPSU Central Committee with orders to examine the reasons why the Guards Directorate spent so much.

Malenkov supervised the Central Committee employees who were conducting this examination, and, under prompting by Beria, he turned it into an inquisition of Abakumov. The inquiries by the Central

Committee staff interfered with our minister's supervision of the MGB. As often as two or three times a day during the spring and summer of 1951 he was called to the Central Committee building to defend the directorate budget.

Meanwhile, Abakumov was about to be confronted by Stalin with critical questions concerning the deaths of Zhdanov and Shcherbakov. In August 1951 Stalin posed those questions, obtained the admission that the Timashuk allegations had been concealed from him, and jailed Abakumov.

Beria and Malenkov made their next move while Stalin vacationed in Georgia during the autumn of 1951. By then Beria's adversary, Abakumov, had been replaced by a deputy minister whose forte was operational activities, not political infighting. By then Stalin began reacting to the news of Beria's syphilis. He opened the offensive in November 1951 with the Mingrelian Conspiracy.

A CPSU Central Committee letter on the MGB was read aloud at a meeting of MGB Party activists in December 1951. The letter departed from custom in that it bore a signature, Malenkov's. We heard the Central Committee accusation that Abakumov was guilty of overspending, specifically that everyone in the service received excessively high pay. (An across-the-board decrease hit our paychecks soon afterward.)

The bulk of the letter related to the Guards Directorate: it was serving its own self-interests, it had "lost touch with reality," and it "engaged in materialistic practices." Guards officers at the meeting immediately forecast hard times ahead.

So did my boss Goryshev when I informed him of the letter.

"Now we'll see what Beria has in store for us," he said. "I've just been told of his creating an Independent Commission to take up where the Central Committee left off in questioning Abakumov. . . . But the Independent Commission will go farther and recommend whether to cut the bodyguards' budget next year. I'm absolutely sure that we'll have less money in 1952. The issues really are where to cut and what amounts to cut."

"But maybe the commission will like what it sees, once it delves into our work," I said.

"'Petr Sergeyevich Deriabin, MGB officer and champion optimist'—that's what they ought to put on your tombstone."

"No grounds at all for any optimism?"

"None whatsoever," said Goryshev, "not with Comrade Beria heading the commission and not with the other two on it, also Politburo members. The second commissioner is—can you guess?"

"Georgiy Maksmilianovich Malenkov."

"Naturally. The third person on the Independent Commission is Nikolay Aleksandrovich Bulganin."

"Bulganin! Why, with Zhdanov dead, he's the sole drunkard left in the Politburo."

Stalin bestowed on Bulganin the military rank of marshal and the title of deputy premier in recognition of his service to the Party within the Red Army. Bulganin became defense minister in 1947, succeeding Stalin. Never having fired a shot in anger or led a combat unit, he was not up to the job, and Stalin replaced him as defense minister with a qualified military officer in 1949. Bulganin, however, did have some background in State Security, for he had worked in the Cheka from 1919 to 1921.

"You see, Petr Sergeyevich," my boss said, "it makes sense to me that Beria put Bulganin on the Independent Commission. He can be counted on to follow the path of least resistance. Beria will put forward a motion, Malenkov will second it, and the motion will pass three votes to zero by the Politburo comrades."

"Did I ever tell you about Bulganin and my mother-in-law?"

Goryshev had not heard the story. Prior to the Great Patriotic War Bulganin held a number of civilian positions, one managing a factory where my mother-in-law was employed as an accountant. He propositioned her. She declined and, rather than suffer the indignity of more overtures by Bulganin, resigned.

"That's a good one," my boss said with a laugh. "Well, I wonder what the Big Chief will think when he's told about the Independent Commission. He insists on being told about anything as significant as that."

By naming himself to the commission, Beria created the opportunity for his first officially sanctioned entree to the MGB since 1946.

Beria presented Stalin, still away in Georgia, with a fait accompli. The Independent Commission to investigate the Guards Directorate was in existence, and Stalin could not dissolve it. His recourse would be to monitor the investigation—and Beria's return to State Security territory—

by adding a fourth person to the commission. He needed someone conversant with the Central Committee staff's procedures, someone compliant, someone with no political stake in the outcome, someone outside the Politburo.

Stalin added the fourth man to the commission at the turn of the year. He was Inspector Semen Denisovich Ignatyev from the Central Committee staff, who totally lacked experience in State Security matters. Ignatyev had been a Party *apparatchik* since 1938.

All four commissioners had additional Party duties, and Beria continued to manage the atomic weapons program; yet he was the sole member to visit MGB headquarters throughout the life of the commission. The uniformed sentries—personnel from the bodyguards—told us that he often came to our main building.

Beria reviewed Guards Directorate files and interviewed Guards officers, using a suite on the fourth floor of Dom Dva. The suite had been his as commissar of State Security from 1938 to 1941. It was kept vacant throughout the five-year tenure of Minister Abakumov, whose offices were in the adjacent suite. Odd of Abakumov, we thought, and all the more so considering the shortage of space in the Center.

Colonel Shatalov, chief of the Surveillance Department in the Guards Directorate, traded notes with colleagues about their interviews by Beria. He told me that they were much alike, one interview to the next. Shatalov said his went like this:

Beria:	What's the size of your department?
Shatalov:	About 3,000 men.
Beria:	You have so many people on the Arbat that I can't spit between them. Why so many?
Shatalov:	We need them to protect the Big Chief and other leaders, including yourself, Comrade Beria.
Beria:	But who would want to harm our dear Comrade Stalin, Shatalov? Everybody loves the Big Chief.
Shatalov:	Yes, sir.
Beria:	Now here's what you're to do. Take yourself and your best 1,500 men and move over to the Surveillance Directorate. [That directorate was separate from Shatalov's department and fulfilled assignments against different targets.]

Shatalov:	What about the other half of my men, Comrade Beria?
Beria:	Send them somewhere else, away from Moscow. If a man doesn't want to be relocated, fire the son of a bitch.

"And that's the way it was," Shatalov said. "Comrade Beria gave me my orders, not the Big Chief or our acting minister or General Vlasik. Orders from Comrade Beria, who hasn't been in State Security for all these years. But I'll do as instructed by Comrade Beria. He seems to be running the show. It's not like the old days, Petr Sergeyevich."

By March of 1952 Stalin had implemented the Independent Commission's recommendations about the Guards Directorate budget. None of the expenses for the leaders' lifestyles were touched—not even the monthly bribes to keep them from blackmarketeering and exchanging foreign currency. Instead, the newly honed financial axe chopped outlays for operational activities.

Altogether 6,000 of our operations officers were reassigned. Because openings in Moscow could not be found for a large number of them, the majority were scheduled to take positions in Siberia. The squads of personal bodyguards were most seriously affected. Stalin was persuaded that half the number of bodyguards would suffice for himself and the rest of the leadership.

He assented to replacing other Guards personnel around him. The next commander of his detail of bodyguards would come from Beria's squad, and there would be a new chief of security at his dacha in Kuntsevo. Stalin exercised kindness and the principle of noblesse oblige with his personal staff—the drivers, cooks, servants, and groundskeepers. Regardless of his temper tantrums, they admired and adored him. Now his three chauffeurs were reassigned, as were most servants at the Kuntsevo dacha.

Goryshev expressed apprehension over Stalin's safety. "Soon something very bad is going to happen," he predicted. "The Big Chief is being deprived of protection, Petr Sergeyevich, and I'm afraid they will soon liquidate him." His words in Russian *("I ya boyus' chto ego skoro likividiruyut")* can also be translated, "And I'm afraid that soon he will no longer be." Either way, both of us knew that not everyone loved Comrade Stalin.

Shortly after Abakumov's arrest in 1951, I had been given the choice of two new assignments within the Guards Directorate: chief of the personnel section for the Kremlin Guards or Party boss for the entire Guards Directorate Personnel Section. Either of these positions held grave consequences for the holder at this point in Soviet history, and on the advice of Goryshev, I chose neither.

Instead, my boss and other associates urged me to leave the Guards Directorate, to get out while I could, before anything worse happened. Already I had lost my sense of job security and any sense of being insulated from purges—nothing less than a bloodless purge was occurring in the bodyguards. How long it would stay bloodless no one I knew would venture to estimate.

Again I looked to my friend Volodya Petrochenkov for help, and again Volodya did not let me down. He scouted around the MGB Foreign Operations Directorate, where he had recently been assigned as a senior personnel officer. Volodya combined my smattering of German with my wartime service against Hitler's armies into a strong recommendation for employment by the Austro-German Department. I left the Guards Directorate to join that department in early April 1952.

Despite my transfer, the Deriabin family was allowed to continue to reside in the Chkalov Street apartment building for Guards officers. Neighbors there kept me abreast of events, commencing with startling, unannounced personnel actions by Stalin later in April. Nearly all of these changes came from Beria's work with the Independent Commission.

Vlasik had neglected to destroy his copy of a memorandum relating to the Timashuk-Ryumin letters. The memorandum showed that not only Abakumov but also Vlasik and Poskrebyshev knew about the allegations of murder by doctors affiliated with LSUK. Vlasik, by having a general responsibility for LSUK, and Poskrebyshev were as guilty as Abakumov in concealing Timashuk's allegations from Stalin.

Beria unearthed the memorandum in Vlasik's files. He saved his secret until the end of April 1952, when the commission was about to be disbanded, and gave it to Stalin. Whatever he felt toward Beria, Stalin had to accept this documentary proof that Vlasik and Poskrebyshev had participated in the conspiracy with Abakumov.

Stalin immediately fired both of them and all deputy chiefs of the Guards Directorate, Goryshev included. He placed Poskrebyshev and the first deputy chief under house arrest.[2] Vlasik and the other deputy chiefs received orders to leave Moscow for assignments to the supervisory staffs of labor camps.

A handful of Guards officers went to the train station to see Vlasik off to a labor camp near Sverdlovsk, beyond the Ural Mountains in Siberia. The well-wishers were accompanied by Stalin's son, Vasiliy, who had grown up having Vlasik around the household. Until a few days before, they and Poskrebyshev had been drinking companions. Drunk, his fears for the safety of his father heightened by the departure of Vlasik, Vasiliy shouted, "They're going to kill him! They're going to kill him!"

The identities of the Guards officers at the train station were reported to the Center. Upon returning to Dom Dva they were advised of their dismissal from the bodyguards and placement in the pool of former directorate personnel who awaited transfers to MGB jobs in Siberia.

Six years earlier, after Stalin had dismissed him from the Guards Directorate the first time, Vlasik won back his position by personally arguing his case. Vlasik tried to repeat that turnabout after he left the labor camp to collect his personal effects in Moscow during the summer of 1952. While on this authorized trip, he attempted to pay Stalin a visit in the Kremlin. Vlasik approached the Spasskiy Gate entrance, but Guards sentries—his subordinates only of two or three months earlier—intercepted and detained him. They phoned higher authorities for instructions, which were to arrest Vlasik and take him to the Lubyanka Prison.

Goryshev phoned me in June at the Foreign Operations Directorate. "I'm on my way and calling to say goodbye."

"Hello, Serafim Vasilyevich. I had hoped to say goodbye in person," I replied.

"Yes, well, this latest by the Big Chief was—er, not anticipated, was it? I'd like to ask a favor. Could you place your car and driver at my disposal this afternoon?"

I had grown rather fond of this man who had often helped me in the past, but I hesitated—it might be dangerous for me to help a person in his shoes—but then answered, "I'll send them whenever and wherever you tell me."

"Many thanks, Petr Sergeyevich. I have lots of luggage to drag to the station." He gave specifics for his transportation.

"Before hanging up," I said, "I want to thank you for all you've done for me."

"Let's just leave it at two comrades who assisted each other. I look forward to seeing you again some time. Till then, goodbye, Petr Sergeyevich. Goodbye."

The driver reported delivering my former boss to the station in plenty of time to catch the train to Siberia. That was the last I heard about Goryshev, nor did I hear any more about the other former deputy chiefs of the Guards Directorate.

The eight months beginning in August 1951, when Stalin imprisoned Minister Abakumov and his deputies, encompassed the broadest shake-up in State Security since the Revolution. Toward the end of this period Beria, through his Independent Commission, enticed Stalin into loosening his security. Then the removal of Poskrebyshev and the Guards Directorate chiefs cost Stalin additional loyalists in important positions.

Guards officers wondered why Stalin decided that he did not need as many or the same bodyguards and personal staff. He was a suspicious person, he knew Beria well enough to suspect his motives, and after the news of Beria's syphilis, he began purging the Georgian Republic of Beriaites at the time the commission was formed. But apparently Stalin believed that the directorate, although weakened, could still stave off would-be assassins.

Thus Stalin expelled aides who had served him well, notably by keeping Beria's hands off State Security. He surrendered unswerving loyalty and managerial experience at a time when the Independent Commission gave Beria entree to the MGB. These changes, coupled with the change in their personal relations, virtually guaranteed that Beria would contest Stalin for control of the MGB. Control of the MGB would position Beria for his attempt to succeed Stalin.[3]

10

Battleground: The MGB

By ousting Poskrebyshev, Stalin sacrificed his most trusted, knowledgeable personnel consultant, and no one replaced his longtime chief of staff. Bizarre personnel appointments were made as soon as Poskrebyshev left the Kremlin. Stalin's selections disconcerted the MGB officer corps, because they were so obviously detrimental to the future of our service.

After the arrest of Abakumov, Stalin had managed to get by with an acting minister of State Security. Now he demoted this general to a supernumerary position and, without publicly announcing it, named CPSU Central Committee Inspector Ignatyev to be the minister. Also in April 1952, Colonel Martynov, who had been in charge of sentries at the Central Committee building, succeeded Vlasik as chief of the Guards Directorate.

Neither man possessed the experience that his job required. Ignatyev's MGB background consisted of a subordinate role in the investigations of the Guards Directorate, whereas always before that position had been filled by a State Security general. (In another break with tradition, Stalin made no public announcement of the appointment; *Pravda* reported it one year afterward.) No one I talked to considered Ignatyev qualified for the job. His outstanding attribute was loyalty to Stalin. Ignatyev, we judged, would not be a strong deterrent if Beria tried to move beyond the Independent Commission beachhead.

The selection of their new Guards Directorate chief stunned my neighbors in the apartment building at 48/A Chkalov Street. Replacing Vlasik was a little-known colonel. Colonel Martynov had not served in the front office of the Guards Directorate before being promoted to chief, and he quickly proved himself incapable of handling a ticklish problem. Guards officers who were affected by the reductions in the directorate grew restive waiting for their promised transfers. Martynov could not placate them.

My neighbors told me that Stalin chose him on the basis of Malenkov's recommendation. They agreed that Martynov did not have the professional background for the job, just as Ignatyev did not for his.

The upshot was unique in State Security annals. About 250 jobless Guards officers staged two protest demonstrations outside our main headquarters building. They marched up and down shaking their fists in the air, yelling demands for immediate employment in Moscow, not away from the Center, and occasionally chanting a slogan in praise of Stalin.

The second demonstration took place at the Dzerzhinskiy Square entrance to Dom Dva, and Ignatyev watched from his office on the fourth floor. Evidently in a panic, Ignatyev went to the adjacent suite for Beria's advice on dealing with the protesters. In effect Beria told Ignatyev, "Let them think you're knuckling under. Send them away with your word that they'll be at the top of the list of officers being reassigned to jobs here in the Center. Call them back tomorrow individually. Tell each one that he will either leave Moscow and work for the MGB in Siberia, or quit the MGB." Ignatyev tricked the protesters in the manner suggested, and most of the former Guards officers chose Siberia.

Stalin blamed the embarrassing protests on Guards Directorate Chief Martynov. After scarcely one month in office, Martynov was removed. The way Stalin took care of this vacancy stunned Guards officers. He added the responsibility of personally managing the directorate to Ignatyev's duties as minister.

"You and I are lucky being where we are," my pal Volodya said as we compared notes in a private corner of a bar.

I agreed that as long as we had to be somewhere in the Center during the summer of 1952, both of us had the good fortune of having offices in the Foreign Operations Directorate. It did indeed seem safer for us in a separate complex, 15 minutes by car from Dzerzhinskiy Square.

"Oh, I don't mean just our office location, Petya. Our directorate is focused on people and activities externally. We don't get involved with internal politics, in particular not with having to side with either the Big Chief or Beria."

"True enough," I said. "Eventually one will lose, and all of those supporting the loser will be punished by the winner."

"A man needn't have come right out and supported the loser, either," said Volodya. "The slightest suspicion and at minimum a fellow gets a train ride to Siberian labor camps."

"But siding with the winner isn't any insurance."

"No," Volodya said, "Beria is the equal of the Big Chief when it comes to forgetting who his loyalists were."

Our glasses were empty. Boisterously, we faked an argument over whose turn it was to pay for the next round of drinks, but the bartender knew us too well to fall for our bit of acting. With laughter and full glasses we returned to the private corner.

"Going back to your point about our directorate," I said. "It's almost as if there are three Ministries of State Security—the Big Chief's, Beria's, and the neutral parts, like we are."

"Oh, yes. A year ago we couldn't conceive of that. A year ago Comrade Stalin and only Comrade Stalin called the tune."

"A year ago, Volodya, the Big Chief had Abakumov. Four months ago he had Poskrebyshev and Vlasik. Now he has Ignatyev, who is still on lesson one in the MGB training manuals."

"Ignatyev doesn't poke his nose into our directorate at all," Volodya said, "and I hear that he doesn't with most other outfits in the Center."

"How can he? The Guards Directorate by itself is enough to keep him busier than the village whore on May Day."

"Besides, Petya, there are quite credible rumors Ignatyev is the messenger boy between the Big Chief and Sled-Chast'."

I too had heard rumors about the Stalin's keen interest in Sled-Chast'. A few weeks would pass before I confirmed them and my suspicions that "Little Mishka" Ryumin was involved.

"Assuming the rumors are based on fact," Volodya said, "the Big Chief can count on Ignatyev—"

"Certifiably impotent."

"And Sled-Chast'—"

"Its former chiefs sit in prison, and a lot of former Sled-Chast' officers are slaving in labor camps."

"And the Big Chief can count on his bodyguards."

"The depleted bodyguards. . . . Now," I said, "what is Beria relying on?"

"In the MGB, I'm not sure. I am certain, though, that Beria has more than Malenkov voting with him in the Politburo. Things in the Politburo can't be any other way. When we used to get an *instantsiya* there was no doubt who originated it, the Big Chief. These days every important order I read is signed by the Politburo collectively. Of his own free will the Big Chief wouldn't abdicate exclusive control of the MGB."

"Of course not," I said. "To complete your thought, then, nobody except Beria has the wherewithal to cross swords with the Big Chief in the Politburo."

"Nobody except Beria," Volodya said.

With midnight near, the management began to close the bar. We gulped down one last round of drinks and went outside. After I turned down Volodya's invitation to his apartment for "a final vodka," he commented on another advantage of our working in the Foreign Operations Directorate.

"Why on earth would we want to work in the neighborhood of Dom Dva, Petya? Some bosses over there dedicate most of their hours to internal politics. Against the time when the Big Chief and Beria break into open warfare, they're covering their flanks with excuses for not making decisions. No decisions, no action. No action, no mistakes. No mistakes, no future punishment by the Big Chief or by Beria, whichever wins."

As a headquarters desk officer for West Germany, I saw my department in the Foreign Operations Directorate proceeding routinely in the summer of 1952—the usual rotation of officers between the Center and Berlin, the continued exploitation of captured Nazi documents for leads to potential agents, the sporadic interrogations of high-ranking German prisoners of war, the extension of agent networks in the two Germanies.

From my old State Security friend Major Landyshev I obtained signs of Beria burrowing deeper into the MGB. Kolya invited me to have supper with him and his wife after I told him of being a temporary bachelor—my wife and daughter had stayed an extra week at our dacha that August. Landysheva left to wash the dishes, and Kolya and I started to talk about his work.

"You know I've left Sled-Chast', don't you, Petya? No?" He mentioned the names of two mutual acquaintances in Sled-Chast' who had recently transferred with him to a different part of the Center. At present the three investigators were in the Department of Records and Archives, "Department A."

On organizational charts the department was one level below the MGB directorates, but its chief reported directly to our minister, currently Ignatyev. Department A ranked second in size only to the Guards Directorate among all Center components.

"That's not a demotion for you, I trust."

"The reverse, Petya, the reverse." With each passing of the brandy bottle after supper, Landyshev's voice had risen in volume, and his face turned a deeper red. "Twelve of us are in a special group, in separate rooms where ordinary Department A personnel aren't admitted."

"It must be fairly secret work," I said.

"Absolutely, Petya, absolutely." He leaned across the table and lowered his voice. "We're reviewing old files, old operational files and old investigative files from Sled-Chast' and other places. They go back to the 1930s and early 1940s."

"Well, that doesn't sound like exciting stuff for someone with your experience as an investigator. Are you sure you haven't been demoted?"

"Oh, stop needling me." Landyshev was slightly angry. "It's exciting, all right. We're there to uncover the cases of people who should be rehabilitated."

"Rehabilitated! Will they be absolved of crimes whether they're dead or alive?"

"They're mostly dead, from what we've found so far.

"You mean to tell me, Kolya, that you're looking at the files of enemies of the people—enemies of the Big Chief—every citizen he's ever purged?" I was amazed by this reopening of cases of MGB officers, military leaders, Party *apparatchiki,* and others Stalin had punished.

"Not every citizen. The records aren't that complete."

"Will the names of these citizens be announced?"

"The officers I work with believe so," Landyshev said.

"I cannot, absolutely cannot, understand why the Big Chief is thinking about rehabilitation at this late date," I said.

"He isn't, Petya. The Big Chief isn't. . . . Look, already I've told you too much. Don't try to coax out information that could cost a friend dearly."

"Please let me get this straight. The Big Chief isn't behind the rehabilitation project because he doesn't know what your special group is doing. Correct?" Landyshev nodded. "The Big Chief doesn't know because Ignatyev doesn't know. Correct?" Landyshev nodded. "Ignatyev doesn't know because the chief of Department A hasn't told him. Correct?" Landyshev nodded again.

"See, Kolya, you're not telling me anything that I couldn't have surmised. . . . So your department chief hasn't told Ignatyev, which shows that your chief takes orders from someone else.

"I didn't say—"

"You didn't need to. And we both know who that is."

Once more Landyshev nodded. "Someone else" was Beria. He now had influence in the MGB, the cunning, the nerve, the incentive—the combination to establish a rehabilitation project aimed at destroying the myth of Stalin.[1]

During 1952 Beria spread his influence within the MGB stealthily. Stalin still remained alert to any attempt to usurp his authority over State Security, and Beria was not yet prepared for a showdown. MGB officers who supported Beria, either by choice or by threat, had at least a general notion of their part in a conspiracy against Stalin. Accordingly, they concealed their clandestine activities on Beria's behalf.

Stalin, meanwhile, was playing his MGB cards close to his chest. Knowledge about the secret orders he gave to Minister Ignatyev and Sled-Chast' was tightly restricted. I learned, however, that the orders called for an in-depth investigation aimed at verifying Dr. Lydiya

Timashuk's allegations. Now Stalin wanted evidence—no matter that it might be fabricated or extracted by torture—to implicate as many persons as possible in the conspiracy he was certain existed.

Investigators led by Ryumin sifted through record after record and conducted interview after interview. General Sakharov, who had headed the detail of Zhdanov's bodyguards, told me about his interview while I was visiting Dom Dva.

"Even now, four years after Comrade Zhdanov died," he said, "that twerp Ryumin is still trying to make something out of nothing. He's an obsequious bastard. 'Comrade Major General' this and 'Comrade Major General' that with every sentence he lets out of his mouth."

"'Comrade Major General Sakharov,'" I mimicked, "your chum Ryumin is widely regarded as a pain in the ass."

"That, 'Comrade Major Deriabin,' is slanderous. Ryumin is as much a chum of mine as he is of yours." We both laughed.

"What did Ryumin do to bring this on?"

"Oh, last week he had some questions for me. He's looking into the accusations by that dog-gratifier Timashuk. I told him they're baseless, utterly baseless, but he already knew my opinion from reading my written report to Abakumov about her. That woman isn't all there on the top floor."

"Yes, you told me," I said.

"Ryumin sat where you're sitting, Petr Sergeyevich, asking questions and taking notes. I didn't hold back—why should I? I know doctors didn't knock Comrade Zhdanov off."

"Did anyone?"

"Maybe so, maybe not," Sakharov said. "But that's not the angle Sled-Chast' is pursuing."

Sled-Chast' at first failed to produce evidence to satisfy the purposes of Stalin. In the past, lack of evidence never prevented him from punishing enemies of the people. Now it did not stop his punishment of doctors affiliated with LSUK.

Before the summer of 1952 was out, a number of doctors were under arrest. One was Major General of Medical Services Yegorov, chief of LSUK. His background included service under Zhdanov at the Siege of Leningrad during the Great Patriotic War. Another doctor was escorted by four MGB officers from Beijing. Stalin had sent him there to treat Chairman Mao Tse-tung for an illness that Chinese doctors could not alleviate.

Stalin would have Minister Ignatyev and "little Mishka" Ryumin develop these early arrests into a case of widespread conspiracy. As with his latest appointments to MGB positions, Stalin did this without the counsel of Poskrebyshev, but his former chief of staff was indispensable to him in one sphere of contemporary CPSU activity. Amid the turmoil in the MGB, he released Poskrebyshev from house arrest in order to lend assistance with the forthcoming Party congress.

11

The 19th Congress of the CPSU

By indirection, *Pravda* and *Izvestiya* noted a reduction in Stalin's power in the Party on August 20, 1952. This momentous development was not proclaimed in headlines or given a separate paragraph or sentence. Rather, the fact was placed inconspicuously, at the end of an important announcement about the Communist Party of the Soviet Union. The two national newspapers printed identical texts. At a meeting "held recently in Moscow," the announcement read, the CPSU Central Committee "decided to convene the next, 19th Congress" of the Party on October 5.

Stalin signed the announcement, but the most significant item in the entire text was the title that accompanied his signature. Previously he had been the "general secretary," at the pinnacle of the CPSU Secretariat. Now he was merely a "secretary" (as were four others).

Retractions or corrections of the item were out of the question. *Pravda (Truth)* and *Izvestiya (News)*, respectively the official publications of the Party and the government, would not print a substantive or typographical error of this magnitude. Readers could be sure that "Secretary" Stalin stood lower in the Party hierarchy.

Soviet media, always censored, reflected prevailing winds in the Kremlin, but this time they did not allude to the deletion of "general" from Stalin's title. The subject was also avoided at Party meetings of

MGB officers that I led and others that I attended. Doubtless my colleagues felt as cautious as I did about openly commenting, lest Beria loyalists or Stalin loyalists at the meetings tattle on us.

Although supposed to be held every five years, a Party Congress had not been convened since 1939. Stalin rejected proposals to convoke the Congress after the Great Patriotic War. At first he waited for the economic collapse of the capitalist countries, which Marxist-Leninist dogma confidently predicted. Then he postponed the Congress pending clarification of Tito's course in Yugoslavia, resolved in 1948, and settlement of the civil war in China, ended in 1949. Still Stalin marked time.

The 19th Party Congress, however, seemed hurriedly called. In the past the process of electing delegates—1,359 for this one—and discussing the agenda took about six months. In 1952 the process was truncated to 45 days. The announcement of August 20 set in motion local elections of delegates to the all-union 19th Congress who, in turn, would elect the CPSU Central Committee. The Central Committee would elect the policy-making Politburo[1] (or Praesidium, as it was named for a short period) and the policy-implementing Secretariat.

In practice the Kremlin leadership decided the composition of the Central Committee, and Stalin dictated the composition of the other two bodies. Neither the Politburo nor the Secretariat had a fixed number of members. As the Congress opened, the Politburo had had 11 members and one candidate (nonvoting) member since early 1949, and there were 5 members with the title CPSU secretary: Stalin, Malenkov, and Khrushchev, who were also in the Politburo, and two who were not, Mikhail Suslov and P. K. Ponomarenko.

The announcement listed the Congress agenda, which consisted of the "election of central Party bodies" and four reports, none signifying major changes of policy or leadership. Two reports would be presented by second-stringers in the Party and a third by Khrushchev. He had preceded Beria and Malenkov as a Politburo member, and he had joined Malenkov and Stalin in the Secretariat in 1949, succeeding a Zhdanovite.

At earlier congresses Stalin had awarded himself the honor of delivering the fourth report, the prestigious "Report of the Central Committee." At the 19th Congress the "reporter" would be Malenkov.

The substitution seemed to confirm slippage in Stalin's power and to indicate Malenkov's rise in Party affairs.

Soviet republics prepared for the Congress by holding their own congresses beforehand. In Georgia that microcosm reflected an upsurge by Beria in the Party organization of the republic, an apparatus where Stalin had been purging Beriaites in the fabricated Mingrelian Conspiracy. The Georgian Congress of September 1952 hedged bets on the two "fathers" of the republic. Delegates paid their traditional obeisance to Stalin, but actions by local Party leaders implied the revival of Beria's power.

The Georgian Central Committee, when meeting twice in November 1951 and again in April 1952, had adopted resolutions based upon "Comrade Stalin's personal instructions." Beria, however, attended the April meeting. In the aftermath the Georgian Party leaders rediscovered that he was a native hero, not the sponsor of *apparatchiki* who deserved to be purged.

The Georgian Congress approved a public letter to Beria in Moscow, "an outstanding figure in the Communist Party and Soviet state, true disciple of Lenin, and comrade-in-arms of Comrade Stalin." The letter thanked Beria for outlining "practical measures for ensuring a reorientation of our work and success in the struggle to eradicate errors and shortcomings." Delegates sent no communication to native son Stalin.

Stalin had been the putative author of tracts on Communist theory before and after he became the supreme leader. He chose to take the bloom off the forthcoming 19th Congress by going to press with a 15,000-word treatise entitled "Economic Problems of Socialism in the USSR." The CPSU monthly magazine *Bolshevik* printed it on October 2, and *Pravda* reprinted it on October 3 and 4.

"Economic Problems" preempted publicity about the Congress and became a principal theme of the delegates' discussions. It was thoroughly covered at later Party meetings in the MGB. Each of us Party members in State Security received a personal copy, and the CPSU distributed copies broadly elsewhere.

Stalin's purpose in writing "Economic Problems" was at least partially to rebut the leading economist from the Zhdanov faction, secretly executed two years before. Perhaps he also wanted to demonstrate his primacy in Party theory or to distract us from his decreased authority.

In any event, the treatise contained nothing relevant to the agenda announced for the Congress.

Poskrebyshev emerged from house arrest and applied the experience he had gained at the Congress in 1939 by helping Malenkov with administrative preparations for the 19th session. In October Stalin's former chief of staff headed the nine-man Secretariat of the Congress, gave a speech on law, and was elected to the Central Committee.[2]

All the while, Poskrebyshev's wife was under detention for espionage on orders from Stalin. Molotov had the honor of making the introductory speech at the Congress; yet his wife was still in the prison camp where Stalin had sent her in 1949. Neither of these incarcerations nor the dismissal of Poskrebyshev as Stalin's chief of staff had been announced. Unaware of that background, the vast majority of delegates presumably saw nothing unusual in Congress participation by Poskrebyshev and Molotov.

Delegates met in a tsarist palace on the Kremlin grounds for ten days, October 5 through 14, and I was present throughout as one of several hundred MGB officers on guard in the building. With a few others from the MGB, I had the special mission of watching David Zaslavskiy. We were to shoot this 73-year-old *Pravda* correspondent if he pulled a gun or bomb from his pocket.

Stalin had used Zaslavskiy to write criticisms of Soviet industry and individual citizens. The MGB report on him that was given us surveillants to read explained the suspicions about our "rabbit"—questionable loyalty to the Party because he had not joined it until he was in his 50s, and pro-American sentiments because he had written a book about the United States. Unexplained but implicit in the report was another reason for Stalin to be wary of Zaslavskiy: his nationality was "Jewish."

We detected nothing to indicate that Zaslavskiy intended to fire a gun or throw a bomb. During the ten days of speeches, he stared out the window, his facial expression one of boredom. When Stalin spoke, Zaslavskiy showed his sentiments by turning fully sideways to the podium.

From my vantage point in the balcony, a few seats away from Stalin's daughter, Svetlana Alliluyeva, I had a good view of the Politburo members on the platform at the front of the hall. Beria and Malenkov. Khrushchev, short, fat, clad in rumpled coats and pleated trousers.

Bulganin of bulging eyes and a ruddy complexion, his dark blond hair and goatee going gray. Stalin, with thick gray hair styled in a pompadour to make him seem taller, different from the rest by wearing a uniform.

The four formal reports on the agenda and the humdrum addresses that endorsed them—over 75 speakers altogether—lauded Stalin. No speaker at the Congress missed an opportunity to praise Stalin. From the speeches of Beria and Malenkov one would not have guessed that they were planning to depose him. Beria: "With outstanding courage our wise and fearless leader led the Soviet Army and the entire Soviet people... to victory over the enemy." Malenkov: "For the unshakable solidarity of its ranks the Party is indebted primarily to our leader and teacher, Comrade Stalin." Khrushchev chipped in: "Long live the wise leader of the Party and the people, the inspirer and organizer of all our victories, Comrade Stalin." Said Bulganin: "Hail to our leader and teacher, Comrade Stalin."

Stalin did not attend any of the Congress sessions except the first on October 5 and the last on October 14, and he delivered a speech at the latter. In it he paid tribute to no one. When Stalin finished, the delegates gave him a standing ovation interspersed with hurrahs and cries of "Hail Comrade Stalin!"

The delegates met against the background of a stalemate in the Korean War, a stronger North Atlantic Treaty Organization, and wartime commander Eisenhower on the verge of occupying the White House. The militant speech by Stalin in some ways echoed the one Beria had given, for both referred to the Soviet Armed Forces having strength superior to that of the West. Stalin's heavy Georgian accent made him hard to understand despite a clear voice. Beria had a less-pronounced Georgian accent but a softer voice, and he tended to swallow his words.

By a unanimous vote the delegates accepted the four reports. They also agreed without a dissenting vote to have the Party program revised in accordance with Stalin's "Economic Problems." That work was entrusted to an 11-man commission chaired by Stalin and having Beria and Malenkov as members.

In uncontested elections, the delegates named 125 members and 110 alternates to the Central Committee. This outcome cost Beria a prominent supporter in the Central Committee, but otherwise he had no disappointments, nor did Stalin or Malenkov.

Byplay between Stalin and Malenkov indicated bad feelings toward each other. While Malenkov was submitting the Central Committee report on the first day, Stalin left the platform, walked to the section of the hall for observers from 44 "fraternal" parties, and shook hands with Communist Party leaders from France, Italy, Spain, and Czechoslovakia. (Among those he slighted were the six members of the delegation from the People's Republic of China, headed by Liu Shao-chi.) The disturbance was so great that after Stalin returned to the platform, Malenkov interrupted himself and called a recess.

On the occasions when Stalin approached him, Malenkov displayed an attitude unlike the subservience everyone normally accorded Stalin. Stalin stood; Malenkov sat. Stalin spoke to him; Malenkov responded with gestures.

Between Stalin and Beria, nothing so noticeable transpired as I studied them. They were actors behaving as if their relationship stayed on an even keel—ostensibly amicable, noncompetitive, Beria the junior to Stalin.

We MGB officers assigned to protect the leadership at the Congress discerned, however, that Stalin had relinquished at least part of his authority over the Guards Directorate. Always before, the minister of State Security—Ignatyev since April 1952—had personally supervised the directorate and other MGB headquarters elements guarding Stalin at public appearances such as the Red Square parades. Not Ignatyev but Beria supervised the physical security arrangements at the Congress in October.

Stalin revised the Politburo and Secretariat on October 16, two days after the Congress closed. As with the MGB personnel assignments earlier in the year, he did not consult his one-time advisor Poskrebyshev regarding appointments to these two components at the top of the Party pyramid. Stalin supplemented the Politburo (now, temporarily, the Praesidium) with 16 additional members, including Ignatyev, and the Secretariat with five more men, Leonid Brezhnev being one of the five additions.

Aside from two lesser Party lights who left the Politburo, both bodies contained holdovers. Thus, the old guard remained with Stalin in the Politburo—Beria and Malenkov on the top tier in terms of contemporary influence, Khrushchev and Bulganin on the middle tier, and Molotov, Voroshilov, Kaganovich, and Mikoyan on the bottom tier. In the Secretariat, too, one still found Stalin, Malenkov, and Khrushchev.

The *Pravda* report on the Central Committee's elections showed that Stalin had not been restored to full seniority in the Secretariat. Although his name did come first among the secretaries, followed by the remaining nine in alphabetical order, Stalin lacked the title CPSU first secretary that once was his. The summertime demotion stood. He continued as one of ten secretaries until March 1953, when *Pravda* next printed the title in reporting Stalin's fatal illness and death.[3]

The 19th Party Congress, like shadowboxing before entry into the ring, was a necessary preliminary to a showdown between Stalin and Beria. Stalin required the convocation of the Congress in order to pack the Politburo with newcomers. His plan worked as far as Beria let it work. Congress delegates elected the Central Committee, and the Central Committee elected—that is, Stalin appointed—a Politburo consisting of himself, 16 new members, and 8 from the old guard.

In the reconstituted Politburo Stalin anticipated outvoting the old guard by over a two-to-one margin (17 to 8) on policies related to domestic politics, in particular Beria's thrust for power. These policies would have the aim of igniting a purge on the scale of Stalin's decimation of the CPSU and the Armed Forces in 1937–38. Any citizen of doubtful allegiance to Stalin, everyone conceivably in conspiracy with Beria, would be punished. They were enemies of the people.

Groundwork for the purge had long been under way in Sled-Chast'. It began after Stalin learned in the summer of 1951 about the Timashuk allegations of murder in the deaths of Party leaders Zhdanov and Shcherbakov. Sled-Chast' was far enough along as of August 1952 for Stalin to agree to convening the 19th Congress, with the purge as his ultimate objective.

The case against the doctors accused by Timashuk and against others to be implicated still had not been completed when the Congress closed in mid-October. Stalin needed to move quickly to stop the erosion of his power in the Party and the MGB—to stop Beria—by starting the purge. First, however, Sled-Chast' had to gather evidence against more enemies of the people so that Stalin could bring to light the results of the investigation.

12

"Saboteur-Doctors"

The former chief of Kremlin medical services (LSUK) and several others had been under interrogation by Sled-Chast' since the summer of 1952. After the 19th Party Congress ended, more people were arrested, their families questioned, their homes and offices searched. That raised the total to about 15 men and women currently jailed in the investigation of charges that doctors murdered Party leaders Zhdanov and Shcherbakov.

All of the doctors had been either on the LSUK staff or LSUK consultants. Among them was the 70-year-old Vinogradov, Stalin's personal physician until he was fired in the wake of Beria's contracting of syphilis. Vinogradov was one of five doctors who signed Zhdanov's death certificate; three other signatories also were in prison, and the fifth was deceased.[1]

At first the Sled-Chast' interrogations were relatively temperate by Lubyanka Prison standards, but they failed to produce the confessions desired by Stalin. More than admissions of murdering Zhdanov and Shcherbakov, Stalin wanted the doctors to acknowledge working with Western intelligence services. They claimed, however, that they neither misprescribed medicines nor collaborated with foreigners.

The question of Zhdanov's cause of death is complicated by the fact that the five doctors who signed his death certificate also signed the death certificate of Bulgarian Communist Party General Secretary Georgiy Dimitrov in 1949. In 1948 Dimitrov had supported Marshal Tito of Yugoslavia in advocating an East European federation, a proposal that Stalin opposed.

A Guards captain in my apartment building provided an unusual slant involving Dimitrov. Dimitrov, aged 67, died in July 1949 in Moscow's Barvikha Sanitarium, reportedly from cirrhosis of the liver and other ailments.

"I suspect these doctors also killed Dimitrov," my neighbor said. "He died, you see, from medicine they gave him."

"I know the Guards Directorate sent you to Sofia to be Dimitrov's chauffeur," I replied, "but that doesn't make you an expert on how he died in Moscow."

"Well, his wife came here with him, and she and I were . . . ah, shall I say, on fairly close terms, if you get what I mean, Petr Sergeyevich. She told me how Dimitrov died."

"From medicine."

"From medicine, but that could amount to murder, couldn't it?" the captain asked. "Or Dimitrov could have asked the LSUK doctors for an overdose of something that would finish him off. He was very sick and in pain. Regardless, I should probably report my suspicions."

I advised him against it. "You might find yourself in prison for dereliction of duty in not reporting this long ago."

"I guess you're right," he mumbled, and that was the last I heard of the matter.[2]

Stalin then fell back on the cruelty toward recalcitrant prisoners that had succeeded in the past. These interrogation methods were described by Khrushchev in his so-called Secret Speech on the Stalin "cult of the personality" to delegates at the 20th Party Congress in 1956. An extract of the Secret Speech I quote here because it happens to be consistent with information from my MGB colleagues reads as follows:

> [Stalin] personally issued advice on the conduct of the investigation and the method of interrogation of the arrested persons. He said that . . . Vinogradov should be put in chains, another one should be beaten. . . .
>
> Stalin told him [Minister Ignatyev] curtly, 'If you do not obtain confessions from the doctors we will shorten you by a head.'

Stalin personally called the investigative judge [meaning to imply a government prosecutor but referring to Ryumin], gave him instructions, advised him on which investigative methods should be used; these methods were simple—beat, beat, and, once again, beat.3

Under that duress, doctors supplied the confessions sought by Stalin. Yes, they attested to the Sled-Chast' interrogators torturing them, they murdered Zhdanov and Shcherbakov. Yes, they planned to murder others—whoever the interrogators told them to name. Yes, other Soviet citizens were involved—whoever the interrogators cared to nominate. And yes, hostile foreign intelligence organizations took part in their conspiracy.

Stalin rewarded Ryumin with two outlandish promotions. In December 1952, about the time of Stalin's 73d birthday, Ryumin became both chief of Sled-Chast' and our deputy minister of State Security. The letter the lieutenant colonel wrote to Stalin some 18 months earlier had set him on a road to great rewards.

The Petrochenkovs spent New Year's Day 1953 with Marina and me at Chkalov Street. The wives scurried around our apartment chasing and chastising the children when they were not laying out the holiday repast of sausages and special pickles. Volodya and I sat to the side in quiet conversation.

Answering his question, I said that I had not seen much of the new chief of the Foreign Operations Directorate since his first day back in the MGB the previous November. General Yevgeniy Pitovranov had been one of seven deputy ministers arrested with Abakumov in August 1951. Shortly after Stalin released him, Pitovranov and I exchanged greetings at the entrance to the Directorate building. His body was swathed in a black overcoat that came to his ankles; his face looked pale and thin.

"The Big Chief told someone he let Pitovranov out of the Lubyanka because he decided Pitovranov isn't an enemy of the people after all," Volodya said.

"So I hear."

"But that's not the true reason."

"What is?"

"The true reason is Beria. He and Malenkov are in cahoots, and Pitovranov is Malenkov's brother-in-law. So Beria as much as ordered the Big Chief to free Pitovranov."[4]

"That doesn't surprise me," I said. "Beria is throwing his weight around in the MGB, and our weakling of a minister doesn't stand in his way."

"No, Ignatyev devotes day and night to Sled-Chast'."

"Things have reached the stage, Volodya, where colleagues of mine in our directorate and bodyguards here in this apartment building are talking about a Kremlin without the Big Chief. They say it won't be long before Comrade Stalin is forced into retirement and bundled off to Georgia where he came from."

"Nobody would have dared to breathe such a thought until lately," Volodya said. "My contacts in the Center say that Beria and Malenkov have already divided up the pie. Beria gets the MGB—"

"May the saints help us!"

"And Malenkov gets the Party. Beria might not be so bad, Petya. He'd be an improvement over Ignatyev, from a professional standpoint."

"Sure, but. . . ." It wasn't necessary for me to tell my pal that, although neither of us worked against Beria, we might wind up jailed or executed anyway.

"Something else is going on, out there in Siberia."

Marina, assisted by Natasha, tried to break up our tête-à-tête. I asked my wife to lower the heat under the sausages for a couple of minutes while Volodya and I finished our conversation. She frowned but did as I requested.

"What were you saying, Volodya?"

"They've finished slapping together new labor camps in Siberia. The bastards. If I were religious, I'd pray for an abscess of every last one of their teeth."

"You know damned well Siberian labor camps are hardly a recent phenomenon," I said. "So what?"

"The camps are for Jews, you see. For Jews! All the Jews in Moscow are going to be sent to internal exile there."

"Why? When?"

"Ask the Big Chief," Volodya said. "The secret order came from him."

The children were asleep, the food was ready, the wine was poured, and the wives were impatient. Volodya and I adjourned to the table, but after a while his black mood got the better of him. He predicted that the new year would bring more than its share of bad luck. I asked why.

"Take a look at the calendar, Petya. Thirteens everywhere. 1953. First digit one, last digit three. Thirteen."

Natasha told him that he was talking nonsense.

"In February we have a Friday the 13th," Volodya persisted. "In March we have a Friday the 13th."

"Our superstitious grandmothers would go along with foolishness like that," I said. "I don't, and you shouldn't—it's against Party rules."

"Screw the Party," said Volodya, laughing. The rest of us laughed too, and we turned to more pleasant subjects.

But perhaps Marina, Natasha, and I should have given a little credence to Volodya's concern about the number 13 in the year 1953. It was on the 13th day of January when we read the rudiments of Stalin's dreadful plan for a purge.

The story disseminated by the Telegraph Agency of the Soviet Union (TASS) exemplified the prevailing journalistic style that mixed bombast and propaganda. Typically, what was left unsaid had as much or more importance than what was said, but readers were accustomed to filling in blanks, to deciphering code terms, to unraveling intrigues barely hinted at in the media.

As published by *Pravda* on January 13, 1953, the story drew extensively upon confessions that Sled-Chast' had extracted from the doctors under torture. Thus, this affair was constructed out of fabricated evidence.

The name by which the affair has become popularly known, "The Doctors' Plot," is misleading—the plot was Stalin's, against the doctors. The full text of the story follows:

ARREST OF GROUP OF SABOTEUR-DOCTORS

Some time ago agencies of State Security discovered a terrorist group of doctors who made it their aim to cut short the lives of active public figures of the Soviet Union through sabotage medical treatment.

Among the participants in this terrorist group there proved to be: Prof. M. S. Vovsi, therapeutist [specialist in treating illnesses]; Prof. V. N. Vinogradov, therapeutist; Prof. M. B. Kogan, therapeutist; Prof. P. I. Yegorov, therapeutist; Prof. A. I. Feldman, otolaryngologist; Prof. Ya. G. Etinger, therapeutist; Prof. A. M. Grinshtein, neuropathologist; and G. I. Maiorov, therapeutist.

Documentary evidence, investigations, the conclusions of medical experts, and the confessions of the arrested have established that the criminals, who were secret enemies of the people, sabotaged the treatment of patients and undermined their health.

Investigation established that the participants in the terrorist group, taking advantage of their positions as doctors and abusing the trust of patients, by deliberate evil intent undermined patients' health, deliberately ignoring the data of objective examination of the patients, made incorrect diagnoses which did not correspond to the true nature of their illnesses, and then doomed them by wrong treatment.

The criminals confessed that, taking advantage of Comrade A. A. Zhdanov's ailment, incorrectly diagnosing his illness and concealing an infarct of his myocardium, they prescribed a regimen contraindicated for this serious ailment and thereby killed Comrade A. A. Zhdanov. Investigation established that the criminals likewise cut short the life of Comrade A. S. Shcherbakov by incorrectly employing strong drugs in his treatment, prescribing a regimen which was mortal to him and thus brought him to his death.

The criminal doctors sought above all to undermine the health of leading Soviet military personnel, to put them out of action and to weaken the defense of the country. They sought to put out of action Marshal A. M. Vasilyevskiy, Marshal L. A. Govorov, Marshal I. S. Konev, General of the Army S. M. Shtemenko, Admiral G. I. Levchenko, and others, but arrest disrupted their evil plans, and the criminals did not succeed in attaining their aim.

It has been established that all these murderer-doctors, who had become monsters in human form, trampling the sacred banner of science and desecrating the honor of scientists, were enrolled by foreign intelligence services as hired agents.

Most of the participants in the terrorist group (M. S. Vovsi, B. B. Kogan, A. I. Feldman, A. M. Grinshtein, Ya. G. Etinger, and others) were connected with the international Jewish bourgeois nationalist organization "Joint," established by American Intelligence for the alleged purpose of providing material aid to Jews in other countries. In actual fact this organization, under the direction of American Intelligence, conducts extensive espionage, terrorist, and other subversive work in many countries, including the Soviet Union. The arrested Vovsi told investigators that he had received orders "to wipe out the leading cadres of the USSR"— received them from the USA through the "Joint" organizations, via a Moscow doctor, Shimeliovich, and the well-known Jewish bourgeois nationalist Mikhoels.[5]

Other participants in the terrorist group (V. N. Vinogradov, M. B. Kogan, P. I. Yegorov) proved to be old agents of British Intelligence. The investigation will soon be concluded.

The "saboteur-doctors" story actually announced that Stalin had a purge brewing, and that Jews would be among his victims. Not only did *Pravda* specifically mention Jews and "Joint," but 8 of the 11 accused had Jewish names. The three Gentiles who were cited had signed Zhdanov's death certificate.[6]

If any doubts existed that the story heralded a purge, *Pravda* removed them on January 18. An editorial that day referred to a speech of March 1937 in which Stalin signaled the two-year purge that cost thousands of lives.

Those of us who knew about the current relationship between Stalin and Beria understood that Stalin's purge must have Beria as a principal target. Our conclusion received support from the *Pravda* story itself, because Soviet Jewry was a constituency with which Beria sympathized. Stalin, of course, did not.

Beyond that, the accused and Beria seemingly cooperated. At least two of the five military officers whom the "saboteur-doctors" allegedly intended to kill—Deputy Minister of Defense Konev and Armed Forces Chief of Staff Shtemenko—were enemies of Beria. He had tried to undercut them with Stalin by relaying rumors about their disloyalty. Beria's failed effort irked Stalin in the case of Shtemenko, who was his

favorite military officer. When the German Army marched to the out-
skirts of Moscow in 1941, Stalin and Shtemenko bunkered together two
levels below ground in the Kirovskaya subway station; the rest of the
General Staff stayed in a command post one level below ground in the
Byelorussian metro station.

The alleged involvement of British intelligence pointed toward
sharpening another nail for Beria's coffin. Before he joined the CPSU,
and before the Soviets overthrew the Mussavat government ruling
Azerbaijan in 1920, Beria was an employee of the Mussavat police.
Separately, *Pravda* claimed that the Mussavat government "operated
under the control of British intelligence organs."

Vinogradov and Yegorov, two of the three Gentiles named by *Pravda*,
were said to be "old agents of British intelligence." Stalin had fired
Vinogradov as his personal physician on grounds that he concealed
Beria's syphilitic condition. One who did engage in this conspiracy of
concealment from Stalin had been the officer heading LSUK, and that
was Yegorov.

Finally in the bill of particulars against Beria, there was the year of
death of one person whom the doctors were accused of killing. In 1945,
when Zhdanov's brother-in-law Shcherbakov died, the Beria protégé
Merkulov was in charge of State Security. Within State Security was the
Guards Directorate, and under the Guards Directorate was LSUK and its
affiliated doctors. Guilt by association made Beria a party to that
alleged murder.

The story adapted scripts from the 1930s. Where Stalin's purge in
1937–38 decimated the officer corps of the Armed Forces, draining it of
competence while Hitler prepared to launch the Great Patriotic War, the
opposite tack was now being taken: "The criminal doctors sought above
all to undermine the health of leading Soviet military personnel...."
This time Stalin appeared to be soliciting the support of the Armed
Forces. He needed it, given Beria's newly won strength in the MGB and
the CPSU.

The charges showed lack of imagination on Stalin's part, for they had
been manufactured twice before. The commissar of State Security from
1934 to 1936 "confessed" at his trial a few years later that he had
arranged the murder of the famous Russian writer Maxim Gorkiy. On

his orders, the commissar said, doctors in 1936 prescribed fatally incorrect medication for Gorkiy. After the trial this commissar, a Jew who had begun his career as a pharmacist, was executed.

Moreover, two "doctor-poisoners" were tried for the murder in 1935 of Politburo Member Valerian Kuybyshev, after whom the industrial city on the Volga is named. An expert witness on behalf of the prosecution in 1937 was the Vinogradov of this affair in 1953. The testimony of Vinogradov was false, the two doctors were innocent, but they were found guilty and sentenced to be executed. Having ingratiated himself, Vinogradov became Stalin's personal physician.

Muscovites' reactions to the story varied according to individual gullibility, prejudice, or vulnerability. Medical practices suffered due to the opinion of many that doctors not cited by *Pravda* might be "saboteurs." Some patients discharged themselves from hospitals, and a large number stopped seeing physicians. Jews went to Jewish doctors, but few Gentiles did.

Certain MGB officers gloated over Jews being in trouble, but otherwise my colleagues were circumspect in voicing opinions. To speak out might put a person on the losing side, Stalin's or Beria's. An exception occurred at the first weekly Party meeting of my department following the *Pravda* report. Holding up the newspaper to show the story, one officer said, "Here's a good example of the Big Chief's vigilance." In contrast to earlier days when everybody seized every opportunity to sing Stalin's praises, the rest of us remained silent.

On the day *Pravda* printed the story, the general who had headed Zhdanov's bodyguards took flight, presumably in fear of imminent arrest. Sakharov, as he told me long before, had rejected the possibility of doctors murdering Zhdanov and had gone on record with his conclusion. Now he became the object of a nationwide manhunt. The MGB apprehended him in Stalingrad Oblast during the following week. Sakharov was taken to the Lubyanka Prison for interrogation by Sled-Chast'. That was the last I heard of him.

Annually on the anniversary of Lenin's death the government announced the names of recipients of the Order of Lenin, the country's highest honor. Dr. Lydiya Timashuk's name was on the list that *Pravda* published on January 20. Nowhere did the media cross-reference her honor to the story on the "saboteur-doctors," nor did the media mention her status as an MGB employee working for the Kremlin medical organization LSUK.[7]

Timashuk was virtually unknown outside the MGB. Her sole achievement on public record had been an article on myocardial infarcts, the type of heart condition that doctors certified was the cause of Zhdanov's death. The article appeared in the medical journal *Klinicheskaya Meditsina* on October 3, 1952.

Whether Timashuk wrote the article attributed to her is a dubious proposition—she was a radiologist, who ranked far down in the structure of LSUK and who had little professional standing among her peers. Doubtless Sled-Chast' planted the article in order to authenticate Timashuk's credentials, for she was to be an "expert witness" at the trial of the doctors whom she accused of murder. The analogy with Vinogradov testifying at the trial of the two innocent "doctor-poisoners" in 1935 is clear.

Sheep-like, government spokesmen and the press took their cue from the *Pravda* story and replayed its theme with variations. For example, the assistant prosecutor-general wrote that American intelligence had financed "this vile Zionist spy organization" Joint via philanthropic channels. In this article published by *Bloknot Agitatora* on January 30, he linked American intelligence to "the Gestapo agent Tito" of Yugoslavia. The article went on to enumerate economic crimes in various parts of the country, and it quoted Stalin on the virtues of vigilance.

Each day in January after that Friday the 13th, my MGB colleagues and I read *Pravda* in expectation of reports about Minister Ignatyev, Deputy Minister Ryumin, and Sled-Chast' stepping up the tempo of Stalin's purge. *Pravda* was the official mouthpiece of Stalin and of the Politburo, and we awaited reports of more arrests on newly minted charges. After all, the final paragraph of the original *Pravda* story on the "saboteur-doctors" had promised rapid fulfillment of a promise. "The investigation," it said, "will soon be concluded."

13

Spying on Chairman Mao

While domestic events were brewing, one of Stalin's finest foreign operations was about to come to an end. Chinese Communist Party Chairman Mao Tse-tung would finally uncover and bring to a halt an MGB operation that had given Stalin an intimate look into Mao's thoughts. It is generally thought that Comrade Stalin warmly loved the Chinese people, but Mao knew the opposite was true.

In the postwar years the MGB sent advisors abroad to guide counterpart services in organizing intelligence and security work for fledgling Communist governments. The Guards Directorate participated by training bodyguards for foreign Communist leaders, such as Marshal Tito of Yugoslavia. Agreement to train Mao's bodyguards was reached while Stalin and Mao negotiated the 30-year treaty of Sino-Soviet "friendship, alliance, and mutual aid." They signed the treaty in February 1950.

Mao's victory and Chiang Kai-shek's evacuation of the Kuomintang forces to Taiwan in 1949 brought no abatement to MGB operations in mainland China. Quite the opposite, we had been informed at a secret briefing for MGB Party activists by the senior lecturer of the CPSU Central Committee. The lecturer, German Sverdlov, departed from his notes to fill us in on a Politburo meeting at Stalin's dacha in Kuntsevo.[1]

With the government of the People's Republic of China barely two months old, Chairman Mao left Liu Shao-chi in charge and came to Moscow in December 1949 for medical treatment and face-to-face negotiations with Stalin.[2] He and his entourage were put up at another of Stalin's dachas in the vicinity of Moscow, on Dmitrovskoye Highway. Giving him the first day to rest from the journey, Stalin went there on the second day to greet Mao. This show of hospitality flew in the face of Stalin's prior instructions to the Guards Directorate: the housekeeping staff's duties included collecting information on the Mao delegation, and microphones should be concealed in every room. Considerable fanfare attended the signing of the 30-year Sino-Soviet Friendship Treaty near the end of Mao's visit to Moscow. He returned to Beijing in February 1950.

The Politburo meeting in Kuntsevo took place shortly afterward. The lecturer Sverdlov told us that when Politburo members started congratulating Stalin on his successful talks with Mao, Stalin interrupted. "Comrades," he announced, "the battle for China isn't over yet. It has only just begun."

All had not gone well in his bargaining with Mao, Stalin explained. Mao had sought more aid for agriculture, industry, and the military than Stalin thought the USSR—still recovering from wartime losses and beginning to build against its new "main enemy," the United States— could or should provide. Where Mao had been insistent, Stalin had been adamant. Outwardly, they had displayed "the fraternal friendship expected of leaders of peaceloving nations." That facade misled the Politburo as much as us readers of *Pravda*'s sugarcoated articles on their talks.

Stalin told the Politburo that the Soviet Union would not be safe from the People's Republic of China as long as Mao coveted our resources. One means of blocking Mao, he said, would be to convert the Chinese territories of Sinkiang Province, Inner Mongolia, and especially Manchuria into independent states. Separated from China, they would act as buffers between the two great Asian powers. To accomplish this objective, Stalin thereupon ordered the CPSU Central Committee and the MGB to step up the clandestine organization of pro-Soviet

Party cells in all three territories. The lecturer Sverdlov commented that this activity, under way since the Japanese defeat and departure from the mainland, was receiving the highest priority.

It seemed to me at the time that Sverdlov had been indiscreet in revealing Stalin's strategy to us MGB Party activists, trusted though we were. He went too far, considering the relief to be taken in the West if such evidence of a Sino-Soviet split trickled out. Were Mao to learn of the joint operation by the CPSU Central Committee and MGB in lands he placed within his domain, the split might escalate to warfare.

Stalin had three aces up his sleeve during the long-running contest with Chairman Mao. On the surface Stalin and Mao were cordial, but each knew that the other stood in the way of winning higher stakes. Among the prizes were supremacy on the Asian mainland and sole leadership of the international Communist movement. Probably never before now could Western observers appreciate how much of an edge Stalin maintained over Mao. I can now disclose that Stalin had the great advantage of MGB agents and technical operations through which the USSR acquired strategic intelligence information and manipulated Chinese Communist policy.

One ace was Liu Shao-chi, whom Stalin personally recruited in the 1930s, after Stalin gave him safe haven in Moscow and a seat on the governing body of the old Communist international trade union organization Profintern.[3] Another ace was Kao Kang, the Communist king-pin in Manchuria, who volunteered himself to Stalin in the 1930s. (Stalin continued to meet openly and officially with both Liu and Kao, while the MGB received their reports and gave them clandestine assignments.) Their worth as Soviet agents can be imagined from the positions they held. Both belonged to the People's Republic of China's Politburo and Central Committee. Liu rose to become Mao's second in command before and after the Communists defeated the Kuomintang forces of Chiang Kai-shek. He succeeded Mao as PRC head of state in 1959. Kao had been Vice-chairman of the Central People's Government Council since the PRC came into existence in 1949. He was perhaps most valuable to Soviet interests for holding sway as Party secretary and government chairman in the pivotal territory of Manchuria until 1954.

The third ace was a technical penetration of Mao's offices and residence in Beijing. Judged by the locations of the equipment and the resources that the MGB threw into the operation, it must be presumed to have produced intelligence data of the highest quality.

Guards Colonel Anatoliy Nechayev, along with his wife, an MGB captain, left for Beijing with two or three dozen subordinates later in 1950. At least in the beginning Nechayev met resistance by Chinese bodyguards to his suggestions for protecting Mao, but I heard nothing else about him until a Sunday in January 1953. A neighbor of mine in the Guards Directorate apartment building broke the news to me about a "monstrous scandal" involving this particular group, one of several advisory units which the MGB had sent to Beijing.

"The Chinese," the major said, "kicked them out at the beginning of this month. Nechayev is back in the Center, but none of the others from our directorate returned to Moscow—maybe the Big Chief had the crew of the Trans-Siberian Railroad off-load them at a labor camp beyond the Urals."

"What went wrong in Beijing?" I asked.

"We got caught red-handed in an operation against Mao. Our people were listening in on Mao's private conversations."

"Technical operations are a strange sideline for Nechayev. He was supposed to be there on a training assignment."

"Training took second place to eavesdropping on Mao," the major said. "The Big Chief valued the eavesdropping reports very highly, and now he won't have them anymore. But if you think that's bad, Petr Sergeyevich, listen to the rest. Mao personally protested to the Big Chief about the operation."

"Protested! Our relations with the Chinese are getting worse and worse."

"Well, the Big Chief tried to patch them up. He wrote Mao a letter of apology in which he claimed not to have known about the operation. Of course, that wasn't true—the Big Chief relished reading what Mao said in private."

"Mao would have to be crazy to believe a statement like that," I said. "The Big Chief should have known better."

"So should our minister, but Ignatyev recommended telling Mao that whopper, and the Big Chief bought it. Nobody I've talked to thinks that Mao is foolish enough to believe him."

Pravda presented Mao's eulogy to Stalin three months after the Chinese detected the MGB technical operation. Sergey Tikhvinskiy rounded out the story for me during the summer of 1953 at a time when we shared a Foreign Operations Directorate office in Dom Dva. Then in his mid-30s, Tikhvinskiy had already reached the rank of colonel. He went to China on his first State Security mission at the age of 21 and over the years registered a string of successes with agents there.[4]

Tikhvinskiy often stressed China's importance to the USSR. He pointed out that the collective leadership was appointing Panyushkin, who had worked in China during the 1920s and 1930s and again as ambassador there, to be chief of our directorate. He cited the names of several officers who had risen high in State Security thanks to their excellent work in China operations. Among them was Mikhail Kapitsa, who Tikhvinskiy said still figured in the MGB operation with Liu.[5]

Tikhvinskiy boasted that Stalin personally recruited Liu and Kao Kang. The book *Samoye Pamyatnoye* (published by Nauka in Moscow in 1972) contains one version of a story about Kao that Tikhvinskiy recounted to me in 1953.[6] The book quotes Kao as saying that, after Stalin expressed interest in his background, "I took my shirt off and showed him my back, which had been scourged by a whip. Catching sight of it, I. V. Stalin approached me, excused himself for touching on this question, embraced me, and said that everything was clear to him...." The full story from Tikhvinskiy was that Stalin interrogated Kao to ascertain his reliability as a future secret agent, and Kao proved his trustworthiness by showing Stalin the scars where he had been whipped by the Kuomintang.

According to Tikhvinskiy, Guards Colonel Nechayev reported from Beijing that his group of advisors was free of local escorts and surveillance. "The Chinks[7] made the mistake of letting your friends from the bodyguards roam around Beijing unescorted," said Tikhvinskiy. Out of that information grew the plan for the MGB to dispatch technicians to Beijing under the guise of belonging to the Guards Directorate. The technicians installed microphones in Mao's office and bedroom.

"The operation surpassed our expectations," Tikhvinskiy said. "The intelligence product from the microphones was first rate, I can tell you. Comrade Stalin wanted the information faster than the time it took for the recordings to reach Moscow by diplomatic pouch and to be processed here. We scoured around for Chinese linguists, who would go out there to handle the translating as soon as anything of interest was heard. They had to be able to pass themselves off to the Chinks as Guards Directorate officers. Well, we found a few who qualified. Off they went to Beijing. Next came a request for additional code clerks in Beijing—the volume of enciphered traffic was shooting up to keep pace with the translators' work out there. Off to Beijing went more code clerks. Transcripts of Mao's conversations landed on the Big Chief's desk every week, and he couldn't have been happier."

"Couldn't have been happier until last January."

"Yes, until New Year's Day, Petr Sergeyevich. We think that in celebrating the holiday, some MGB officer in Beijing drank too much and gave the operation away to the Chinks."

"Like the proverb, 'What's on a sober man's mind is on a drunken man's tongue,'" I said.

"I'd like to pull that drunkard's tongue out. We knew—the Big Chief knew Mao's plans and hopes and peculiarities, and he directed our policies in the Far East accordingly. Then, suddenly, nothing. The Chinks had torn Mao's rooms apart, found the hidden microphones, and traced the connecting wires as far as the walls of the area where the Guards officers worked."

"And drew the correct conclusion."

"And drew the correct conclusion," Tikhvinskiy repeated. "Then Mao ordered the MGB advisors to his bodyguards sent home."

"I heard that an exchange of letters followed."

"More stupidity by that idiot who used to be our minister. Specialists on China like myself urged the Big Chief to ignore Mao's letter. He should carry on as if the microphones never existed. Not Ignatyev, though, and the Big Chief listened to him. He apologized to Mao and compounded the error by claiming he hadn't known about the operation. Mao had learned a lot from the Big Chief and didn't believe him. A high-level agent of ours reported that Mao didn't."

So productive was the eavesdropping operation on Mao, Tikhvinskiy later added, that the MGB would try another. For this purpose Colonel Ivan Raina, an engineer trained in the United States during the 1940s, left Moscow later in 1953 to take charge of MGB activities in Beijing, as the MGB legal resident. His position in the Foreign Operations Directorate had been the deputy chief for technical operations.

The MGB operations with Kao and Liu sputtered to a close after I defected to the United States. Kao, accused of trying to create an "independent kingdom" in Manchuria, was arrested for treason in 1954. He died about a year later. Liu was deposed in 1968 on allegations of revisionist opposition to Mao. He died in prison, reportedly a suicide. Kao was regarded as "a true friend of the USSR." In his memoirs Khrushchev called Liu "second only to Mao in power and influence" and "the number one casualty of the Cultural Revolution" in the PRC.[8]

14

A Policy Defeat

It is often written that nature struck down Stalin in the fullness of his power. That is not true. I witnessed Stalin being systematically stripped of his defenses during the last months of his life: his fantastic guard force cut back; his most faithful protectors sent away, or imprisoned, or killed; his hands removed from the levers of control. Even as he was building up another blood purge, he was losing the power to carry it through—and was exposing himself to murder.

The story of Stalin's downfall, as I know it, has an ironic twist. No one understood better than he how to protect himself against plotters. No one was more concerned for his own safety. He had built around himself a protective system unequaled in history, largely outside the formal framework of the state, a mysterious apparatus the capabilities of which were not fully known to any but the top bodyguards themselves and to a few of Stalin's closest associates. It was able to protect him not only against the people but also against his own courtiers. It spied on other leaders, blackmailed them and, striking out from the dark, murdered or discredited any who—in Stalin's growingly suspicious eye—might oppose him. Yet the final plot against him did succeed—and it did so by dismantling, before his very eyes, that inner circle of protection.

Such a plot could only have succeeded against the aged Stalin, rendered vulnerable by his very suspicions—and even so the outcome was in doubt until the very end. For while the plotters were moving against Stalin, Stalin was moving against them. He might still have undone them before they could undo him.

In this tense, urgent, two-way struggle lay a great drama, still knowable only in bits and pieces, still hidden by today's survivors: the elimination of Josef Stalin.

The prediction of an early end to the case of the "saboteur-doctors" proved wrong. *Pravda,* the bellwether of Kremlin internal politics, did not announce any more arrests, and publicity about the case petered out.

Observers accustomed to reading between the lines had concluded (correctly, as later evidence confirmed) that Stalin dictated the contents of the announcement of January 13. Now it appeared that his plans for a purge might have been sidetracked. If so, the policy-making Politburo had inflicted a defeat on Stalin for the first time in his long reign.

Beginning in late January I saw signs that this had occurred and that Stalin was in retreat. At that time, during a visit to Dom Dva, I met Colonel Dmitriy Nosarev with whom I formerly served in the Personnel-Security Department of the Guards Directorate. He was one of the few senior officers to retain his position in the bodyguards, with responsibility for the Kremlin Kommandatura. This regimental-sized garrison stationed uniformed sentries inside and outside the Kremlin buildings, around the Kremlin Wall, and at the Lenin Mausoleum.

"How are things?" Nosarev asked.

"Oh, about as usual."

"Really? I thought you'd be looking over your shoulder as soon as the charges against the doctors came out in the open."

"I am, but I have trouble when I look into the shadows."

"There's nothing to worry about in the shadows, Petr Sergeyevich. Nothing, rest assured."

"Oh? What's going on?"

"Sled-Chast' is tapering off the investigation. The doctors are still in the Lubyanka, though, and a few more are being arrested. The Big Chief nevertheless isn't able to go further."

"Very interesting, Dmitriy Nikolayevich." Nosarev was saying in a veiled way that Stalin's purge would not materialize. "What else is going on?"

"Keep this under your hat, too: I expect there'll be big changes at the top."

"At the top—you mean our minister?"

"Yes, and higher up as well."

I questioned whether he was right about State Security Minister Ignatyev, pointing out that MGB officers had recently elected Ignatyev to a seat on the Moscow City Council (Soviet). Nosarev told me to wait and see.

A few days afterward, my friend Volodya Petrochenkov reinforced Nosarev's statement. Against the possibility that monitors were listening as we talked on the telephone, Volodya chose his words carefully. "New winds are blowing, Petya," he said, and then implied that the new winds would waft Stalin away.

The new winds blew stronger in February, and they affected Stalin's inner circle, his son Vasiliy, and others close to him.

Vasiliy Stalin was commissioned a captain in the Air Force while a teenager. In under ten years he rose to the rank of lieutenant general and assumed important assignments. He received credit for flying combat missions and was awarded two Orders of the Red Banner to go with lesser decorations. In fact, Vasiliy was a failure—guilty, among other things, of rash disregard for safety, substandard performance, insubordination, and drunkenness on duty. As long as his father held the power that he did, the Ministry of Defense swept the negative reports under the rug. In February the ministry brought Vasiliy's career to a halt. He was dismissed as the air commander of the Moscow District and dishonorably discharged.

Five more links in the chain of loyalists around Stalin broke during February 1953. On the 13th the Jew Lev Mekhlis, one of the last of Stalin's old comrades from the Revolution, died at the age of 64 and was buried in the Kremlin wall, an honor normally reserved for higher-ranking leaders. Mekhlis had been hospitalized following his retirement for reasons of health in 1950.[1]

Beria's foe and Stalin's favorite general, Armed Forces Chief of Staff Colonel General Sergey Shtemenko, also lost his job in February.[2] The Politburo took this action at the insistence of Beria, after consultation with former Defense Minister Bulganin. Only later did Stalin learn of it. In addition, the Politburo fired Minister of Public Health Dr. Yefim Smirnov, who had been serving simultaneously as Stalin's personal physician.

Lieutenant General Nikolay ("Fat Kolya") Spiridonov and Major General Petr Kosynkin had been commandant and deputy commandant, respectively, of the Kremlin Kommandatura since 1939. Of the two, General Kosynkin was on more intimate terms with Stalin. He spent less time supervising Kommandatura subordinates than standing at Stalin's elbow and fulfilling his requests for personal services.

The obituary for Kosynkin said that he died "unexpectedly" of a heart attack, in the line of duty, on February 17.[3] On the next Saturday I happened to see Colonel Nosarev's deputy for Kommandatura Personnel-Security as we left the main MGB headquarters building. Hailing this lieutenant colonel, I caught up with him, and we walked together for a block or two.

"Too bad about Comrade Kosynkin," I said.

"Yeah, too bad. It hit Colonel Nosarev and me pretty hard."

"Well, it's a severe blow to the Big Chief too. I often saw Comrade Kosynkin opening the car door when the Big Chief's limousine drove up to the Council of Ministers building."

"Yeah, Comrade Kosynkin was always there," said the lieutenant colonel.

"And almost always the Big Chief would smile at him and say a few words. By the way, was it known that Comrade Kosynkin had a heart condition?"

"Petr Sergeyevich, I'm skating on thin ice when I tell you this. The only heart condition he had was that it stopped beating. Comrade Kosynkin died from being shot in the head."

"Executed?"

"You could say that." The lieutenant colonel paused. "It's making a difference in Comrade Spiridonov. 'Fat Kolya' says that hereafter he'll answer only to the Politburo as a group. He won't answer to a single individual anymore."[4]

"Whereas till now he answered strictly to the Big Chief."

"Yes, that's right. Strictly to the Big Chief till now."

When we separated at the corner he urged me not to repeat his remarks.

From late January through February 1953 the indications of a drastic shift in power accumulated. They led us in the MGB to believe that in the Politburo as well as in State Security Stalin had lost the struggle with Beria. The fabricated case against the "saboteur-doctors" was Stalin's last stand. If the case mushroomed into a purge that destroyed rivals, Stalin would have been restored to his positions as CPSU general secretary and de facto chief of State Security. Obviously, the gamble failed.[5]

I imagine Beria putting forward two arguments to persuade a majority of Politburo members to join him in a rebellion against Stalin. The first argument would have been this: Stalin intended the purge to envelop the entire Politburo old guard—Malenkov, Khrushchev, Bulganin, Voroshilov, Mikoyan, Kaganovich, and Molotov besides Beria. After that, and following his pattern of the past, it was only a matter of time before Stalin purged some or all of the 16 new members whom he appointed in October 1952. To cancel the purge, the eight old guard members (including Beria) needed five new members for a majority of 13 votes to 12 (including Stalin's). Assuming a democratic process at work in the Politburo, Beria won a majority over to his side, against Stalin.[6]

Second, Politburo members needed no persuasion that Stalin *should not* repeat the pattern of past purges. Where Politburo members needed persuasion was on the point that Stalin *could not* repeat the pattern. Beria may have argued that Stalin had lost the capability to conduct a purge because he no longer controlled the MGB—Beria did. Beria had been building influence in the MGB since the last months of 1951, and Stalin and Minister Ignatyev had not succeeded in stopping him. With nothing to fear from an MGB no longer answering to Stalin, the Politburo majority joined with Beria to terminate the purge.

Whether or not the Politburo was actually polled, it did rebel against

Stalin and then faced the problem of how to dispose of him. Explaining the removal of "the beloved leader" to the Party and to the public at large presented grave difficulties. The Politburo had to be prudent in letting it be known that Stalin had been unseated—to disclose the mutiny clumsily might stir up violence and cause the shedding of Politburo blood. Telling the truth was not feasible—to declare at this time that the doctors' plot was a fabrication by Stalin might open Pandora's box. Not only would the truth raise questions about the legitimacy of the post-Stalin regime, the truth could spark a counterrevolution against everyone in the Kremlin, including Stalin, or a counterrevolution led by Stalin against his successors. While it sought a solution, the Politburo had no choice but to keep Stalin on as the titular head of the Party and government.

Kommandatura Deputy Kosynkin, who died in mid-February, had been a Stalin loyalist in the mold of Kremlin chief of staff Poskrebyshev, Minister Abakumov, Guards Directorate Chief Vlasik, Vlasik's deputies, and the chief of bodyguards for Stalin—all dismissed in 1951–52. Stalin's personal physician and the chief of the Armed Forces General Staff were both dismissed in February 1953. Also, during that 21-month period the number of Stalin's bodyguards was cut in half, many of his personal staffers were reassigned, and the inexperienced Ignatyev took charge of the Guards Directorate. Gradually the means for protecting Stalin's life had withered.

In the 30 years since Stalin had been named CPSU general secretary, the quality of MGB protection for his life was never worse than toward the end of February 1953. The stripping of Stalin's personal security and his increased vulnerability were apparent.

- Personal chief of staff and aide in directing MGB activities: position vacant since Poskrebyshev's removal in April 1952.
- Minister of State Security: the inexperienced Ignatyev since April 1952.
- Chief of the Guards Directorate: none since April 1952.
- Personal bodyguards: reduced by half in mid-1952.
- Chief of personal bodyguards: replaced in mid-1952 by a colonel lacking command experience in this specialty.
- Personal chauffeurs and bodyguards: also replaced in mid-1952.
- Personal servants at the dacha in Kuntsevo: cut back in mid-1952.

- Chief of physical security at the Kremlin office and unofficial doorman: none since February 1953.
- Minister of Public Health and Stalin's personal physician: dismissed in February 1953.
- Chief of the Armed Forces General Staff: dismissed in February 1953.
- Miscellaneous physical security units around Moscow: reduced in size and dispersed to other organizations in mid-1952.

Stalin was now in greater isolation than ever in his Kremlin office. Bodyguards noticed that after *Pravda* printed the saboteur-doctors story on January 13, Stalin behaved more cautiously than ever before. He ceased entertaining leaders at his dacha in Kuntsevo, he had Guards officers employ more stringent security measures for his trips by limousine between Kuntsevo and the Kremlin, and he received Politburo members only in his Kremlin office, never seeing Beria alone. Stalin, it seemed, feared that revealing his intentions about the purge intensified his opponents' incentives to assassinate him.

15

The Assault and the Cover-Up

The Council of Ministers building lies within the walls of the Kremlin, which separate it from the Lenin Mausoleum and Red Square.

Empress Catherine the Great reigned during its construction in the years 1776 to 1787, and it was originally known both by the name of its architect Kazakov and as the Senate Building. After the 1917 Revolution, Lenin lived and worked there until his death in 1924. Stalin followed suit, up to a point.

The building has two wings set at a 30-degree angle, and the exterior looks plain by comparison with the Kremlin cathedrals and towers. On the ground floor of one wing was an apartment for Stalin. He had not occupied it since his dacha in Kuntsevo had opened, making redundant the round-the-clock staff of Guards Directorate servants. The top floor of the wing was vacant.

Stalin had offices on the second (middle) floor of that wing. Visitors passed through the anteroom where Poskrebyshev sat, and they met Stalin in the outsized, oblong inner room. In the far left corner stood his heavy wooden desk, perpendicular to a conference table, which was equipped with pencils and pads. Both the desk and the conference table were made of the same light yellow Karelian birch. At the rear of the inner room was a corridor leading to three smaller rooms: a servants' room that had an exit (always guarded), a room where snacks were stored and eaten, and a room where Stalin rested. In this last room were a couch that he used, a bed that he did not use, a small table, and two chairs. Stalin could enter this room either through the corridor or through a sliding panel concealed in a wall of the inner room.

He was alone in the inner room Friday evening, February 27, 1953, when Beria and Malenkov arrived. He was alone for many hours after they left. His personal bodyguards, who remained on the ground floor, eventually grew concerned by Stalin's silence. They peeked into the inner room, saw him lying beside the desk, and went to his aid. However, they were unable to rouse him.

The first doctors to reach the scene were summoned from the small LSUK clinic within the Kremlin. They were told that Stalin had fallen and struck his head against a corner of the desk.

This much of events inside the Kremlin on the night of February 27–28 I learned from separate accounts given to me in confidence by two Guards officers. They were Colonel Dmitriy Nosarev and his deputy, the personnel-security officers for the Kremlin Kommandatura that guarded the Council of Ministers building. Their statements received partial corroboration from a neighbor of mine in the Guards Directorate apartment building. He served on the detail of Malenkov's bodyguards.

As I left for work at about 9:30 on Saturday morning, February 28, he returned to Chkalov Street at the end of his night shift. "Last night," my neighbor said excitedly, "they found the Big Chief in a coma on the floor of his office." He told me that he had learned this from overhearing a conversation of Malenkov's wife a few hours before.

What happened to Stalin while Beria and Malenkov were in his office that evening can be inferred from the remainder of Colonel Nosarev's account to me. Through the evening and night hours of February 27–28 it was his turn to be the duty officer for the Kommandatura. Checking physical security measures, duty officers circled outside the Kremlin Wall and the Lenin Mausoleum, walked around the buildings inside the Kremlin, and received verbal reports by sentries. If sentries heard a commotion inside the Council of Ministers building or elsewhere, they had orders to report this to the duty officer.

On that night they made no such report to Colonel Nosarev. He himself, however, witnessed something significant.

"I was standing in darkness near the Supreme Soviet building," Nosarev told me, "and I saw Comrade Beria and Comrade Malenkov come out of the Council of Ministers building. Their cars and drivers were waiting for them in the courtyard. They walked toward Comrade Beria's car. They talked to each other, but I couldn't hear what they said.

"Comrade Beria had a blackjack in his hand, in full sight of Comrade Malenkov. They stopped beside the Beria car, the bodyguard who had been sitting with the driver opened the door, and Comrade Beria tossed the blackjack on the back seat. They talked a little bit more, still out of earshot. Then they got into their cars and left."

Answering my questions, Nosarev said that he was by himself that night, that he had not been observed, and that he had not reported the blackjack scene through official channels nor did he expect to report it.[1] About being observed, Nosarev remarked, "I probably wouldn't be standing here if I had been seen, Petr Sergeyevich." He meant that he probably would have been killed.

Stalin was overmatched in defending himself against an assault by the two Politburo members, one armed with a blackjack. Beria and Malenkov were younger than he by 19 and 21 years, respectively, and both outweighed him. Stalin's left arm had been partially immobilized since his youth from an injury inflicted when his father struck him with a shoemaker's last, and in later life his health had deteriorated.

Guards officers said prior to the assault that Beria beat people with blackjacks in order to obtain cooperation or to vent anger. Either could have been his purpose in striking Stalin, but it seems equally possible that Beria meant to kill him. Whether the assault was premeditated is also open to debate.

I heard from two high officers of Stalin's protective forces—who may have heard directly from the bodyguard who first found the stricken Stalin—that Stalin was not stricken in the dacha nor in his Kremlin living quarters, but in his Kremlin office. Major Ilyin was the chief of the Personnel-Security Department of Stalin's personal bodyguard (Okhrana Number One), and Lieutenant Colonel Pesochnikov was deputy chief of personnel-security of the commandant of the Kremlin. Both were close and longtime colleagues of mine in the personnel work of the bodyguards, and they spoke to me separately and on different occasions. As far as I can imagine, neither of them knew nor cared that the other had told me or would tell me. The matter does not seem to have been especially sensitive, at least within the inner circles of the bodyguards. (The leaders had not yet begun to issue contrary stories.) Ilyin and Pesochnikov had no reason to mislead me, and they had a very good reason to tell the truth. The Kremlin was no place to spin dangerous lies.

They told me that Stalin was found lying on the floor alongside his desk, as if he had been stricken either at the desk or getting up from it. One said that he thought Stalin had been trying to reach a buzzer or phone and may have lain there for hours. (I presume he was calculating from the last prior bodyguard sighting of Stalin.)

The guard notified the proper people. Soon afterward, on highest authority—meaning Beria and Malenkov; it could not have been done otherwise—Stalin was carried down to the door (either by his elevator or by the short staircase, both known well to me personally) and bundled into his car, as usual two steps from the outside door. Then he was driven out to the dacha for the five-day agony. (As I remember, this happened on Saturday night, 28 February.)

Why was Stalin moved to the dacha? Why was he not taken to the Kremlin clinic or treated where he was? One reason might be the fear that in the Kremlin or in the Kremlin clinic, where many people worked, the news might leak and cause a panic. (The leaders showed in many ways in those next days how frightened they were of the people's reaction.) By moving Stalin to the dacha they revealed—as they did again by not calling a doctor immediately—that their motive was not Stalin's survival, but their own.

If the statements by Guards Directorate personnel are truthful—and I have no reason to doubt them[2]—the facts are these: During the evening of Friday, February 27, 1953, Beria and Malenkov visited Stalin in his offices on the second floor of the Council of Ministers building. Beria hit Stalin with a blackjack and rendered him unconscious. Malenkov witnessed Beria's assault on Stalin, but no one else was present. Beria and Malenkov left Stalin alone, perhaps for dead.

They did not call for medical assistance. Stalin's personal bodyguards did so much later that night, and their assumption, stated to the doctors, was that the Big Chief had been hurt in falling against his desk. There must have been a head wound, at least an edema, for the bodyguards to have said this; yet never have Soviet officials referred to an injury to Stalin of that sort, or to any injury at all.

The dissident Soviet scientist Andrey Sakharov accused the KGB of injecting him in 1984 with a substance that induced the symptoms of a stroke. (The larger the dosage of this poison, presumably the likelier a fatality sooner rather than later.) While I was in MGB headquarters, until 1953, the MGB operated a secret laboratory in the Lubyanka Prison that developed and experimented with new poisons and tested them on inmates. The formula for the poison injected into Sakharov might have been discovered by the Lubyanka laboratory 30 years earlier. (The commandant of the Lubyanka Prison, Major General Blokhin, was one of the few MGB generals in the Center whom Beria did not purge during the March–June 1953 period.)

Conceivably, Beria administered a substance that produced stroke-like symptoms in Stalin—although it appears more likely that the cause was a blow to the head. Whether from poison, the blackjack beating, or a combination of both, Stalin lapsed into a coma. Unintentionally, then, Stalin's bodyguards set the stage for the cover-up that protected Beria and Malenkov.

On Saturday, February 28, Stalin was found unconscious in his office. Beria and Malenkov, who had not expected Stalin to survive their visitation of the night before, arranged for Stalin to be transported out of the Kremlin and taken to the Kuntsevo dacha. This relocation, away from the unwanted attention that Stalin's condition was certain to attract, could have taken place anytime during the 24 to 36 hours after Stalin was found.

February 28 is the birthday of Svetlana Alliluyeva, Stalin's daughter. Stalin meticulously marked the birthdays of those close to him. His daughter's memoirs, however, make no reference to her birthday in 1953 or to having been in touch with Stalin on that date in 1953. No sources have made available any details concerning Stalin's health, whereabouts, or activities during the daytime hours on this Saturday.

According to Khrushchev, on Saturday night Stalin was host to Beria,

Malenkov, Khrushchev, and Bulganin at a late dinner party in Stalin's dacha, and his illness began following the dinner party.

By Sunday night, March 1, Stalin had neither died nor regained consciousness. Beria and Malenkov called Khrushchev and Bulganin to the dacha, where they put together the alibi of the dinner party on the previous night. (The alibi was a bargaining chip of blackmail for Khrushchev and Bulganin as they brokered themselves into a piece of the collective post-Stalin leadership.) Only then was medical assistance sought for Stalin.

The team of specialists saw the injury from the blackjack beating. Discretion being the better part of valor, they swallowed their suspicions and disregarded this evidence. They attested that Stalin suffered a stroke and certified that the stroke was the single cause of his death.

In her book, published in the West but not in the USSR, Stalin's daughter wrote that she was first notified of her father's illness on Monday, March 2.[3] She was called to the dacha in Kuntsevo at that time to be at Stalin's bedside. The leaders present there with her were Beria, Malenkov, Khrushchev, and Bulganin.

Ms. Alliluyeva also wrote of having tried on March 1 (Sunday) to phone Stalin—presumably at the dacha, although she did not specify—and the bodyguard who took her call telling her after checking, "There's no movement right now." (Of course there was no movement; Stalin was unconscious.) Svetlana interpreted the response to mean that Stalin could not be disturbed.

Stalin never regained consciousness, or at least never regained speech—he was unable to accuse Beria of assaulting him and Malenkov of being an accessory.

A government announcement broke the news to the public on Wednesday, March 4, about "the grave illness of Comrade I. V. Stalin." Dated March 3, signed by the CPSU Central Committee and Council of Ministers, the announcement read in part:

> During the night of March 1–2 [sic, i.e., 48 hours after the assault occurred] Comrade Stalin, while in his Moscow apartment [sic], had a hemorrhage of the brain, which affected vital parts of his brain. Comrade Stalin lost consciousness.

Paralysis of the right arm and leg developed. Loss of speech occurred. Serious disturbances developed in the functioning of the heart and breathing.

The best medical personnel have been called in to treat Comrade Stalin. . . . [Titles, names, and specialties of eight doctors were listed; none of the names was recognizably Jewish]. Treatment of Comrade Stalin is under the guidance of Comrade A. F. Tretyakov, USSR minister of Public Health, and Comrade I. I. Kuperin, chief of the Medical Office of the Kremlin.[4]

Treatment of Comrade Stalin is under the constant supervision of the Central Committee of the Communist Party of the Soviet Union and the Soviet Government. . . .

The next passage predicted Stalin's "more or less prolonged" incapacitation. That would necessitate his "withdrawal from leading state and Party activity."

No additional medical particulars concerning Stalin's death were officially released after the government announcement dated March 3. Its statement about a brain hemorrhage seems accurate as far as it goes, but a blow or blows to the head could have caused this result. The existence of a head injury was not mentioned.

Another area of conflict is the time when Stalin was found unconscious. The announcement on March 3 said that Stalin's illness began "during the night of March 1–2," a Sunday. My conversation with my neighbor took place on the previous Saturday morning, February 28. That makes my neighbor's time of February 27–28 more acceptable than March 1–2.

My neighbor at that time had no reason to distort or withhold the truth, no reason to worry about punishment for telling me these details. The official version, which conflicted with his, *was not released until the following Wednesday, March 4.*

The announcement lied about the date and place of Stalin being stricken. Khrushchev later offered almost as many versions about the night when Stalin was found unconscious as the number of times he told the tale.

Official versions say Stalin was stricken ill in his private quarters. According to Khrushchev on several occasions, the illness began in the dacha in Kuntsevo. The announcement dated March 3 said that Stalin became ill "while in his Moscow apartment."

Noting its discrepancy with the Khrushchev claim, i.e., the Kuntsevo dacha, I fault the March 3 announcement by the Central Committee and Council of Ministers on an additional count. Stalin had not used his "Moscow apartment," on the floor below his office, since World War II. (The Russian word for apartment, *kvartira*, cannot be construed to mean office, for which the Russian word is *kabinet.*) It is clear, therefore, that the official versions contradict each other, and that in all probability Stalin was not found ill in his "Moscow apartment."

But this does not indicate that Khrushchev was correct in placing the onset of Stalin's illness at the dacha in Kuntsevo. To the contrary, four Guards officers made identical statements to me that disputed not only Khrushchev's claim but also the official announcement. They said that Stalin was found unconscious beside the desk in his Kremlin office.

In my opinion the general conclusion has been wrong and Khrushchev lied. In speaking to Westerners while heading the Soviet regime and in dictating his memoirs while retired, Khrushchev never got straight his elaborate tale about the night Stalin was found unconscious.

The version that Khrushchev most often paraded began with Stalin hosting him, Beria, Malenkov, and Bulganin at a late dinner party in the Kuntsevo dacha on Saturday night, February 28. Stalin became ill after his guests left. Upon being notified many hours afterward, Khrushchev and the other three leaders hurried back to the dacha. Then the doctors arrived.

Among other things wrong with this version is that, following the *Pravda* announcement of the doctors' plot on January 13, Stalin refused to entertain anyone at the dacha.

One relevant part of the Khrushchev account is that Khrushchev lied about where and when Stalin was found unconscious. Another relevant part is his claim that the guests attending Stalin's dinner party were Beria, Malenkov, Bulganin, and himself, Khrushchev. The account brings these four together at a crucial moment in Soviet history.

There had been a delay in obtaining medical assistance, Khrushchev said. *Pravda* reported that the specialists treating Stalin were "under the guidance" of the (newly appointed) minister of Health, Aleksandr Tretyakov, and the "chief of the Kremlin medical office," Ivan Kuperin (an MGB major general who had been head of LSUK for under a year). Neither of Stalin's recent personal physicians participated in his treatment. He had imprisoned Dr. Vinogradov in 1952, and Dr. Smirnov was relieved of his position as minister of Health in February 1953. The attending physicians thus had no personal familiarity with the medical background of their patient in the dacha.

Doctor of Historical Sciences Sergo Mikoyan is the son of the late Anastas Mikoyan, a Politburo member immediately before and after Stalin died. Sergo's version of Stalin's death appeared in *Komsomolskaya Pravda*, the official national newspaper for younger people preparing to join the CPSU. Published on February 4, 1988, the pertinent extract reads as follows:

> It was nighttime on 1 March 1953. Stalin, who had high blood pressure, went for a bath. He was left alone in the room, where a bed had been prepared on a couch. He never used to get up before 12 or sometimes even 1 in the afternoon, and nobody could enter his room unless asked.
>
> Two o'clock came and went, three, four, five o'clock. The alarmed security guards did not know what to do. Finally they called the cook, a simple elderly Russian woman who had long worked for the Big Chief (perhaps one of the few people whom he still trusted). She knocked on the door. No answer. She knocked louder. Finally they decided to break the door down.
>
> The Big Chief was lying on the floor near the couch. He had suffered a major stroke and was completely paralyzed, having lost even the power of speech. He just looked angrily at those around him and the physicians [new ones!] who had arrived, and at the Politburo members, informed by Malenkov, who had come to the dacha. Three or four days went by.
>
> It was the end of an era. . . .

Thus in 1988 Sergo Mikoyan replayed fictions from the government announcement 35 years before and from Khrushchev's tale.

In the end, the March 6, 1953 issue of *Pravda* reported Stalin died in the evening of March 5, 1953, according to an announcement by the Central Committee, the Council of Ministers, and the Praesidium of the Supreme Soviet.

Stalin died 51 days after *Pravda* printed the first article on the doctors' plot. Without any more than *Pravda* and hunches to go by, the public East and West concluded that Stalin's death explained why Beria and others were not purged. Khrushchev confirmed this general conclusion at the 20th Party Congress in 1956. He claimed that death prevented Stalin, his power absolute, from culminating the doctors' plot in a purge.

Material from Soviet sources about the cause of Stalin's death wasn't convincing, least of all for MGB officers. In the West skepticism arose from three factors: the history of Soviet leaders distorting the truth, the inconsistent and contradictory statements about the circumstances of death, and Stalin's loss of power before the end of February.

Stalin could not be permitted to live, I believe, due to the risk that he would attempt a countercoup. The Politburo, therefore, overthrew Stalin in February 1953 to avert a purge. Stalin's timely death was the solution—Beria's, Malenkov's and possibly others'—to the problem of disposing of the deposed Stalin. Discounting the information from official Soviet sources, I conclude that Beria was responsible for the death of Stalin, Malenkov was his accomplice, and Khrushchev and Bulganin were accessories after the fact.

Colonel Nosarev told me in 1953 that the cover-up puzzled him. It did not do so insofar as the guilt of Beria and Malenkov was concerned—the reason was as evident then as it is today—but it did regarding where and when Stalin lost consciousness. Clearly Stalin was moved from the Kremlin office to his dacha by someone. He probably was not moved by Guards officers, or else Nosarev would have known and said so.

16

The Status of Stalin

Stalin's death removed a threat to my MGB career that I myself created, but there would not have been that threat without the meddlesome Valya Orlik. A denunciation by Orlik got me in trouble with MGB Minister Ignatyev. The outcome was not as Orlik intended, however, and by accident she led to my discovering of the new regime's attitude toward Stalin after he died.

Orlik was a clerk who worked for me in the Austro-German Department of the Foreign Operations Directorate. She was an old hand there, and her command of German helped officers like me who had only a smattering of the language. Nevertheless, we did not get along well. Orlik's work remained sloppy regardless of my demands for improvement and despite the critical evaluation that she knew I had placed in her personnel file. By the fall of 1952, I had had enough—at my request, she was transferred.

Meanwhile, Orlik listened as avidly as everyone else in the department to my tales of serving with the bodyguards. I was surprised by my new colleagues' ignorance about the Kremlin leaders and their relatives, facts that Guards Directorate officers knew as a matter of course. It was not known, for example, that Politburo Members Zhdanov and Shcherbakov were brothers-in-law or that Stalin's daughter Svetlana had married Zhdanov's son, Yuriy.

Their high interest carried me, I admit, beyond the bounds of propriety into making disclosures about the Stalin family. I related anecdotes from the bodyguards that revolved around son Vasiliy's drinking binges, daughter Svetlana's love affairs, the cigarettes packaged exclusively for the Big Chief, his specially bottled wine, the efforts to make him seem taller than he really was. That is where the trouble started.

In January 1953, less than eight weeks before Stalin died, I was called in for an interview by the chief investigator of officers' infractions of MGB rules. The colonel treated me politely. Volodya Petrochenkov had helped him get that job, and perhaps the colonel knew I was Volodya's friend.

He said he was checking a complaint that I had spread "unhealthy rumors" in the Austro-German Department about people around Stalin. The complaint was sent by letter to Minister Ignatyev from a self-described "devoted Party member." Ignatyev had passed the letter to the colonel with a handwritten cover note that read, "Investigate and report."

This was a serious matter, I knew, particularly with our minister having the chief investigator's ear. For misdeeds less consequential than mine, MGB officers had been punished severely. Some were sentenced to prison camps.

"Is the accusation correct, Major Deriabin, that you've been gossiping in your office about the Big Chief and his children?"

"Anything I might have let out of the bag was truthful."

"Truths or falsehoods aren't the point," the colonel said. "Generally, do you remember the nature of your rumors?"

"Oh, probably something about the Big Chief's son being an alcoholic. That's an open secret around the Center, isn't it?"

"What else, Major?"

"Well, I've spoken quite a bit about Comrade Stalin's daughter—her being pregnant at the time of the first marriage, to Morozov. He's a Jew, you know. So the Big Chief. . . ."

"You ought to be careful about what you say," interrupted the colonel.

I promised that I would, then asked whether the Orlik woman was my accuser. The colonel broke the rules. He confirmed my guess, showed me her letter with Ignatyev's cover note, and asked why I had suspected Orlik. I told him the background.

"Although I'd like to sweep this complaint under the rug," he said, "you've seen that our minister wants it investigated. I'll get back to you as soon as he's made a decision."

Two months passed, Stalin died, Beria succeeded Ignatyev at the head of State Security, and I had heard nothing more about my case. As Petrochenkov realized, I still worried about the charge outstanding against me. In mid-March he advised me to phone a different colonel about my case, a new chief investigator appointed by Beria a few days earlier.

"Greetings, Comrade Colonel. This is Major Deriabin."

"Oh? What can I do for you?"

"I understand you've taken over my case."

"Your case?"

"Yes, the Orlik letter to Minister Ignatyev. The one concerning my statements about Comrade Stalin and his family."

"Oh, that case!" The colonel laughed. "Forget it, Major. Comrade Beria doesn't want us bothered with trifles like that."

"Well, it's a great relief to hear that."

"I'm pleased to say that our minister has ordered me to drop the whole senseless affair. I've tossed your case in the wastebasket where it belongs. Get back to your job, and good luck."

"Thank you, Comrade Colonel," I said.

"You can thank Comrade Beria." The colonel hung up.

This brief conversation told me as distinctly as anything could in those early days of the new regime that Beria had set about destroying the idolization of Stalin. There was no other explanation for his verdict in my case, nor for Beria so soon paying attention to a matter so seemingly minor among the hundreds of pressing items on his agenda.

After Beria was deposed in June and another reshuffle of the leadership occurred, I began to worry again about Valya Orlik's complaint. A chance to test where I stood arose in July.

At the top of the CPSU structure in the MGB was a Party committee closely attuned to the nuances of Kremlin politics. This committee of generals and colonels had veto power over postings to foreign countries, and it interviewed each candidate. In July my turn for an interview came as a result of an impending assignment abroad. The Party secretary spent several minutes reading my record aloud to the other committee members. No mention of Orlik's letter was made.

"Any questions?" the Party secretary asked the panel. The rest of the members shook their heads.

"Any objections to Comrade Deriabin's next assignment?" A second round of head-shaking.

"Well, then, Comrade Deriabin," the Party secretary said, "I congratulate you. We expect you to be the exemplary Communist that you always have been in the past. That will be all."

"Thank you, Comrades," I said, "but there's one more point I'd like to raise."

Better now than later to determine whether the denunciation by Orlik was expunged from my record. I summarized the investigation and its origin.

The generals and colonels exchanged smiles, and the Party secretary, grinning, replied that nothing of this sort appeared in my file. Even if it did, he added, it would be irrelevant. The committee members nodded. The Party secretary told me I could leave, and leave I did, relieved that the trouble instigated by Orlik was definitely over.

The reactions of the MGB Party committee showed that these high-ranking MGB officers, with excellent connections to the Kremlin leadership, did not give a damn about Stalin any more. Clearly, then, the CPSU Central Committee and the Politburo didn't either. Soviet citizens, I realized, no longer were expected to pay lip service to Stalin or the myth about him.

Thirty-one months would elapse before this stance on Stalin became official policy for the CPSU at large. It was in February 1956 that Khrushchev delivered the remarkable Secret Speech at the 20th Party Congress on Stalin's "cult of the personality."

17

"I Am the Politburo"

All of Moscow seemed subdued by shock. In the sunshine and bitter cold of March 10, 1953, some 30,000 of us in Red Square watched three dozen leaders—our own and those from foreign Communist parties—assemble on the platform at the Lenin Mausoleum in front of the Kremlin. Below the platform, below a simple banner bearing two names, Lenin's above Stalin's, reposed the massive ornate casket of Iosif (Josef) Vissarionovich Stalin.

Moscow Radio had interrupted the playing of dirges to announce his death: At 9:50 P.M. on Thursday, March 5, Stalin, "chairman of the USSR Council of Ministers and secretary of the Central Committee of the Communist Party of the Soviet Union, died after a grave illness."

Although an earlier report had forewarned us of the seriousness of Stalin's condition, the news stunned the nation. A typical reaction was that of my mother-in-law. Tearfully she ran around her apartment saying over and over, "What shall we do now that Comrade Stalin is dead? What shall we do?"

She was not alone in her apprehension. Everyone wondered about a future without Stalin, the man whom MGB officers called the Khozyain, the Big Chief. Colleagues of mine in the MGB expressed concern about changes under the new regime. A reign of nearly 30 years had ended, and we could be sure of nothing else.

For three days the body lay in state at the Hall of Columns in the House of Trade Unions, three blocks from the Kremlin. On the first day hundreds died in the crush of thousands pushing forward, not knowing that admission to the hall was by ticket. People wanted to check for themselves that the unthinkable had happened, that their god had died.

Mourners with tickets went into the hall through the rear entrance, 50 at a time, and shuffled past the casket. They weren't allowed to pause and gaze at the remains of Stalin. Some wept quietly. Some sobbed aloud.

Friends of mine in the MGB honor guard let me enter the hall through the front entrance on two of the three days when the body was on view. I joined the orderly queues filing past the casket, but it was raised so high that only the tip of Stalin's nose could be seen. This made little difference to me. I was there partly out of curiosity, partly to be able to say that I had seen the Big Boss in death as well as in life. My eyes were dry. The indecencies of the deceased would not permit me sadness; yet fears and uncertainty about the coming days, about life ahead, would not permit me joy.

Only a favored 10,000 dignitaries and 20,000 of us on the MGB security detail were allowed into Red Square for the funeral ceremony. We listened to loudspeakers broadcast eulogies by three Politburo members speaking from the Lenin Mausoleum platform—first Georgiy Malenkov, the successor to Stalin as chairman of the Council of Ministers and a secretary of the CPSU Central Committee; last Vyacheslav Molotov, the Politburo elder who was minister of Foreign Affairs; in between Lavrentiy Beria, head of the newly reconstituted State Security service.

Of the three eulogies, I considered Beria's the best, even though he took liberties with the truth. "The peoples of the Soviet Union," he declared, "can continue to rely with complete trust on the Communist Party, its Central Committee, and their Soviet Government.... Our Party... is united and unshakable."

Beria praised one living person, "the talented disciple of Lenin and loyal comrade-in-arms of Stalin," Malenkov. As for Stalin, he was "the inspired continuer of Lenin's works... a man who is near and dear to all Soviet peoples.... The grief in our hearts is unquenchable, the loss is immeasurably heavy." Beria closed his funeral oration with the words,

"Eternal glory to our beloved and dear leader and teacher, the great Stalin."

What hypocrisy! For more than 30 years "our beloved and dear leader and teacher" had set a standard for bloodletting and cruelty that made reigns of the tsars seem benign. This was no secret, certainly not to the Big Chief's former collaborator Beria.

In the realignment of the Kremlin power structure after Stalin died, the Politburo old guard acquired almost all of the important Party and government positions. The leaders sought to keep the public calm by moving quickly to exhibit unity and smoothness in the transition. They announced the realignment on March 7, two days after Stalin died and three days before his funeral.

The largest share of power went to the Beria-Malenkov alliance. Guards officers for many years had remarked on the affinity of the two men; no other Politburo members displayed a closer friendship, and they had been in league on many things (including, most recently, the fatal assault on Stalin). Now Beria assumed primacy in one center of power, the so-called "organs of State Security," and Malenkov assumed primacy in the other, the CPSU. Both gained power beyond what they had amassed toward the end of Stalin's reign.

Organs of State Security were consolidated under Beria by the merger of the MGB with the regular police, the Ministry of Internal Affairs (MVD). The hybrid organization took the name of the MVD, and Beria took the title minister of Internal Affairs. Malenkov continued as a CPSU secretary, but in addition he succeeded Stalin as premier, i.e., as chairman of the Council of Ministers.

The remaining principal ministries were allotted to Molotov (Foreign Affairs), Bulganin (Defense), and Mikoyan (Foreign Trade). Each was returning to a job held before being dismissed by Stalin in 1949. Voroshilov assumed the chairmanship of the Praesidium of the Supreme Soviet, which meant that he headed the ruling body in the powerless national legislature.

In the revised Party lineup, 14 of Stalin's 16 recent appointees to the Politburo were left out. The eight old guard members who stayed on—Beria, Malenkov, Khrushchev, Bulganin, Voroshilov, Molotov, Mikoyan, and Kaganovich—made a solid majority. The current crop of CPSU secretaries consisted of two holdovers besides Malenkov—Khrushchev and a nonmember of the Politburo—and three newcomers, including former minister of State Security Ignatyev. By title, the six secretaries were equal, for none was designated general secretary as Stalin had been until the previous year.

It looked as if Malenkov were indeed the heir to Stalin that proceedings at the 19th Party Congress in October 1952 had indicated he would become. Like Stalin, Malenkov simultaneously held the positions of premier, Politburo member, and CPSU secretary, the latter encompassing (as before) oversight of Party cadres and Beria's MGB-MVD. This arrangement, however, was only temporary. It lasted one week.

Pravda waited seven more days and *Izvestiya* eight days to print the official statement that showed how Malenkov had been taken down a peg or two. The newspapers reported that the CPSU Central Committee on March 14 granted his "request" to be released from the Secretariat. He was relinquishing a position that provided him with considerably greater power than did his chairmanship of the Council of Ministers.

Khrushchev benefited from Malenkov's setback. In retrospect it had been a bad omen for Malenkov when on March 10 Khrushchev gave up his duties as secretary of the Moscow Party Committee in order to "concentrate on work in the Central Committee" of the CPSU. He was pushing deeper into Malenkov's realm. From March 14, Khrushchev stood preeminent in the Secretariat by virtue of Politburo membership, which the other four secretaries did not have, and by seniority in length of service. Besides being first among equals in the Secretariat, he garnered greater power by taking on Malenkov's responsibility for oversight of Party cadres and the State Security organs.

My MGB colleagues concluded that in the jockeying for power among the post-Stalin leadership, Beria abruptly tilted away from Malenkov and toward Khrushchev. When it fit his plans, Beria severed the alliance that had been vital in the struggle with Stalin. Doubtless Beria favored someone less likely than Malenkov to challenge him for dominance, someone such as Khrushchev, whom he judged to be more maneuverable.

To get Khrushchev's support in downgrading Malenkov, Beria apparently made concessions. MGB officers noted the allegiance of two generals who were given assignments just below Beria in the combined MGB-MVD. Directly under him were three deputies. The previous minister of Internal Affairs, General Sergey Kruglov, became first deputy minister and day-to-day supervisor of the MVD side of the business. General Ivan Serov of the MGB was promoted to deputy minister without portfolio. Both he and Kruglov were Khrushchev protégés. The deputy minister for the MGB, General Bogdan Kobulov, belonged to the Beria faction.

Anticipating Stalin's death, his successors needed and sought acceptance by the citizens of a country where one man had monopolized power during most of the previous 29 years. The government announcement of March 3 on the illness of Stalin reflected Kremlin concerns about internal political stability.

> The Central Committee and the Council of Ministers express confidence that our Party and the whole Soviet people in these difficult days will display the greatest unity and cohesion, staunchness of spirit, and vigilance, will redouble their energies in building Communism in our country, [and] will rally closer around the Central Committee . . . and the government. . . .

The leadership repeated this thought in reporting that Stalin had died, and it was seen again many times during the following weeks. Behind the appeals lay anxiety that, with Stalin gone, citizens would rise in rebellion.

From its inception in 1917, State Security had been officially described as "the sword and the shield of the Revolution." It was the institutional weapon to prevent or put down counterrevolutions. The post-Stalin leadership thus relied on Beria and his combined MGB-MVD to save the new regime.

Although the inflammatory word "counterrevolution" was not used, the subject was the theme at an emergency meeting of MGB Party activists during the week after Stalin was buried. The CPSU Central Committee notified us that our "main purpose at this time is to maintain tranquillity." Nobody was fooled by the phrase—"to maintain tranquillity" was a loftier, softer way of saying "to prevent counterrevolution."

Beria and Deputy Minister Kobulov mobilized the MGB to quell any popular uprisings that might occur. Uniformed MGB troops massed around Moscow, and several thousand MGB officers were moved from East Germany to major cities in the provinces. Against the possibility of attempted coups by military units, MGB personnel responsible for security in the Armed Forces were placed on alert status.

If citizens had been inclined to revolt, these measures succeeded in pacifying them. The people remained passive. There was no storm for the Kremlin to ride out or sink under, and Beria was the savior. Molotov was overheard asking another Politburo member, "What would we have done without Comrade Beria?"

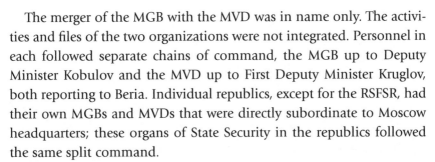

The merger of the MGB with the MVD was in name only. The activities and files of the two organizations were not integrated. Personnel in each followed separate chains of command, the MGB up to Deputy Minister Kobulov and the MVD up to First Deputy Minister Kruglov, both reporting to Beria. Individual republics, except for the RSFSR, had their own MGBs and MVDs that were directly subordinate to Moscow headquarters; these organs of State Security in the republics followed the same split command.

Beria brought in to run the MGB a number of arrogant, floundering generals whose principal qualification was loyalty to him. Besides Kobulov as deputy minister, Beriaites who arrived in the Center were Kuzmichev, chief, Guards Directorate; Vlodzimirskiy, chief, Sled-Chast'; Goglidze, chief of the Directorate for counterintelligence and security in the Armed Forces; and Ryasnoy, chief, Foreign Operations Directorate.[1] In two republics, Beriaites became chiefs of the combined MGB-MVD, Dekanozov in Georgia and Meshik in the Ukraine.

The most competent and experienced Beriaite general, Merkulov, chafed at the bit waiting to take a job in the MGB. He had been Beria's successor and Abakumov's predecessor as commissar of State Security but was now Minister of State Control. It was a secondary post, one of the supervising bureaucrats who checked on adherence to industrial production quotas.

Even in that ministry, Merkulov performed a service for Beria. It was imperative to get "little Mishka" Ryumin, until March 7 the deputy minister of State Security and chief of Sled-Chast', out of the way quickly. Beria arranged Ryumin's demotion on March 15. Now he was a department chief and dropped into the Ministry of State Control, where Merkulov kept an eye on him.

Deputy Minister Kobulov purged scores of MGB generals and colonels on evidence or suspicion of being disloyal to Beria. He carried out Beria's orders to have them executed, jailed, reassigned to Siberia, or retired. Lower down in the ranks, we worried that the purge would eventually reach us.

My friend Volodya Petrochenkov was a lieutenant colonel, one step above me. "In times like these," I told him, "I wish for a job on a collective farm."

"Me too. In all my years in State Security, I've never gone through anything like it. One day a boss is here, the next day he has disappeared. That used to happen when the Big Chief was alive, but not with such regularity."

We were taking a stroll during the afternoon break on a spring day in 1953. The mood around the Center was a mixture of pessimism and stagnation, so we walked away from the glum atmosphere in the MGB buildings around Dzerzhinskiy Square.

"There are more vacancies here and abroad than my department can fill," Volodya said.

"Don't I know it! Just try to get operational cables out of the Center. When I do locate a boss who has the right to approve my cables, as likely as not he won't sign off."

"Afraid of the consequences." Volodya stopped and squared around to face me. "Aren't you afraid, Petya? Before answering, let me tell you that I am."

"Yes, I am afraid," I said. "I've never openly criticized Beria or secretly collaborated against him, but that wouldn't prevent a malicious complaint from poisoning my life. Secretaries of MGB Party cells like I've been for quite a long time often have to make decisions that stunt careers."

"So do MGB personnel officers like me, and like you used to be in the Guards Directorate."

"And as a result of doing our job, we've alienated officers, Volodya. One of them might take it into his head to denounce us, and Beria would make sure that we were punished. He's not bothering with State Security tribunals to consider the evidence. Just a whisper about disloyalty, and the man is dead."

"Think of all the bosses who've disappeared," my pal said. "Their disloyalty to Beria was only conjectural in some cases."

"According to friends of mine in the bodyguards, certain Politburo members are beginning to feel nervous. They are having second thoughts about our minister of Internal Affairs."

"Maybe they yearn for the good old days under the Big Chief."

I laughed at Volodya's black humor, and we turned back toward Dzerzhinskiy Square.

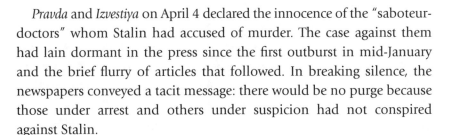

Pravda and *Izvestiya* on April 4 declared the innocence of the "saboteur-doctors" whom Stalin had accused of murder. The case against them had lain dormant in the press since the first outburst in mid-January and the brief flurry of articles that followed. In breaking silence, the newspapers conveyed a tacit message: there would be no purge because those under arrest and others under suspicion had not conspired against Stalin.

The item was printed beneath the headline "Communique of the USSR Ministry of Internal Affairs." Notices that convey important ramifications routinely came from the CPSU Central Committee, the Council of Ministers, or at least the Supreme Soviet. The communique was without precedent.

Identification of the MVD as the source signified that Beria considered the doctors innocent, had approved the wording of the text, and had authorized its publication. He was also absolving himself of guilt in this particular conspiracy against Stalin.

The communique read

> The USSR Ministry of Internal Affairs has carried out a thorough verification of all the preliminary investigation data in the case of the group of doctors accused of sabotage, espionage, and terrorist acts against active leaders of the Soviet state.
>
> The verification has established that the accused in this case [15 doctors' names listed but not all-inclusive] were arrested by the former USSR Ministry of State Security incorrectly, without any lawful basis.
>
> Verification has shown that the accusations against the above-named persons are false, and the documentary sources [confessions] on which the investigating officials based themselves are without foundation.
>
> It was established that the testimony of the arrested, allegedly confirming the accusations against them, was obtained by officials of the investigatory department [Sled-Chast'] of the former Ministry of State Security through the use of impermissible means of investigation [torture] that are strictly forbidden under Soviet law.
>
> On the basis of the conclusion of an investigatory commission especially appointed by the USSR Ministry of Internal Affairs to check this case, the arrested . . . [doctors' names] and others accused in this case have been completely exonerated of the accusations against them of sabotage, terrorist, and espionage activities, and . . . have been freed from imprisonment.
>
> The persons accused of incorrect conduct of the investigation have been arrested and brought to criminal responsibility.

Certain allegations in the original *Pravda* report about the "saboteur-doctors" were not specifically retracted. Presumably, however, American intelligence and British intelligence were as innocent as the accused doctors in this case; "leading Soviet military personnel" had not been the doctors' intended victims; and Politburo Member Zhdanov and his brother-in-law Shcherbakov did not die from medications deliberately misprescribed.

In a separate article on the same day, *Pravda* reported the disgrace that had befallen the LSUK doctor whose letters about Zhdanov and Shcherbakov were the starting point for Stalin's plan for a purge. In January Lydiya Timashuk had received the country's highest honor, the Order of Lenin, but now *Pravda* said that it had been revoked. The reason was not given, just as the reason for Timashuk having received the award had not been given.[2]

An editorial on April 6, three times longer than the MVD communique, attacked Stalin's minister and deputy minister of State Security, Ignatyev and Ryumin. "...The leaders of the former Ministry of State Security proved unequal to their tasks," *Pravda* said. "Ignatyev displayed political blindness and heedlessness. It turned out that he was led around by such criminal adventurists as Ryumin...who directed the investigation and who has now been arrested."

The editorial, expressing a stance that had always been Beria's, also criticized the past persecution of Jews as follows:

> Despicable adventurers of the Ryumin type tried, through their fabricated investigation, to inflame Soviet society...with feelings of national antagonism [anti-Semitism], which are profoundly alien to socialist ideology. For these provocational ends they did not stop at mad slander of Soviet people. Careful investigation has established, for example, that an honest public figure, USSR people's artist Mikhoels [a Jew], was slandered in this way.

Left unsaid was the fact that on Stalin's orders, the MGB killed Mikhoels in 1948 by running him over with a truck. Ryumin had had no part in the assassination by Operod of the Guards Directorate.

One day after the editorial appeared, *Pravda* said that the CPSU Central Committee had "released" Ignatyev from the Secretariat. Beria ordered the arrest of Ignatyev and Ryumin. While MGB officers were en route to take Ignatyev into custody, he suffered a heart attack—or so Beria was told—and gained a reprieve. Ryumin, however, went to the Lubyanka Prison. Although other Sled-Chast' officers investigated the doctors, and although the editorial indicated that they had, no one else was jailed for the frame-up.

I was in the United States when on July 23, 1954, *Pravda* reported Ryumin's trial and execution "by shooting" for his interrogation methods and "unjustified arrests...of a number of Soviet citizens, including prominent medical workers." The doctors, *Pravda* added, had been "fully rehabilitated." Rehabilitation, I knew, had arrived posthumously for some of those falsely accused—for Mikhoels and at least two doctors.

Shortly after the release of the MVD communique, I had opportunity to gain further insight into the public pardoning of the doctors. The Moscow City Party Organization assisted the Guards Directorate in the recruitment of personnel for the bodyguards by screening the files of CPSU members for candidates. During my years of recruiting for the directorate I met weekly with a district Party official named Petr Demichev.[3]

He often gossiped about his superiors, including Ekaterina Furtseva, whom Khrushchev later appointed Minister of Culture. "It's common knowledge that she's the mistress of Khrushchev," Demichev told me one day in 1950. "Who can blame them? Furtseva is rather pretty, and she has a stupid husband. Look at Khrushchev's wife—she's fat and ugly."

After leaving the Guards Directorate, I continued to see Demichev socially. We happened to meet again within a few days of publication of the MVD communique about the innocence of the accused doctors, and the subject arose during our conversation. I mentioned that Beria would not allow the doctors, despite their exoneration, to return to the Kremlin medical service, LSUK.

"Comrade Beria does some unusual things," Demichev said. "Now he has the Politburo in an uproar. The members went along with his proposal to pardon the doctors unconditionally, but he turned right around and defied them."

"How did he do that?"

"Well, the Politburo approved the pardons yet overrode Comrade Beria's suggestion to make the decision public. This fact filtered down to us in the Moscow City Party Committee, including to people on the staff of *Pravda*. They were astounded when somebody from your outfit delivered the communique with a note from Comrade Beria saying to publish it."

"That must have put the *Pravda* staff in a quandary," I said. "Either go with the Politburo or go with Comrade Beria."

"The editor showed guts, Petr Sergeyevich. He phoned Comrade Beria and said, 'I understand that the Politburo doesn't want your communique published.' Guess Comrade Beria's answer."

I told Demichev that I had given up guessing whenever Beria was involved.

"Comrade Beria replied, 'Publish it, you son of a bitch. I am the Politburo.'"

"So *Pravda* printed the communique, and. . . ."

"So," Demichev finished the sentence for me, "to all intents and purposes Comrade Beria really is the Politburo."

Independent of the Politburo, Beria set the country on different courses domestically and internationally. He made conciliatory gestures toward Jews, one of the first being to free those, including Molotov's wife, whom Stalin had incarcerated.

Against the wishes of the Politburo, Beria ordered the Praesidium of the USSR Supreme Soviet to issue a decree granting amnesty to nonpolitical criminals imprisoned during the Stalin era.[4] *Pravda* published the decree on March 28, the day after it was signed by Politburo Member Voroshilov as chairman of the Supreme Soviet Praesidium and by a Central Committee member who was the Praesidium secretary.

Beria honored the desire of other nationality groups to have persons of their own blood heading the Party in the republics. Stalin's practice of appointing Party secretaries of the republics and oblasts regardless of their nationality groups had aroused much resentment. Ukrainians wanted a Ukrainian at the head of the Party organization in their republic, Tadzhiks a Tadzhik in their republic, and so on. Beria traveled to Byelorussia, the Ukraine, Latvia, Lithuania, and Estonia, and in each installed a native of that republic—of course, a native who was his handpicked man—as secretary of the Party organization. Beria reversed the practice in several instances but never in consultation with Politburo members. He traveled to the capital of the Byelorussian Republic, Minsk, and personally subjected Party Secretary Nikolay Patolichev to a public indignity.[5] At a session of the republic's Party organization Beria abruptly announced the dismissal of Patolichev as its Party secretary. Secret orders were issued for the MGB-MVD to determine whether lower-ranking Party officials in the republics favored or opposed Beria.

The Politburo also learned, accidentally, that Beria had ordered the

MGB to investigate the factional leanings of the Party secretaries he had not replaced. The MVD chief in the Kamenets-Podolsk Oblast of the Ukraine, Major General Timofey Strokach, let the cat out of the bag. Strokach divulged to the local Party secretary that Beria had ordered him to open an investigation of this CPSU functionary. Alarmed by the news, the Party secretary phoned the CPSU Central Committee to protest. The Central Committee knew nothing of Beria's order and referred the protest to the Politburo, which then ascertained that the investigations of Party secretaries were widespread.

At the same time a purge was under way in Georgia. Eight of the eleven Members of the Georgian Politburo were arrested, as were others whom Stalin had appointed to replace Beriaites during the Mingrelian Affair of 1951–52. It was yet another swing of the pendulum between the two natives of the republic who had risen to power in Moscow. In April the Georgian Party newspaper reported a speech calling Beria "Georgia's best son, the outstanding leader of the great Soviet state."

Beria offered assurances to Czechoslovakia that the USSR would not continue to interfere in Czech internal affairs, and he wrote a personal letter to Marshal Tito apologizing for the manner in which Stalin had treated him. The MGB officer who would carry the letter to Tito showed it to me. The final sentence said, "Let us cast the past aside and look ahead to the resumption of diplomatic relations between our two nations."

Workers in Communist East Berlin staged demonstrations, riots, and a general strike June 17–19, 1953,[6] against the work quotas and compensation scheme of the East German government. Soviet tanks and troops halted the disturbance, killing 16 rioters. On the first day of the disturbances, Beria dispatched Deputy Minister Kobulov with a group of ten MGB officers to conduct on-the-scene investigations. Only after their departure (but before Soviet tanks and troops put down the uprising) was the Politburo told of Kobulov's mission.

Beria told the Politburo that, according to the Kobulov commission, the riots resulted from East Germans' anger at the overwhelming Soviet presence in their country. He stated that 800 MGB officers were being recalled to the USSR, and he insisted that Defense Minister Bulganin withdraw military units in order to pacify the East Germans. The level of the Soviet Armed Forces in East Germany remained at 450,000 men, however, because the Politburo suspended action on Beria's demand. Another, more urgent, internal issue was at hand.

With the MGB and MVD under his command, Beria came within a hair's breadth of seizing control of the country. He planned to become the new Stalin, to achieve absolute power over the Party apparatus from the Politburo down.[7]

Beria imposed unreasonable restrictions on us in the Foreign Operations Directorate. He prohibited our recruitment of members of Communist parties abroad, saying that they had little clandestine value because their Party connections made them automatically suspect to opposition security services. He questioned the loyalty of so-called illegals, Soviet intelligence operatives in Western countries who pretended (and still pretend) to have no ties to the USSR. In doubt that the MGB was getting its money's worth from possibly disloyal illegals, Beria allowed only those of proven merit—Colonel Rudolf Abel in the United States, as one example—to remain in the West.

Two rounds of restrictions as to which officers would be admitted to the buildings in the Center were instituted. For reasons never announced, the Personnel Directorate issued new admission badges in mid-March 1953 and again in June.[8] If an officer did not have the badge insignia to get him past the building guards, he could not be posted anywhere abroad.

The turmoil in the MGB that Stalin started by arresting Abakumov in 1951 continued under Beria. He brought old cronies back to the MGB, into senior positions where most performed as ineptly as they had before Abakumov fired them. During the period from March to June 1953, scores of generals and colonels disappeared from the Center into graves, jails, labor camps, Siberia on reassignment, or retirement. Beria's first shot, literally, was the March 6 execution of Lieutenant Colonel Karasev, who had been in charge of secretly monitoring conversations of the leaders.

The MGB was the platform for Beria's accretion of power in Party and government matters. He acted alone, whereas the ten Politburo members should have been setting policy by majority votes. The threat of MGB reprisals against Soviet leaders served Beria as well as it had served Stalin, for the other leaders stood aside after the reorganizations in March. Beria was, in effect, precisely what he purported to be when he said, "I am the Politburo." The next step would be for him to supplant Politburo members with Beriaites.

18

A Coup Aborted

My wife took our daughter to the Black Sea on vacation in the summer of 1953. Nearly hysterical, she phoned me from a resort there in Georgia on Sunday, June 21.

"Oh, Petya, they're menacing us," Marina said. "I'm worried for Larisa. I think we ought to take the train home tomorrow."

"Wait a minute. Who's menacing you?"

"Georgians. They're accosting Russians everywhere—on the beaches—not just me—everybody they think is Russian."

"I'm surprised at you, Marochka. You shouldn't let drunken Georgian hoodlums scare you. Georgians simply resent Russians. There's no more to it than that."

"They're not drunk," she said, "and they don't look like hoodlums to me."

"How are they threatening you—with clubs and knives?"

"With words, Petya. They say such things as, 'Watch out for us. You Russians are going to be a lot worse off before long.'"

"Georgian hot air. Ignore them."

"Still, shouldn't we come home?"

I told Marina to keep calm, to stay away from Georgians on the beaches, and to call me again on the following Sunday.

Nothing seemed out of the ordinary in Moscow during the rest of that week until the hours before dawn on Saturday. Noise outside our apartment building awakened me. From the balcony I made out silhouettes of tanks and armored personnel carriers moving through the streets. That never occurred except in connection with Red Square parades, and no parade was scheduled for the weekend of June 27–28.

While going to work in the Foreign Operations Directorate before 10 A.M. that Saturday, I saw Red Army vehicles in large numbers. I was wondering why they were in Moscow when I heard someone call my name. It was an acquaintance from my days in the Guards Directorate.

"Hey, slow down," Lieutenant Igoshin shouted from 100 paces behind me. When he reached my side he said, "I've just been told something that will knock you off your feet."

"I don't want to be knocked off my feet this morning. My wife's away, I haven't had breakfast, and I'm getting over a headache from last night's vodka."

"Listen to this, Petr Sergeyevich. Our minister, Comrade Beria, is under arrest."

"Especially this morning I don't like having my leg pulled, Igoshin. Goodbye."

"You know I wouldn't do that. Ugh, your eyes look as if an army of cockroaches took turns pissing in them."

"My ears are perfectly all right," I said, "and I heard something about Comrade Beria and arrest."

"Correct. I'm on my way back from Comrade Beria's house. They wouldn't let me in to check what supplies he needs. They stopped me at the front gate."

"Please be so kind as to tell me who the 'they' are."

"A bunch of military colonels," Igoshin said, "not the Guards personnel on patrol at Comrade Beria's—they weren't anywhere in sight. The Army guys said they ordered our guys away, and I asked why, and they told me, 'We've arrested Beria.' He isn't under house arrest, either, because he's not at home. They told me to go away and not ask any more questions."

Although Igoshin's news might fit with Red Army vehicles being in the streets, everything appeared to be normal in the Foreign Operations Directorate when I reached Dom Dva.[1] From my office on the ninth floor, however, I noticed something else unusual. The second floor windows of the department store at the corner of Kirova Street displayed photographs of all current members of the Politburo. On the morning of June 27 Beria's was missing.

I reported all this news to the acting chief of my directorate and suggested that he look through his office windows to see for himself the blank space formerly filled by the photograph of Beria.[2] The general checked the department store window, returned to his desk, dialed a number, and whispered into the telephone. His hand trembled as it cradled the instrument.

"You're right, Major Deriabin," he said. "I've confirmed that the Red Army arrested Comrade Beria last night."

Marina began our telephone conversation on Sunday morning, June 28, even more distressed than when we had spoken a week earlier. The Georgians had been searching out Russians to make stronger threats such as, "We'll make a St. Bartholomew's Night for you." (The reference was to the slaughter of French Huguenots in the 16th century.)

"You're as safe there on the Black Sea as you'd be here in Moscow," I said. "We've had an important change that will disappoint those Georgians. They won't dare lay a hand on you and Larisa. Now, relax, Marochka. Come back next week with a tan and the little daughter I long to see."

My guess is that something about Beria's plans had spread to Georgia, making the people there more openly aggressive toward ethnic Russians like Marina. If I am right, evidently they did not know about the imminent arrest of their Georgian hero.

A gross oversight stalled Beria in his tracks: he ignored or forgot the capability of his subordinates in the MVD regular police to conduct eavesdropping operations. They secretly installed technical equipment to listen in on Beria's private conversations. Monitors reported his alarming plans to Deputy Minister Kruglov, a Khrushchev protégé. He relayed the plans to Malenkov, then to Khrushchev, then to Bulganin and to Voroshilov, chairman of the Supreme Soviet Praesidium.

On the basis of intercepted conversations, they were informed that Beria was preparing a coup d'etat to take place on the weekend of June 27–28.

Beria had laid groundwork for the coup by manipulating uniformed troops of the Red Army and the MGB. As a precaution against the Armed Forces resisting an overthrow of the Politburo, he ordered units of the Moscow Military District to Byelorussia on field maneuvers before that weekend. Properly speaking, Minister of Defense Bulganin should have issued such orders—one more example of the power that Beria exercised.

Because not every military unit would vacate the Moscow area and go on the maneuvers, Beria required a show of force in the capital. In his capacity as minister of Internal Affairs, he issued orders to the First Dzerzhinskiy Division, the crack MGB paramilitary component directly under him. It was to occupy strategic positions around Moscow on Saturday, June 27.

Unknown to Beria, Bulganin countered by having Red Army units from Byelorussia and an independent armored division preempt those strategic positions on Friday night. These units were what awakened me that night and what I saw the next morning. That night the Politburo lured Beria away from the Kremlin, where members usually met but where the Guards Directorate might intervene to rescue him. A trap was laid by convening the Politburo in the CPSU Central Committee building. Ultimately, the Red Army and the MGB did not exchange shots, and the MGB's First Dzerzhinskiy Division retired to its compound.

While the Red Army started moving toward Moscow on Friday night, two groups gathered separately in the Kremlin. One, the Politburo, convened to discuss a subject for which Beria was unprepared—himself. The second group, six military officers bearing sidearms, had been spirited into the Kremlin for the purpose of following the Politburo's orders to arrest Beria.

In the summer of 1953 I heard the outline of what transpired that night, but 35 years would pass before the details unfolded before the public. Correspondents for two Moscow newspapers reported in 1988 on their interviews with the last surviving eyewitness.[3] He was retired General Ivan Zub, in June 1953 the chief political officer in the Moscow District Air Defense Forces.

Pieced together, the two interviews of Zub tell the following story:

> Bulganin and his first deputy minister of Defense, Marshal Zhukov, organized the military's arrest of Beria. Zhukov, Zub, and four other

officers waited in a restroom near the meeting hall where the Politburo was in session, Malenkov in the chair. At one point they were joined by Khrushchev and Bulganin.

"Do you know why you have been called here?" Khrushchev asked the six officers. "You are charged with Beria's arrest."

"Are you ready?" asked Bulganin.

"That's right, we're ready," all six answered. Of the six officers, only Zhukov[4] had previously known the mission.

Khrushchev and Bulganin explained that when a bell rang, the six officers were to enter the hall in pairs, going through three doors, with pistols drawn. Khrushchev added, "You must bear in mind that if the operation fails, you will become enemies of the people."

When Malenkov sounded the bell, the officers burst through the doors. Some Politburo members jumped up, but the presence and words of Zhukov reassured them. So did the sight of the six officers brandishing pistols and surrounding Beria, who sat motionless.

"Comrades," Malenkov said, "I suggest we examine the questions of Beria once again." (The statement indicated to Zub that Beria had already been a subject of discussion.) "He is such a trickster, so dangerous, that the devil only knows what he could do. So I suggest arresting Beria immediately."

The Politburo, except for the silent Beria, voted unanimously for the arrest.

"Hands up," Zhukov told Beria. "You're under arrest. Follow us."

The officers escorted Beria to the restroom where they had previously waited. The seven men stayed there until four o'clock on Saturday morning, when military personnel replaced the MGB [Kremlin Kommandatura] guards and it was safe to leave.

Meanwhile, Beria tried to wheedle his way out, but Zhukov ordered him to be quiet. Before Beria was given permission to go into a toilet, the officers cut off the buttons of his trousers, forcing him to use both hands to hold up the trousers and thereby preventing any chance for escape.

Zhukov remained behind as the other five officers and Beria piled into a car. They drove through the gates at the Spasskiy Gate of the Kremlin, thence to Lefortovo Prison. Throughout, Beria behaved calmly.

Zub's story omits two significant points. First, it does not disclose the reason why the Politburo had Beria arrested at this time: the imminent coup that he intended to stage. Second, Zub failed to repeat Beria's words after the vote to arrest him. MGB officers told me that he said, "Whatever I may be guilty of, so are the rest of you [Politburo members]."

Out of concern that his former MGB subordinates might try to rescue Beria from Lefortovo Prison, a State Security stronghold, the leadership had him transferred to a more secure location, one under military control. Beria spent the remaining period of his incarceration in an
underground cell in the headquarters building of the Moscow Military
District. MGB officers told me that he went on a hunger strike that was
broken by rectal feedings.

Within a few hours MVD police arrested five of Beria's six principal
protégés: Merkulov, the minister of State Control; Vlodzimirnskiy, the
Sled-Chast' chief; Goglidze, who was chief of MGB counterintelligence
and security in the Armed Forces; Meshik of the Ukrainian MGB-MVD;
and Dekanozov of the Georgian MGB-MVD.

Arresting the sixth, Deputy Minister Kobulov,[5] posed a problem,
because he remained in East Germany investigating the riots. The
Politburo cabled our ambassador in East Germany with instructions to
take Kobulov into custody and return him to Moscow at once. Sensing
trouble, Kobulov declined the ambassador's invitation to the embassy
and tried to call Beria. He was informed that the telephone lines were cut.

Not expected, Kobulov then somehow managed to enter the embassy
and read the Politburo cable. He reacted by driving to an East Berlin
airstrip and trying, but failing, to commandeer a Moscow-bound plane.
Military officers intercepted Kobulov as he headed back to the embassy,
handcuffed him, and shoved him onto an Air Force bomber going to
Moscow.

Deputy Minister of Internal Affairs Serov told me about Kobulov's
reception in Moscow, at Dom Dva. "We were waiting in his office when
Kobulov walked in. He glanced at us and lunged toward his safe, but we
had already confiscated the gun in the top drawer. The bastard put up a
fight—we manhandled him."

"How many of you were there, Comrade General?" I asked.

"Oh, six or eight, but only I and a couple of others were needed to
subdue him," Serov said. "Well, Kobulov started yelling that the MVD
couldn't arrest him because it was against the law to arrest a deputy to
the Supreme Soviet.

"I yelled right back, 'That claim is shit! In your case, Kobulov, the
laws don't apply.' That shut his mouth."

The intercepted conversations of Beria had not made it clear whether commanders in the Moscow Military District and the MGB First Dzerzhinskiy Division were in collusion on the attempted coup. Consequently, over 100 generals and colonels were confined to barracks under armed guard. Investigations lasting into the first week of July established that no military or uniformed MGB officers had conspired with Beria.[6] All were released, but Colonel General Pavel Artemyev, Commander of the Moscow Military District, did not receive a clean bill of health. He was demoted to deputy chief of the Ural Military District and never permitted to return to Moscow on assignment.

Pravda and *Izvestiya* reported the downfall of Beria on July 10, two weeks after the event, but the newspapers did not specify that he and six accomplices were under arrest. The "Information Bulletin" announced the results of meetings of the Central Committee and the Praesidium of the Supreme Soviet.

> Having heard and discussed a report of the Politburo delivered by Comrade G. M. Malenkov concerning criminal activities against the Party and the State—undermining the security of the Soviet Union in the interest of a foreign capital—perpetrated by L. P. Beria and manifested by his treacherous attempts to place the Ministry of Internal Affairs above the Soviet Government and the CPSU, the Central Committee... resolved to expel L. P. Beria from the CPSU for being an enemy of the Communist Party and the Soviet Union....
>
> In view of the criminal activities committed by L. P. Beria against the State that were recently uncovered and that were directed toward undermining the Soviet State in the interest of a foreign capital, the Supreme Soviet... after due deliberation of the report of the Council of Ministers... resolved to:
>
> Remove L. P. Beria from the position of first deputy chairman of the Council of Ministers, and from the position of minister of Internal Affairs;... [and]
>
> Submit the matter of L. P. Beria's criminal activities to the Supreme Court... for consideration.

The Praesidium also removed Beria as a deputy in the Supreme Soviet and stripped him of all titles and decorations.

In companion pieces *Pravda* and *Izvestiya* elaborated. According to *Pravda*,

Beria promoted those employees of the Ministry of Internal Affairs who were personally subservient to him [meaning Deputy Minister Kobulov as well as the Beriaites placed in charge of MGB Directorates, Sled-Chast', and organizations in the republics]....

By devious means, Beria attempted... to sow seeds of discord among the nationalities of the USSR and to reactivate bourgeois and nationalistic elements in the Union Republics [a reference to appointing natives of the Republics as Party secretaries]....

This adventurer and mercenary of foreign imperialist forces planned to take over the leadership of the Party and the nation. His objectives were to destroy our Communist Party and replace the policies created by the Party with a policy of subservience that, in the final analysis, would restore capitalism.

Izvestiya chimed in:

...Although his earlier criminal, anti-Party, and anti-State activities were well concealed and camouflaged, being pressed for time Beria recently cast aside all restraints. He began to reveal his true image, the image of a malicious enemy.... There can be only one explanation for Beria's crimes—international imperialism was to be activated, and so was its secret [intelligence] service.

Beria had piloted the Kremlin leaders through the dangers of counterrevolution and exercised control over the initial phase of certain reforms. *Pravda* gave him no credit, saying it was the Central Committee that "provided a continuous and sound leadership during the past four months since the death of I. V. Stalin. It performed magnificently in uniting the Party and the people behind the task of building Socialism. It strengthened the economic and military potential of our Motherland. It improved the standard of living for workers, peasants, the intelligentsia, and the whole population of the USSR."

With his influence over domestic and foreign policies great and growing greater, Beria seems to have been impatient. His circumstances were unlike Stalin's. No one was challenging Beria for control of Ministry of Internal Affairs, and the MGB had cowed the Politburo as well as other leaders, including the military high command.

Beria, I think, could have won all the power that once was Stalin's if he had continued in the vein of the period from mid-March to late June 1953. Domestically, he had earned the support of Jews and of the people of outlying republics; Beriaites occupied the upper echelons of the Party in certain republics; and in the future Beriaites could have been dominant in the CPSU Central Committee, Secretariat, and the Politburo. In Eastern Europe Beria had taken steps to ameliorate relations with Czechoslovakia. His arrest occurred before the conciliatory letter to Marshal Tito of Yugoslavia could be delivered and before he could reduce tensions in East Germany.

Despite the error of action too hasty and too drastic, the coup probably would have succeeded had it not been for Beria's mistake of overlooking the monitoring capabilities of the MVD. First Deputy Minister Kruglov's proof of an imminent coup could have reminded Politburo members of the recent plan by Stalin to purge the old guard.

In regard to the attempted coup, the two volumes of Khrushchev's memoirs contain nothing about Kruglov, the MVD, and their forewarning of Beria's intentions; nothing about Beria positioning MGB troops preparatory to the seizure of power; nothing about the Politburo counterpositioning Army units; nothing about the arrests of Beria's six henchmen; nothing about the intensive investigations of possible complicity by the Moscow Military District. Khrushchev would have his readers think that he was first to divine Beria's motives and that he based his suspicions on recommendations Beria made to Politburo members. The memoirs do describe Beria's arrest, but that is the most to be said for the Khrushchev version of the showdown.

In the Politburo, Beria already had made enemies—at minimum Malenkov, whom he betrayed in March, and Khrushchev, on whose Party preserve he poached so high-handedly. Not much would have been needed for Beria's enemies to persuade the rest. Siding with the Politburo were the Soviet Armed Forces, whose higher-ranking generals Beria, for the most part, had alienated. Closing ranks, Party and military leaders aborted the coup.

19

After Beria

The Politburo followed up Beria's arrest with appointments that consolidated its grip on the organs of state security. Kruglov became minister of Internal Affairs on the day of the arrest, June 26, although disclosure of his promotion to replace Beria was withheld from the public until August. Khrushchev nominee Roman Rudenko took over as procurator (prosecutor) general on June 30. Three judges were added to the Soviet Supreme Court.

Shortly before the media reported the removal of Beria, the Politburo oiled the propaganda machinery by organizing closed meetings of Party activists. Dutifully, the activists went on record with speeches and resolutions endorsing the charges against Beria. Also dutifully, *Pravda* quoted the stream of invective.

Thanks to our special status as MGB officers, we received a more explicit recitation of the charges than did other Party activists. Some of the charges presented to us in a letter from the Central Committee were well founded. Beria had, in fact

a. tried to "grab power" (although neither then nor at any time since have authorities revealed details of the attempted coup and the measures that aborted it);

b. gathered secret reports on Politburo members (his office safe contained information collected by the MGB on Khrushchev, Malenkov, Bulganin, and Molotov); and

c. attempted to "sabotage collectivization" in agriculture (but only to the extent of opposing Khrushchev's unpleasant proposal to force peasants to work on collectivized farms).

There was not, however, any truth in the Central Committee allegation that Beria tried to set Abakumov free. If Beria had wanted to release the former minister of State Security, he would have done so. After all, the Politburo could not stop Beria from taking many other actions between March and June 1953; besides, the handling of Abakumov fell more within Beria's purview than did, say, his independent initiatives in policy affairs. The closest Beria came to freeing Abakumov was to take him out of solitary confinement in the Lubyanka Prison once, for several hours of interrogation. The claim regarding Abakumov apparently was an effort to portray him as an ally of Beria. On the contrary, throughout his tenure Abakumov had done whatever was necessary to eradicate Beria's influence in the MGB.[1]

The Central Committee letter criticized Beria for helping Merkulov to hide his family origins in tsarist nobility. Lineage like that should have, but did not, automatically disqualify Merkulov from membership in the CPSU and from positions of trust that he held, such as commissar of State Security 1941 to 1946. According to the letter, Merkulov returned the favor—he wrote a false biography of Beria for the *Great Soviet Encyclopedia.*[2]

An intriguing charge in the letter revived and updated the old accusation that Beria had been an agent of a foreign intelligence service. The Mussavat government ruled the country of Azerbaijan before the USSR annexed the territory in 1920; the Soviets contended that British intelligence controlled the Mussavat government; and Beria was once an employee of the Mussavat police. In the 1920s and 1930s allegations of spying for the Mussavat police sprang up against Beria, but at that time Stalin disregarded them.

Pravda's original article on the "saboteur-doctors" in January trotted out their putative involvement with British as well as American intelligence. It seemed then that Stalin planned to link British intelligence to

Beria via the long-defunct Mussavat intelligence organization. Now the Central Committee indicated that Beria worked for a foreign intelligence service as of 1953. Conceivably, the charge gained new life from contemporary evidence appearing in conversations of Beria that Kruglov's MVD monitors intercepted.

At the beginning of December 1953 the Central Committee released a new, secret letter about Beria to all Party members. It dealt mainly with his sexual escapades and emphasized that he preyed on women and young girls, one an 11-year-old. There was a long passage about Beria infecting women with syphilis and spreading the disease even after doctors urged him to practice celibacy.

Minister Kruglov assembled MGB Party activists, directorate chiefs, and department chiefs in the auditorium of our officers' club toward the end of July. We were disappointed that he spoke about Beria for less than three minutes and that he told us no more than what we already knew. Kruglov then introduced his two new deputies, both of whom gave bland, uninformative addresses.

The junior deputy minister was Army General Ivan Serov, a Khrushchev man who by title remained at the same level he had held under Minister of Internal Affairs Beria. The selection for first deputy minister surprised us, not because he was the choice of Malenkov, who again was rising in power, but for other reasons. Nikolay Shatalin brought to the MGB-MVD no background in intelligence, security, or police affairs. As with former Minister Ignatyev, his experience lay entirely in the Party apparatus. He told us that he was continuing as one of the five CPSU secretaries; it was a time-consuming position that should leave him little time for State Security matters. Shatalin made a strongly negative impression with his effeminate movements, puckering lips, and sprays of saliva. My fellow officers exchanged glances and shrugs while he spoke.

Immediately after this meeting, some 250 employees on the staff of the Central Committee—many identifiable as Khrushchev supporters—assumed senior positions in MGB headquarters. All reported to Shatalin in the CPSU Secretariat, assuring tighter Party control of State Security, and to Serov on routine operational and administrative matters.

Their presence, their indecision, their lack of experience further battered our morale.

Of the 250 Party *apparatchiki,* 100 entered the Foreign Operations Directorate to watch over 6,000 of us officers, who were stationed throughout the world. Foreign Minister Molotov arranged to have Aleksandr Panyushkin, former ambassador in Washington and Beijing, appointed chief of our directorate with the rank of general. Malenkov interceded to have his brother-in-law, Pitovranov, brought out of the paid leave-of-absence that Beria had imposed. Pitovranov soon left Moscow to head the huge MGB organization covering the two Germanys from a base in East Berlin.[3]

In the MGB that summer we discerned the outlines of an alliance among Khrushchev, Malenkov, and Bulganin. Khrushchev ranked first in the triumvirate by virtue of his strength in both the CPSU and the MGB-MVD. He belonged to the Politburo and was the senior of five Party secretaries. He could count on Minister Kruglov and Deputy Minister Serov of the MGB-MVD for support.

Next in line came Politburo member Malenkov, chairman of the Council of Ministers. He had regained some influence in State Security through the appointment of First Deputy Minister Shatalin. Politburo Member Bulganin, a hard-drinking womanizer with little say in Party matters and none in the MGB-MVD, won a place for having used his position as minister of Defense to direct the Red Army in forestalling Beria's coup.

This new distribution of power after the arrest of Beria first entered public view in September 1953. At that time Khrushchev became first secretary in a so-called "collective leadership" with Malenkov and Bulganin. The MGB and the MVD separated in March 1954, with Serov becoming chairman of what was now named the KGB and Kruglov remaining minister of Internal Affairs. Shatalin, Malenkov's line into State Security, received a demotion—from secretary of the CPSU to secretary of a small Party organization in the Soviet Far East.

Later Khrushchev eased Malenkov, and then Bulganin, out of the triumvirate. Except for Mikoyan, he discarded the last of the old guard from the Politburo—Malenkov, Molotov, and Kaganovich in 1957,

Bulganin in 1958, and Voroshilov in 1960. Loss of position was the punishment suffered by these Politburo members, punishment for disloyalty to Khrushchev or opposition to his policies. None faced trial and execution or incarceration. Khrushchev remained in power until Leonid Brezhnev unseated him in 1964, and he died in retirement seven years afterward.

From March to December 1953 Marshal Ivan Konev led the team of Armed Forces personnel who interrogated Beria. As he did on the night of his arrest, Beria maintained that all Politburo members were equally guilty of many of the charges against him.

Andrey Zhdanov, Josef Stalin, and Mikhail Kalinin *(left to right)* in 1934. It was Zhdanov's suspicious death in 1948, by "incorrectly prescribed medication," that began the Doctors' Plot, one of Stalin's reasons for another major purge.

The chief of the Kremlin Guards Directorate Nikolay Vlasik with Stalin at Potsdam in 1945.

His power slipping away, Stalin addresses the 19th party Congress in October 1952.

The dictator in death.

A composite photograph of the Soviet Union's top leaders taken at Stalin's bier. *Left to right:* Vyacheslav Molotov, Kliment Voroshilov, Lavrentiy Beria, Georgiy Malenkov, Nikolay Bulganin, Nikita Khrushchev, Lazar Kaganovich, and Anastas Mikoyan.

Lavrentiy Beria *(extreme right)* and *(opposite him)* Georgiy Malenkov are the lead pall-bearers at Stalin's funeral.

With Stalin dead, Beria *(center)* and Malenkov *(right)* take center stage. Molotov is *at the left.*

Peter Deriabin, Jr.

Author Deriabin's identity cards. *The top one* permits "Korobov" to enter the headquarters of the Commission for Soviet Property in Austria. *The second from the top* did the same for "Smirnov." *The third* allowed Deriabin to enter Vienna's Imperial and Grand Hotels. *At the bottom* is Deriabin's official identity card from the Soviet consulate in Vienna.

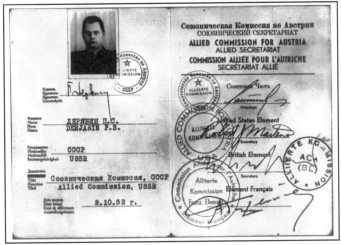

Peter Deriabin, Jr.

The author's travel permit from the Allied Commission for Austria, granting the counterintelligence agent unrestricted travel without presentation of other documents.

Peter Deriabin, Jr.

Peter Deriabin at Niagara Falls in 1965.

PART TWO

FIXING THE GUILT

20

Trials of State
Security Chiefs

The Politburo made sure that sympathizers in the MGB could not rescue Beria before his trial. Soviet political prisoners before and since always have been held in custody by the organs of State Security. Beria, however, was jailed in the basement of the Moscow Military District headquarters building, under guard by officers from the Armed Forces. Military officers also guarded the six codefendants.[1]

By the same token, not State Security but the military conducted the interrogations, with Marshal Ivan Konev in charge. Somewhere on the fringes stood the newly appointed senior civilian prosecutor, USSR Procurator General Roman Rudenko.

Konev also chaired the eight-member "Special Judicial Body of the USSR Supreme Court" that tried Beria in closed proceedings that began on Friday, December 18, 1953, and ended five days later.[2] The trial took place at the same military building where Beria had been incarcerated since June. Until the sentence was imposed and carried out, tanks and armored cars ringed the building. The Politburo was taking no chances if Beria's allies tried to save him.

The arrests of Beria and his six protégés in June 1953 were, of course, tantamount to conviction at their trial in camera the following December. What better way to demonstrate Beria's guilt than to assert that he confessed? Two announcements printed by *Pravda*—one the day before the trial, one the day after—imply that Beria as well as the six others did exactly that.[3]

Said the first announcement: "Exposed at the [pretrial] inquiry by the testimony of various witnesses and by authentic documentary data, the accused pleaded guilty of committing a number of most serious State crimes." The seven names of "the accused" appeared two sentences earlier.

The second announcement contained a longer passage about confessions, saying:

> The guilt of all the accused in the charges made against them was fully proven in the trial by authentic documents, material evidence, *depositions signed by the accused* [emphasis mine], and by the testimony of numerous witnesses. The accused [names of Beria and the six others], convicted by the evidence, at the inquiry [trial] confirmed the testimony given by them in the preliminary inquiry and pleaded guilty of committing a number of most serious State crimes.

Here again, then, Beria is lumped together with the other six.

At no place in either announcement is it said specifically that Beria confessed. Rumors within the MGB had Beria refusing to admit to more than a general statement of guilt that he shared with the rest of the Politburo. The rumors did have his codefendants confessing. The accuracy of the confession rumors can be questioned because the MGB played no active role in the pretrial inquiry or in the trial.

In the USSR the public record on Beria's confession would have rested with the December 1953 announcements by *Pravda* had it not been for *glasnost*. When *glasnost* at last permitted circulation of a first-hand account of Beria's imprisonment, an eyewitness stepped forward. He was Major General (retired) Ivan Zub. Thirty-five years earlier he had been one of the six military officers present at Beria's arrest, and he then had been assigned to the detail guarding Beria throughout his imprisonment and trial. For these services Zub received a promotion and the Order of the Red Banner.

The Moscow weekly magazine *Nedelya* published an interview of Zub that contained the following exchange:

[Reporter]: One last question. Later you were one of those responsible for Beria's fate until the trial. How did he behave in his imprisonment beforehand?

[Zub]:   He did not confess to anything. . . .

To this Zub added that Beria went on a hunger strike lasting ten days. "We made considerable efforts to make that villain 'hold out' [survive] until his trial where he would have to answer for his crimes."[4]

For the Soviet leadership, one problem with *glasnost* is that media reports sometimes run contrary to official positions on issues. Zub's remarks on the absence of a confession by Beria presumably did not sit well in the Kremlin. They evidently did not sit well with the Armed Forces, either. The military had participated in the arrest, conducted the interrogations, and chaired the trial of Beria. Less than a month after *Nedelya* published the Zub interview, the military newspaper *Krasnaya Zvezda* (Red Star) went to press with a three-part series containing an amendment to the public record on Beria's confession. It was based, the newspaper correspondent wrote, on information that he obtained from Zub.

The pertinent extract reads as follows:

> Continuing to refuse to make a statement, Beria declared a hunger strike and refused food for 11 *[sic]* days. This did not do him much harm, given his health and build.
>
> At one of the interrogation sessions, [Procurator General] Rudenko showed Beria a document and asked, "Is this your signature?" Beria looked, looked again, and finally muttered, "Yes."
>
> After this he started making statements. When the investigation was finally concluded, Beria had to read all the depositions from beginning to end and sign every page. He started reading, then gave up: "I can't!"
>
> . . . Beria started making statements when he was shown a document containing direct evidence against him. Only then, under the effect of evidence, did he become talkative. And even though Beria's followers tried to do much in the course of the investigation to cover up traces and prevent any further exposures of his crimes, which were at the same time theirs, there was no shortage of testimony from witnesses.
>
> . . . Ultimately Beria signed all his statements.[5]

Without indicating that the interrogators were military officers on a team led by Marshal Konev, *Krasnaya Zvezda* said this about the manner in which the interrogation of Beria was conducted: "... Beria's victims repeatedly retracted testimony extracted from them by blackmail, threats, and physical force. An admission of guilt by the person under investigation and a denunciation were sufficient to transform a man into 'camp dust.' In his [Beria's] case, however, the investigation was conducted according to altogether different principles."

The declaration that the Armed Forces did not torture Beria is credible. Torture to extract his confession could have been ruled out because the prosecution had sufficient evidence—to say nothing of the ill will aplenty on its side—to be sure of convicting him. The evidence probably incorporated confessions by all, or at least some, of the codefendants.

Available data, in summary, make debatable the official claim that Beria confessed to the charges filed against him.

The indictment against Beria mentioned his "profound moral degeneration" only in passing, although pretrial investigators gathered a substantial amount of material on his raping women and teenage girls. The impediments Beria placed in the way of Khrushchev's plan to force peasants onto collectivized farms received little attention in the indictment. Omitted were prior allegations by the CPSU Central Committee that Beria collected information on Politburo members, that he tried to release former minister Abakumov from jail, and that he helped coconspirator Merkulov hide his relationship to tsarist nobility.

At the trial the seven defendants faced charges under Articles 58-1-b (treason), 58-8 (relations with foreign countries for counterrevolutionary purposes), and 58-11 (conspiracy) under the RSFSR Criminal Code. By himself, Beria was also charged under Article 58-12 (collaboration with counterrevolutionary governments during the Civil War of 1919–20).

The two *Pravda* announcements of December 1953 focused on alleged espionage by Beria and on the effort to seize power six months previously. About the latter, *Pravda* withheld details but presented the claim that the conspirators had the objective of "restoring capitalism and the domination of the bourgeoisie." The inference for readers to draw was that hostile foreign intelligence services had supported or sponsored the attempted coup.

Again the public read of Beria's status as a "secret agent" for British intelligence dating back to the civil war. Now *Pravda* was bringing his espionage activity forward "right up to his arrest" and extending it beyond collaboration with British intelligence.

> It has been established...that also in subsequent years Beria maintained and expanded his secret, criminal contacts with foreign intelligence services through spies sent by them, whom he sometimes succeeded in protecting from exposure and who deserved punishment.
>
> Acting as a traitor to the Motherland and as a spy, Beria, who had sold himself to foreign intelligence services, throughout his criminal activity also maintained, with the help of his accomplices, secret contacts with . . . agents of a number of foreign intelligence services.

Except for the British, *Pravda* failed to identify the other service or services.

When *glasnost* in April 1988 linked Beria to another intelligence group, it was said to consist of "representatives of Hitler's Germany." An attorney involved in the pretrial investigation of Beria stated on Moscow television that

> This was proven because I personally questioned the person who formed the link between Beria's people and people of Hitler's Germany. This was the ambassador of one of the neutral states in Moscow through whom the talks were conducted. The talks themselves—the very fact of such talks during wartime—were a betrayal of the homeland, treachery.
>
> I went abroad to talk to this ambassador, now an ex-ambassador who is retired. He told me everything, including who were the intermediaries from Beria's side, here in Moscow. He told me their code names...[which] were later discovered in Moscow.

The attorney admitted the blunder of not striking while the iron was hot. He did not get the ambassador to sign the statement on the spot, and when the ambassador came to the Soviet Embassy the next day, he refused to put his name on the document. "However," the attorney added, "when I asked him whether what he had said the day before and what was written there was true, he said that all of this was absolutely true."

The presence of "code names," "intermediaries from Beria's side," and a third-country embassy in the affair suggest that State Security represented Beria in these contacts. The likeliest Soviet participants would have been Merkulov, the head of State Security during the Great Patriotic War; Merkulov's chief of foreign operations; and a Russian-German interpreter.

Although the talks were held in secrecy, the interpretation that they were treasonous is not necessarily correct. An analogy might lie in the contacts of Allen Dulles of the U.S. Office of Strategic Services in Switzerland; he was in touch with high-ranking Germans who wanted to depose Hitler and surrender. That might have been Beria's intention, too, but it is hard to imagine him negotiating toward these goals without the knowledge of Stalin. On the other hand, what Dulles had in mind for Hitler and the German military might have been what Beria had in mind for Stalin and the Soviet Armed Forces.

The indictment addressed crimes to silence opponents of the conspirators: "a criminal intrigue" against one, "terroristic murder of persons," and persecution of "honest officials" of the MGB-MVD who refused to carry out Beria's orders. By limiting the indictment in this way, the Kremlin minimized the full range of his actions against individuals and groups of citizens. Nowhere, furthermore, did the two *Pravda* announcements hint that many crimes were committed with Stalin's acquiescence.

The final section of the announcement on December 24 gave the verdict by the Special Judicial Body of the Supreme Court.

> To sentence Beria, Merkulov, Dekanozov, Kobulov, Goglidze, Meshik, and Vlodzimirskiy to the highest criminal punishment: death by shooting, with confiscation of their personal property and deprivation of military titles and awards. The sentence is final and not subject to appeal.
>
> Yesterday, December 23, the sentence...was executed.

As soon as the sentences were passed, guards took the seven prisoners to the basement of the Moscow Military District headquarters building where the trial had taken place. Beria "pleaded for mercy, crawling on his knees," the widow of the executioner told a *Nedelya* interviewer. "My husband found it insulting" that Beria lacked the courage to take the punishment he deserved.[6] The corpse was covered with gasoline and burned.

After all this time it still seems important to the Kremlin that it prove and prove again Beria's guilt. But the case against Beria is carried one step further. Whether they are open critics or open defenders of Stalin, whether they speak as officials or as private citizens, everyone quoted in Soviet media shifts from Stalin to Beria the blame for many crimes by State Security in the postwar years. It is as if Beria were an influential link on the MGB chain of command during that period.

Precisely the opposite was true from 1946 to 1951. Abakumov was minister of State Security then, and he rigorously adhered to Stalin's hands-off-the-MGB orders regarding Beria. Earlier and later, personally and through State Security, Beria did commit criminal acts. Stalin, however, bears the ultimate guilt for all that occurred while Abakumov headed the MGB.

The case of the "saboteur-doctors," later known as the Doctors' Plot, was off-limits to Soviet media for 15 months. Not since a flurry of *Pravda* items in early April 1953 had information about it been released to the public. Most citizens knew only the outlines: the case was supposed to trigger a widespread purge, but the doctors were declared innocent, "criminal adventurists" such as Mikhail Ryumin of the MGB bore responsibility for victimizing them, and Ryumin went to prison.

Pravda broke the silence on July 23, 1954. Since then, nothing else about Ryumin has been disseminated in the Soviet Union. As compared with the magnitude of Ryumin's (and Stalin's) intentions, the report was relatively short. At the beginning of July, it began, "the Military Collegium of the Supreme Court of the USSR examined at a [closed] session the case of M. D. Ryumin, accused of a crime envisaged by Article 58-7 of the Criminal Code of the RSFSR."

Article 58-7 dealt with "the undermining of State industry, transport, trade, monetary exchange or the credit system . . . in the interests of their former owners or of capitalist organizations interested in them. . . ." The statute did not apply to Ryumin's crimes in any way. While handling the investigation for Stalin, he had not been operating in the interests of "former owners or of capitalist organizations." The prosecution thus resorted to a trumped-up charge, and doubtless it did so in order to secure the maximum punishment upon Ryumin's conviction.

The court determined that Ryumin, "a concealed enemy of the Soviet

State," forged evidence. This evidence formed the basis for "provocation cases" and "unjustified arrests . . . of a number of Soviet citizens, including prominent medical workers."[7] According to witnesses (presumably the falsely accused doctors), Ryumin employed investigative methods forbidden by law. He "forced the arrested people to slander themselves and other individuals [concerning] the commission of State crimes: treachery, sabotage, espionage, etc. . . . These charges were completely unfounded. . . ."

Ryumin was sentenced to "death by shooting," and the *Pravda* report ended by saying: "The sentence has been carried out."

Ryumin's positions as a senior investigator in Sled-Chast' and then as chief of that MGB component were given in the report, but not his last MGB title of deputy minister. Also missing was mention of former Minister Semen Ignatyev, the go-between in conveying Stalin's orders on the investigation of the doctors. In April 1953 the Soviet leadership did dismiss Ignatyev from the job of CPSU secretary that he had held for one month; yet he suffered no additional punishment for the saboteur-doctors case.

Ryumin alone paid a higher price, the full price. Naturally, the Kremlin gave no credit to the one person who forestalled Stalin's plan to use the fabricated plot as the springboard for a purge. Politburo members skipped the fact that a year earlier Beria saved their lives and, without question, the lives of hundreds or thousands of others.

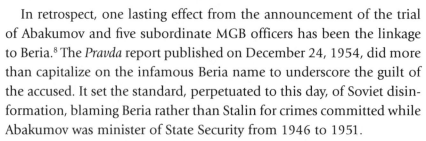

In retrospect, one lasting effect from the announcement of the trial of Abakumov and five subordinate MGB officers has been the linkage to Beria.[8] The *Pravda* report published on December 24, 1954, did more than capitalize on the infamous Beria name to underscore the guilt of the accused. It set the standard, perpetuated to this day, of Soviet disinformation, blaming Beria rather than Stalin for crimes committed while Abakumov was minister of State Security from 1946 to 1951.

A second noteworthy aspect, not at all surprising in light of the political niceties involved, is the absence of Malenkov's name from the report. The "Leningrad Affair" is the single specific matter cited in condemning Abakumov's crimes, and all six of the MGB officers took part in this bloody purge of the Leningrad Party Organization, four of the six directly. While wreaking vengeance on CPSU *apparatchiki* for Stalin, the Leningrad Affair also served Malenkov well: it liquidated and otherwise eliminated the Zhdanov faction, which was rivaling him for power second to Stalin's in the Party. Malenkov, moreover, traveled with Abakumov in 1949 to launch the purge in Leningrad.

At the time of the trial Malenkov formed the triumvirate (or *troika*, as it was referred to in those days) with Khrushchev and Bulganin that ruled the USSR. He had earned this position by working with them to abort Beria's coup and by virtue of his longstanding prominence in the upper echelons. It would scarcely have served the triumvirate well to implicate Malenkov in the Leningrad Affair. They needed stability to consolidate power. It would serve historical accuracy well to do so, and yet as far as the official version of Soviet history is concerned, Malenkov is not portrayed as a participant.

The trial lasted from December 14 to 19, 1954. It was conducted away from Moscow, in Leningrad, probably to make it easier to obtain testimony from witnesses to the central charges against Abakumov. Since the trial was open, a second reason for the venue selection may have been to put the trial beyond the reach of Moscow-based diplomats and foreign correspondents, who were subject to travel restrictions.

Pravda named the members of the Supreme Court who heard the evidence, as it had in the Beria trial but not in the trial of Ryumin. In a departure from the reports on the two preceding trials, *Pravda* identified Abakumov's prosecutor (Procurator General Rudenko) and defense attorneys (four members of the Moscow City Collegium of Lawyers). The accused had been indicted on charges of "crimes envisaged under Articles 58-1-b, 58-7, 58-8 and 58-11 of the Criminal Code of the RSFSR."

The rest of the report was as follows:

> The court inquiry fully confirmed the material of the preliminary inquiry and the indictments made against the accused.
>
> The accused Abakumov, nominated by Beria for the post of minister of State Security of the USSR, was a direct accomplice of [Beria's] criminal

conspiratorial group and carried out the hostile tasks of Beria directed against the Communist Party and the Soviet Government.[9]

Committing crimes similar to those of Beria, Abakumov trod the path of adventures and provocative political acts. Abakumov trumped up cases against certain officials of the Party and Soviet apparatus and against representatives of the Soviet intelligentsia, then arrested those persons and, using criminal methods of investigation forbidden by Soviet law, together with his [three Sled-Chast'] accomplices . . . extracted from those arrested false evidence and confessions of guilt of serious state crimes. [True for the Leningrad Affair and for other cases as well.]

In this way Abakumov falsified the so-called "Leningrad Case" in which a number of Party and Soviet officials were arrested without grounds, having been falsely accused of most serious state crimes. [True.]

The court inquiry established many other cases of the falsification of trials and criminal violation of Socialist legality by Abakumov and his accomplices.

The persons who were falsely accused by Abakumov and his confederates have now been fully rehabilitated. [But for some rehabilitation came posthumously.]

In order to cover up the crimes he had committed, Abakumov forbade the arrested persons' statements and complaints to be forwarded to addressees in the CPSU Central Committee and the Soviet Government. [Certainly true with reference to the few doctors who were the first to be arrested in connection with Zhdanov's death.]

The Military Collegium of the Supreme Court of the USSR, recognizing the charges made against Abakumov and his accomplices to be fully proven, sentenced the accused I. A. Chernov to be sent to a corrective labor camp for a period of 15 years; the accused Ya. M. Broverman to be sent to a corrective labor camp for a period of 25 years; and the accused Abakumov and [names of the three Sled-Chast' officers] to suffer the highest degree of punishment: death by shooting.

The sentence was met by all those present with great satisfaction.

The sentence has been carried out.

The lighter sentences for Chernov and Broverman probably stem from their parts in the Leningrad Affair having been indirect. They stayed behind in Moscow when the rest went to Leningrad.

With one exception, Soviet media have yet to disclose that seven of Abakumov's deputy ministers went to jail with him in August 1951, that the head of his personal bodyguard detail and dozens of Sled-Chast' officers were arrested later, or that the arrests resulted from Stalin's discovery of information being withheld from him on allegations about the cause of Zhdanov's death. It was Stalin who ordered the arrests, and it was Stalin who set free the single deputy minister whose arrest has been made public under *glasnost*. The deputy minister was Yevgeniy Pitovranov, but *glasnost* has not revealed the actual reason for Pitovranov's release: he and Malenkov were married to sisters.

Once again in a report on the trial of MGB officers Stalin's name and criminal legacy did not appear. The Soviet public would have to wait until *glasnost* in the 1980s for the media to begin reporting some of the crimes of Stalin. Delegates to the 20th Party Congress in February 1956, however, would hear Khrushchev announce facts that previously had only been whispered.

21

Khrushchev: Accuser and Defender

Khrushchev's memoirs and the Secret Speech he delivered at the 20th Party Congress in February 1956 contribute uniquely to the study of post-Revolution history. They partially dispel the secrecy that shrouds Soviet regimes at the apex. For the first time a Soviet leader described to wide circles of outsiders the crimes that his peers had perpetrated against citizens of the USSR. Khrushchev's successors have not been as candid on this matter.

In retirement Khrushchev dictated his autobiography, "hoping that this record of mine will fall into the hands of objective scholars."[1] The manuscript was smuggled to the West, and from it was extracted material for the three volumes of memoirs that appeared in print after he died.[2] The autobiography, meanwhile, is nonexistent as far as the Soviet public knows. Other than extracts, the complete text has not been printed there.

The background on the 20,000-word Secret Speech is not as murky. By Khrushchev's account, he was the driving force behind the special Pospelov Commission, assigned in 1954 to investigate abuses of power that had claimed innocent victims during the reign of Stalin. Khrushchev then took the initiative for excerpts from the commission's report to be conveyed to the 20th Party Congress delegates while they were cloistered in the Kremlin.[3] His address amounted to an exposé of certain evils fostered by Stalin's "cult of the personality."

In the speech he explained why his speech should have restricted distribution: "...We cannot let this matter get out of the Party, especially not to the press. It is for this reason that we are considering it here at a closed Congress session. We should know the limits; we should not give ammunition to the enemy; we should not wash our dirty linen before their eyes."

The speech contained material too rich and items too fresh for the delegates to keep it to themselves. After all, a Soviet leader had uttered things that would have been punishable until recently, when adulating Stalin was the uniform practice.

As gossip about the speech spread through the Soviet elite, references trickled out in telephone conversations between Moscow and East Germany. At the East German end, in East Berlin, clandestine taps on the Soviet phone lines connected through a tunnel to a monitoring station in West Berlin. There American (CIA) and British (MI6) technicians recorded these guarded conversations. Analysts soon pieced together enough information for officials in Washington and London to learn the outlines of Khrushchev's denigration of Stalin.[4]

The report from the Berlin tunnel operation confirmed rumors that such a speech had been delivered at the Party Congress. A scramble by Western nations to obtain the transcript intensified. This effort was successful in June 1956, when the U.S. Department of State took the extraordinary step of releasing the text. Khrushchev in his memoirs and the authors of an article in an American journal agree that the transcript reached the West via sources in Poland.[5]

Although the CPSU circulated copies to Communist parties in "fraternal countries," over three decades went by before the average Soviet citizen could read the text. The CPSU Central Committee published it in April 1989, nine months after the speech appeared in the weekly newspaper of the Polish Communist Party.[6] Soviet authorities, however, still have not made available to the public the complete contents of the Pospelov Commission's findings on which the speech was based.[7]

Politburo Members Accused

In the Secret Speech and the memoirs, Khrushchev focused on the purges of Party members working in the government, the armed forces, and especially the CPSU apparatus. They suffered at Stalin's hand, of course, but millions more who were excluded from the Party suffered too. Ordinary citizens likewise were punished without real justification.

Quoted or paraphrased, here are Khrushchev's principal accusations:

Against Stalin: [8]

"Stalin himself, using all conceivable methods, supported the glorification of his own person." His cult of the personality was "the source of a whole series of exceedingly serious and grave perversions of Party principles, of Party democracy, of revolutionary legality...." He "abandoned the method of ideological struggle for that of administrative violence, mass repressions, and terror" [speech]. In consequence, the Party suffered "incalculable losses... the annihilation of thousands of people devoted to the depth of their souls to the Marxist-Leninist cause" [Khrushchev Remembers].

The first great purge by Stalin, in 1937–38, wiped out 70 percent of the 139 members elected to the CPSU Central Committee at the 17th Party Congress of 1934. Additionally, thousands of other "honest and innocent Communists have died as a result of this monstrous falsification." After the Great Patriotic War "Stalin became even more capricious, irritable, and brutal.... His persecution mania reached unbelievable dimensions" [Secret Speech].

Turning against Soviet Jewish leaders "with maniacal vengeance," Stalin in 1948 ordered executions and imprisonment [Khrushchev Remembers].

He "personally supervised" the 1949 purge of current and former officials in the Leningrad Party Organization [speech]. "Many people perished" in the Leningrad Affair [Khrushchev Remembers].

In the Mingrelian Affair that began in 1952, he used "falsified documents" to purge Georgian Party officials [speech]. "Those poor fellows were led to slaughter like sheep" [Khrushchev Remembers].

Stalin managed the "ignominious" Doctors' Plot of 1953 but could not bring it to culmination [speech]. Even though they confessed under torture, nearly all the doctors survived this "shameful business" [Khrushchev Remembers].

Against Beria:

Concerning "the tragedy which Stalin inflicted on our Party... one thing is absolutely elementary: Beria didn't create Stalin, Stalin created Beria," just as he created Beria's two immediate predecessors at the head of State Security during the 1930s [Khrushchev Remembers].

Beria, "the rabid enemy of our Party.... This villain had climbed up the Government ladder over an untold number of corpses." During the 1937–38 purge "Beria's gang, which ran the organs of state security, out-did itself in proving the guilt of the arrested and the truth of materials which it falsified." By the time of the Leningrad Affair, he "had murdered thousands of Communists and loyal Soviet people" [Secret Speech].

With reference to the Leningrad Affair, Beria "'suggested' to Stalin the fabrication by him and by his confidante," State Security Minister Abakumov, of evidence against these Party officials. "When Stalin received certain material from Beria and Abakumov...he ordered an investigation of...[star Leningrad Party Organization graduates] Voznesenskiy and Kuznetsov. With this, their fate was sealed" [speech]. "And who directed the investigation? Stalin himself did. But if Stalin was the conductor, Beria was the first violinist...Abakumov, who actually supervised the prosecution, was Beria's man; he never reported to any-one, not even to Stalin, without checking first with Beria" [Khrushchev Remembers].[9]

Against Malenkov:

Malenkov and Beria, "inseparable" since the mid-1940s, conspired to undermine Stalin's confidence in the Leningrad Party Organization; the purge followed. Moreover, while "in charge of personnel for the Central Committee during the purges," Malenkov "played a pretty active role in the whole business. He had actually helped promote people from the ranks only to have them eliminated later on. I'm not saying he took the initiative in repressions and executions...." [Khrushchev Remembers].[10]

Politburo Members Defended

Fear of Stalin and ignorance of his crimes were the two general lines of defense drawn up by Khrushchev for himself (first and foremost) and for others who served in Stalin's Politburo. The Secret Speech is inter-spersed with alibis, such as:

Stalin "practiced brutal violence not only toward everything which opposed him but also toward that which seemed, to his capricious and despotic character, contrary to his concepts....Whoever opposed...or tried to prove his viewpoint and the correctness of his position was doomed to removal from the leading collective [the Politburo] and to subsequent moral and physical annihilation."[11]

"...Stalin, using his unlimited power, allowed himself many abuses, acting in the name of the Central Committee, not asking the opinion of

Committee members nor even of...the Politburo; often he did not inform them about his personal decisions concerning very important Party and government matters."

"...Stalin, as we have been informed by Politburo Members of that time [1937–38], did not show them the statements of many of the accused when they retracted their confessions before the military tribunal and asked for an objective examination of their cases."

Regarding the Leningrad Affair, "...the majority of the Politburo Members did not, at that time, know all the circumstances...and could not therefore intervene." (Two Members besides Stalin who did, Khrushchev indicated elsewhere, were Beria and Malenkov.)

In the Doctors' Plot, Stalin gave the Politburo "the doctors' confessions of guilt....The case was so presented that no one could verify the facts on which the investigation was based. There was no possibility of trying to verify facts by contacting those who had made the confessions of guilt. We felt, however, that the case of the arrested doctors was questionable. We knew some of these people personally because they had once treated us...."

Comparable statements were made in *Khrushchev Remembers;* for example: "All of us around Stalin were temporary people....The moment he stopped trusting you, Stalin would start to scrutinize you until the cup of his distrust overflowed. Then it would be your turn to follow those who were no longer among the living" (p. 307).

And: "I was never really in on the [Leningrad] case myself, but I admit that I may have signed the sentencing order. In those days when a case was closed—and if Stalin thought it necessary—he would sign the sentencing order at a Politbureau session and then pass it around for the rest of us to sign. We would put our signatures on it without even looking at it. That's what was meant by 'collective sentencing'" (p. 256).

On the other hand, *Khrushchev Remembers* acknowledges that some old-guard Politburo Members were not entirely unaware when crimes were being committed by and for Stalin. The old guard was presiding when the special Pospelov Commission reported to the Politburo on "perversions of Party principles, of Party democracy, of revolutionary legality" during the Stalin era. Did this 1956 report cover territory familiar to everyone in the old guard? Not at all, Khrushchev claimed.

The evidence gathered by Pospelov's commission came as a complete surprise to some of us. I'm speaking about myself [and] Bulganin... Molotov and Voroshilov were the best informed about the true dimensions and causes of the Stalinist repressions... Mikoyan... must have known what had been going on... (p. 345).

So Khrushchev exonerated Bulganin and himself.

Bulganin, however, had been the last to enter the Politburo old guard, in 1948, whereas Khrushchev became a member in 1939. Malenkov and Beria joined in 1946, all the rest—Kaganovich, Mikoyan, Molotov, and Voroshilov—entered in 1934.

Khrushchev's case for the defense of certain Politburo members rested there. A court of public opinion would question his credibility, for Khrushchev could not have risen so high or survived so long in the Soviet system had candor been an element in his makeup. More than that, additional evidence makes Khrushchev's defense unconvincing, just as it shows his bill of particulars against Politburo members to have been incomplete.

22

Stalin: Family Murderer

As I reflected on the purges and the hundreds of thousands of Soviet patriots who died in them, I remembered a remark by one of my high school teachers. "Every revolution," he said, "kills its own heros." Then I thought, Stalin's victims included even a member of his own family.

A widower and father of one son, Stalin in 1919 chose a bright, energetic, equally diminutive (as himself) senior high school student to be his second wife. She, too, was from the Republic of Georgia. Nadezhda Alliluyeva readily adapted to life in Moscow at the side of a Soviet leader, joining the Communist Party and assisting in the management of Stalin's office. With more study and experience, she came to dispute some of her husband's opinions openly. Stalin countered by verbally abusing her.

In the fashion of that day among "liberated" women in the Soviet hierarchy, Nadezhda went by her maiden name, Alliluyeva (a name later to be taken by her younger child and only daughter, Svetlana). She made friends among other Kremlin wives, many of whom followed the same maiden-name practice and several of whom were Jewish. One was Polina Zhemchuzhina, the wife of Molotov.

An official announcement in November 1932 said that Nadezhda succumbed during an emergency operation. The announcement implied that her death should be attributed to natural causes. In all the years since, Soviet authorities have never publicly retracted this misleading information about the reason she died.

It was misleading indeed, my colleagues in the MGB said. The circumstances of Nadezhda's death, as well as the aftermath to her death, were described to me in the late 1940s by several MGB officers who served with the organization of bodyguards for Stalin and other leaders. One officer, Colonel Strekachev,[1] had been assigned to the detachment of bodyguards for the Kremlin at the time Nadezhda died.

On the heels of a heated argument with her husband over his policies, Nadezhda left a banquet in the Kremlin celebrating the anniversary of the Great October Revolution of 1917. She retired to the couple's Kremlin apartment. Stalin followed her to the apartment later that night, evidently still in a rage over their dispute. It was there in the bedroom of the apartment, MGB officers told me, that Stalin shot and killed Nadezhda.[2]

Strekachev's immediate superior, the Latvian Rudolf Peterson, chief of the detachment of Kremlin bodyguards, was one of the first to be called to the bedroom by servants who discovered the body of Nadezhda. Stalin had the detachment chief executed in 1935, and he also ordered the executions of the doctors who signed Nadezhda's death certificate. It was a procedure of eliminating witnesses and their damaging testimony that Stalin later would often follow.

Aside from one single, yet crucial, fact, Stalin's daughter confirmed the details of that night, right down to the presence of Strekachev's boss in the bedroom. Svetlana Alliluyeva gave a version of the death of her mother as it was told to her many years later by one of the servants and by Molotov's wife, Polina Zhemchuzhina.[3] The difference between this version and that by bodyguards who spoke to me is the difference between suicide and murder.

Where I was told that Stalin shot Nadezhda, their daughter wrote that she died of a self-inflicted wound from her own pistol. I cannot accept Svetlana's version. It contradicts information I received from knowledgeable sources. But more than that, it disagrees with two additional facts. First, Stalin established a regulation long before World War II that prohibited anyone near him except his personal bodyguards from bearing lethal weapons—including the State Security chief—and, consequently, Nadezhda could not have had a pistol in the Kremlin apartment. Second, Strekachev and other officers said that the gun used to kill her was Stalin's.

Under *glasnost* it was permissible for Soviet citizens to hint—but no more than hint—publicly at the true circumstances of Nadezhda's death. Historian Dmitriy Volkogonov, enjoying access to certain government records heretofore restricted, took up this subject in a four-part series published in 1988–89.[4] He wrote that

> "The evidence which we possess indicates that . . . the leader's behavior was (indirectly? *or was it?*) the cause of his wife's death. . . . Arriving in the morning to awaken Alliluyeva, Karolina Vasilyevna Til, the family house-keeper, found her dead. A 'Walther' [pistol] lay on the floor. Stalin, Molotov, and Voroshilov were summoned. The deceased would obviously have left a farewell letter, but of this we can only surmise: *there always are and will remain in the world secrets large and small which will never be guessed."* [Emphasis mine.]

Volkogonov added: "Having bade farewell to his wife at a civil funeral, Stalin did not go to the cemetery."

As his bodyguards indicated in conversations with me many years afterward, Stalin appeared to have had a change of heart toward Nadezhda following the Great Patriotic War of 1941–45. At the last minute, they said, he would frequently order a detour from routes of his daily travel between the Kremlin where he worked and his dacha outside Moscow, so that the caravan of cars could stop at the Novo-Deviche Cemetery.

Each time the hour was daybreak, the cemetery deserted. Each time Stalin sat alone on the marble seat beside the grave of Nadezhda, smoking a cigarette or a pipe. More than once the bodyguards over-heard him say, "I am very sorry."

Long before Nadezhda's death Stalin had gathered great power, power to intimidate as well as to compel praise by underlings. For example, the eulogies that I heard at his funeral on Red Square in 1953 echoed the adulations by Party Politburo Members on the occasion of Stalin's 50th birthday in 1929: members such as Kliment Voroshilov and Lazar Kaganovich, who, despite Stalin, would manage to stay alive through the rest of his reign; members such as Sergey Kirov and Valerian Kuybyshev, who would not.

Stalin's power helps to explain why the death of Nadezhda was officially (although still secretly) ruled a suicide. The verdict was but one outcome of an emergency meeting of the Party Politburo, de facto the highest tribunal in the nation, that was held in November 1932 on the day after Nadezhda was slain. Colonel Strekachev, who once headed security at Communist Party headquarters, provided me with details.

Politburo Member Stalin was absent from the emergency meeting where two items were on the agenda: his resignation and the homicide. Molotov pled the case for Stalin, saying that Stalin was carrying forward the work of Lenin and had wrought improvements in Soviet society. To arrest Stalin for murder would necessitate his removal as head of the CPSU, a terrible blunder. It would weaken the Party and its position in the vanguard of the international Communist movement. Molotov's implicit message was that weakening the Party brooked the possibility of a counterrevolution in which all of them in the Politburo might be overthrown.

The Politburo accepted his argument. The members voted to retain Stalin, to drop the homicide charge, and to utter the lie about the cause of Nadezhda's death. Thus Stalin escaped punishment for killing his wife. Thus the remaining nine members of the 1932 Politburo became accessories to the crime.

Kirov, Kuybyshev, and two more in that 1932 Politburo died violent deaths before the decade was out, all of them very likely victims of Stalin's orders to liquidate potential opponents. A fifth member died in 1946, reportedly of natural causes, while a sixth (his eyesight failing) left the Politburo in 1952 and outlived Stalin. The three remaining members—Molotov, Kaganovich, and Voroshilov—had continuity in the Politburo until after Stalin died. As Stalin doubtless knew, none of the latter five members had the ambition and support, much less the courage, to challenge him.

The 1932 Politburo conspiracy to conceal the killing saved Stalin from criminal charges and forestalled a possible counterrevolution that helped Stalin consolidate power. Having conspired once to protect him and themselves, Politburo members conspired again and again for the same purpose. They and the Communist Party they ruled fell entirely under Stalin's control.

Stalin then mastered the other two centers of Soviet power. One was the State Security service, which became his instrument of terror against not only the Party at large and the people but also the third power center, the Armed Forces. Stalin purged the Party starting in 1935. State Security so intimidated our military that it rarely summoned the will to figure in internal politics. Stalin had destroyed it as a power center. He deprived the Armed Forces of the majority of the officer corps in the sweeping purges of 1937–38. As one consequence, the Red Army lacked enough adequately trained commanders to repel Hitler's invading troops at our western border in 1941.

Using a term coined by Lenin, Stalin defined an "enemy of the people" as anyone who assailed or questioned the Party line that he himself laid down. In practice, an enemy of the people was anyone capable of posing a threat—real or imagined, alone or (the far more common allegation) as part of a conspiracy—to Stalin's power. He thought he saw enemies of the people everywhere, even among his own in-laws. "The USSR must be rid of this scum," Stalin said. Three relatives of Stalin's first wife, four of his second wife, and a daughter-in-law were jailed. Two of them died before a firing squad.

So my countrymen suffered mass arrests, tortures of prisoners, and either trials on trumped-up charges or no trials at all but instead permanent disappearances without trace, the victims' fates forever hidden. For millions there ensued executions and terms in prison camps of the kind that Solzhenitsyn spotlighted in *The Gulag Archipelago*. For the lucky ones it was sentencing to internal exile in Siberia. Enemies of the people had been purged, although by Stalin's lights never all of them. Always there were more to be found.

No section of the country escaped the purges. They reached into our farming village in Siberia, in the foothills of the Altay Mountains, closer to China than to Moscow 1,500 miles away. Among Stalin's earliest victims were *kulaks,* a class that hired field hands to work the land. But Stalin broadened *kulak* to mean anyone who refused to enlist in the scheme of communal farming. Famines caused by this "collectivization" and similarly ill-conceived agricultural policies lasted from 1928 to 1938. Kulaks were shot, imprisoned, or resettled in the Siberian wasteland to die of starvation. In 1930, when I was nine years of age, I

saw an armed escort lead four falsely accused *kulak*s away from our village. We never heard from them again.

A year later came the turn of local priests and their parishioners who
continued to practice the faith of our Russian Orthodox Church.
Communist Party members were believers too, but they believed in the
Marxist tenet, "Religion is the opiate of the people." Churches were
shut, and Christians were persecuted. My great uncle fled in fear of
arrest for earning a livelihood by painting Christian icons. He disappeared from us forever.

The Politburo that started by formally acquiescing to murder in 1932
endorsed the purges and policies of Stalin that snuffed out millions
upon millions of lives. No, I could not weep for Stalin when he died.
The eulogies to him by Malenkov, Molotov, and Beria at the funeral on
Red Square bore no resemblance to the hideous realities of his 29-year
regime.

PART THREE

WESTWARD

23

Doubts About the System

My Party work, along with my peasant background and military record, made me seem an ideal Communist. As a youngster I would come home from school and, to my parents' chagrin, recite newly learned Communist slogans. As a teenager I was an enthusiastic member of the Communist youth organization, the Komsomol. As a young soldier I joined the CPSU at the earliest opportunity. Later, MGB colleagues over and over again elected me their Party secretary, the presiding officer of CPSU cells.

For a long time, I suppose I was an ideal Communist. By definition, such a person worshipped Stalin as if he were a god. The hardships of Stalin's making were endured for the welfare of the country, and the purges that Stalin ordered were excused as the handiwork of minions acting without his knowledge or approval. Unquestioningly, the ideal Communist obeyed Stalin. I worshipped, endured, excused, obeyed.

Then came six years in the Guards Directorate, six years of observing Stalin and the Communist system in operation minus the veneer of Party propaganda, his propaganda. I saw how my compatriots had been deceived. I realized that under Stalin my country suffered needlessly from a system combining mismanagement with a lust for power and a streak of sadism. The experience reawakened memories. Possibly I had suppressed them because they ran against the grain of Communist indoctrination.

In my Siberian village of Ovsyannikovo in Altay Kray resided a number of political exiles, all well educated. Due to the shortage of teachers in Ovsyannikovo, regulations were waived so that some exiles could be hired for the faculty in our high school. We had a pitiably small number of titles in the school library, no more than 20, but two exiled teachers had brought to the village their own books that had been published in tsarist days.

The two teachers, Aleksey Shamin and Grigory Kolyshev, risked their lives for my private education. They took the subversive step of letting me, with my strong interest in reading, spend countless hours in their attics, where the collections of books were stored. These books were prohibited from circulation and were not generally available in the USSR. Shamin, who had been wounded while serving as an officer in the tsar's army, spent hours with me outside his classes in Russian Literature. From him I learned about Russian poetry, especially the works of my favorite, Lermontov. Kolyshev, the principal of the school and mathematics teacher, was a relative of the minister of Education under the tsar. He owned a personal library of books, including many suppressed by the regime. In his attic I read translations of *Tom Sawyer*, *Huckleberry Finn*, and *The Arabian Nights*. But mainly I read history, and, in particular, several histories of tsarist Russia.

No other students at the high school—and, I would venture to say, few students anywhere in the country—experienced such an opportunity. That exposure, I think, set me apart many years later and enabled me to appraise the Soviet system objectively.

My self-education in history first came back to mind in 1944–45, while I was enrolled in State Security's Second Higher Counterintelligence School in Moscow. It was drilled into us there that once we had graduated, our mission would be to root out enemies of the people. "They are everywhere," said the instructors, "in the millions."

Even then that imprecise figure of "millions" struck me as an exaggeration, for it contrasted sharply with facts about life in Russia before the 1917 Revolution. My private history lessons in Ovsyannikovo had indicated that under the tsars, the highest total of prisoners—both political and criminal—at any one time was 200,000. I thought of the Russian proverb: "Wicked men will not believe good men exist."

The Guards Directorate, central to protecting the leadership from enemies of the people, proved the truth of the proverb. Service with the bodyguards gave me extraordinary awareness of the meaning of the term enemies of the people. Innocent, they were being purged by Stalin in, for example, the Leningrad Affair. No longer an ideal Communist, I grew disgusted with the Soviet system, but not yet so disgusted as to consider defection.

My disgust was one factor in maneuvering for a foreign assignment. Fear was the second. Under the new regime in the Kremlin, as under Beria and before him Stalin, no one—least of all anyone in the MGB—could be sure what the future held. Enemies of the people were still said to be everywhere. The past had witnessed arrests, tortures, executions, and terms in jails and prison camps on spurious charges against alleged enemies of the people. None of us knew whether or how soon the past would be repeated in, as well as against, the MGB.

Life was definitely safer away from MGB headquarters, out of that maelstrom, and a position had opened in Austria. Gladly I would go there for several years. Amid the disruption and confusion caused by all the personnel changes in Moscow, I spent the summer of 1953 preparing for my new duties.

I was to be stationed at the MGB outpost in Vienna known as the "legal residency," so named because the 80 officers manning it had a legal reason (which is not to say a legitimate reason) for being there.[1] They conducted their clandestine business while posing as Soviet diplomats, trade representatives, and so on—in my case, as a "deputy administrator"—exactly the same as in every MGB legal residency elsewhere abroad. The "legal resident," the chief of the residency, was Colonel Yevgeniy Kravtsov.[2]

It was Kravtsov who came to me, in my capacity as Party secretary in the Austro-German Department, to come up with someone to be the new SK (Sovietskaya Koloniya, translated as the Soviet colony) Chief. We ran through most of the officers on the roster of the Austro-German Department, and Kravtsov rejected all of them. Most did not have the proper experience, some Kravtsov did not like personally or professionally, and a few had been committed to the MGB legal residency in Berlin/Karlshorst. Although I did not care for Kravtsov and his overly demanding style of management, I cared much less for conditions in headquarters. Finally I cast a fly on the water.

"I could be your SK chief," I said, "except for the regulation against former Guards officers being permanently stationed in Western countries. It rules me out."

"That's a pretty fair idea," he responded. "Maybe I can get around that regulation and have you come with me to Vienna."

Kravtsov succeeded, due mainly, I think, to the uproar in the Center. As a member of State Security Kravtsov was my superior and I was his deputy. However, in the Party hierarchy I was in one sense the senior in my position as Party secretary of the Austro-German Section. In turn we each gave the other favorable reviews.

My Party, State Security, and military records, along with my experience with the Altay Kray MGB in 1945–46, commended me for advancement to become the chief SK officer in Vienna. By rank, too, I qualified. I was a major with high seniority awaiting a long-overdue promotion to lieutenant colonel. Personnel procedures had gone haywire in the changeovers of ministers and deputy ministers, and promotion actions were clogged in administrative channels. Ironically, on the day before I defected, Kravtsov told me that a Center telegram certifying my new rank of lieutenant colonel was expected in the next 48 hours.

My specialty was counterintelligence, my MGB title was chief of the section covering SK. The section of seven SK officers handled as many as 40 Soviet and Austrian secret informants, whom the MGB signed on as agents. Besides, all 2,000 of the Soviet civilian employees in Austria belonged to the CPSU, and CPSU members were supposed to be vigilant on our behalf. They were obligated to run to us SK officers with the slightest of suspicions, the flimsiest of rumors about other Soviet civilians. A few did, but never did the accusations amount to more than time wasters for the section.

Our primary SK missions were to prevent Soviets from defecting and to prevent Western intelligence from recruiting our citizens. We watched for telltale signs—disaffection with the system, exceptional workplace or household problems, living or purchasing beyond one's means, friendliness with Westerners. We listened to tattlers. It was my duty to tattle to my boss in Vienna and to my bosses in the Center. The assignment, in a nutshell, called for spying on our countrymen.

Of primary concern to the SK unit were suspicious, meaning unauthorized, contacts of Soviet citizens with foreigners. Our colony had been cautioned to avoid foreigners, Austrians and third nationals alike, however innocent might their purposes appear. Whether it be chatting with shopkeepers, socializing with strangers, or hobnobbing with local hires, we SK officers ordered our informants to pass along every tidbit of discussion whether learned firsthand or from rumor of the wildest sort. I had the authority to investigate anyone in the colony except Kravtsov, and I investigated reports of suspicious contacts unfailingly. All of them proved red herrings, even the lead that involved a full-fledged spy within the colony.

He had patronized the Moulin Rouge nightclub, according to my informant. Western jazz blared into the early morning hours at the Moulin Rouge, seductive waitresses flirted with customers, and the prices were exorbitant—just the kind of decadent place for Western intelligence services to entrap unwary Soviet citizens. My MGB colleagues and I went to the nightclub on our legal residency expense accounts, but anybody else in the colony had to have a good excuse for going there. That applied to the GRU officers, which this particular patron was.

I laid before the GRU legal resident the allegation about his man partying at the nightclub until to two A.M. Did the legal resident already know about it? Oh, yes. Did the legal resident plan disciplinary action? Oh, no—the man went to the Moulin Rouge with his approval. On business? Yes, Comrade Deriabin, on operational business. Thus GRU Major Petr Popov had the good excuse that he needed. I closed the Popov investigation and never had cause to reopen it.

Popov, it later developed, started collaborating with the U.S. Central Intelligence Agency a year before his outing at the Moulin Rouge. The CIA operation with Popov continued in Austria, then in Germany, and finally in Moscow. Arrested by State Security in 1958, Popov was tried in secret and executed.[3]

Not only was my work obnoxious, it was also difficult, in the first place due to the local atmosphere of hostility. The majority of Austrians neither liked nor respected us Soviets. My SK section, moreover, had to cope with the threat to Soviet civilians' security that was posed by the presence of large American, British, and French contingents.[4] Daily I faced dealing with a boss (Kravtsov) whom I despised, with a Moscow headquarters that was in an uproar, and with a community of compatriots who treated me warily because of my work.

I also kept busy with additional duties. Compartmentation between the MGB operational groups broke down under the personnel shortage. Kravtsov allotted me tasks outside the scope of my SK unit and even beyond that of the Counterintelligence Group.

In Moscow I had recognized what these problems would be; yet the Vienna legal residency was preferable to MGB headquarters.

My friend Volodya Petrochenkov was in high spirits during our farewell banquet at a Moscow restaurant in mid-September. "Bring me extravagant presents when you come back, Petya. Other officers returning from capitalist countries do."

"I might bring you presents, or I might not," I said, "depending on how you'll use them."

"Oh, I'll put them in my apartment, or sell them on the black market, except those that I give my bosses. They sit around with hands outstretched, waiting for bribes."

We laughed at that and agreed to write each other. To avoid mail censorship, our letters would be delivered by MGB colleagues traveling between Moscow and Vienna.

Marina, Larisa, and I boarded the train at the Byelorussian Station. Our baggage was light because it was mostly empty—in Austria we planned to purchase better clothing at cheaper prices than that sold in Moscow stores. We arrived at Vienna in two days, on Monday, September 28, 1953. A driver from the motor pool deposited us outside the Grand Hotel, which would be our home.

"Look across the street," said the driver, referring to a main thoroughfare called The Ring. "There's our embassy."

Marina and I saw the Imperial Hotel, topped by the hammer-and-sickle flag against a red background. That summer the Politburo had at last acceded to Austria becoming an independent, neutral country. The Soviet civilian headquarters under Ivan I. Ilyichev, a GRU lieutenant general, once chief of Soviet military intelligence operations and former deputy high commissioner in Germany, was in the process of conversion from high commission to embassy status.

"In there," I reminded Marina, "will be my office."

The embassy conducted legitimate diplomatic and commercial business, of course, but it also served the purpose—some might say the main purpose—of screening activities of Soviet intelligence personnel. The core of the MGB legal residency worked inside, pretending to be employees of other government organizations such as the Ministry of Foreign Affairs. Ostensibly, the incoming chief SK officer was from that ministry, for I had been given the cover position of "deputy chief, Administration Department."

"Now look down the street, beyond the cigarette kiosk," the driver said. "That's the Bristol Hotel. It's part of the American Embassy."

Yes, I thought, my SK work is cut out for me. The Soviet colony and the "main enemy" are in uncomfortably close proximity. We turned toward the shabby Grand Hotel. I would reside there for 20 weeks.

During those first months in Vienna I came across SK cases of back-biting, shoplifting, husbands and wives cheating on each other, and individuals under vague suspicion of being enemies of the people—nothing extraordinary or alarming.

Besides my other responsibilities it fell to me to deal with the Austrian police on petty crimes against the Soviet colony. In one case, Ilyichev was outraged by the theft of copper pipes from the ambassadorial residence, causing water to cascade from top floor to basement. The police failed to identify the culprits in that incident, but they were successful in a second investigation.

Senior embassy officials concluded that Austrian saboteurs had tried to harm Soviet civilians by putting glass shards in a barrel of sauerkraut sent to the Grand Hotel restaurant. Snickering in my face, the police reported their findings. The "saboteurs" were drunken employees at a sauerkraut factory, whose bottle of schnapps smashed when it fell into the barrel.

Two of my SK cases were not so routine. Together with the propaganda spewed by Soviet delegates to the World Peace Council in Vienna, they pushed me toward recognizing the immutability of the Soviet system. That Stalin had died, that Beria had been arrested, that a collective leadership now held sway in the Kremlin made no discernible difference.

Yevlampiy Shvedov and his sister Anna, the children of Russian emigrés in Uruguay, had come to Vienna intending to move on from there to the USSR. Yevlampiy clung to the impossible notion that he would receive a Soviet visa that would allow him to organize collective farms in the Ukraine. Anna wanted a visa to be able to join her husband, but this too was impossible. The man had deserted the Red Army and had taken refuge in Uruguay. The MGB had abducted him in Uruguay, smuggled him aboard an outbound Soviet ship, and taken him "home" to a long term in prison.

The MGB used their visa applications as a lever to recruit both Shvedovs as SK agents. I inherited them. Our clandestine meetings produced little information of value and lots of talk about their future in my homeland. Against my heart, I followed the orders of my boss, Kravtsov, to encourage the Shvedovs to dream their dreams. Against my heart, I lied. "Your visas will come through eventually," I would say. "Meanwhile, continue working with us, but do a better job."

Where the Shvedovs were guilty at worst of naivete about the Soviet system, the Russian Orthodox priest Arseniy Shidlovskiy would have no part of the Soviet system. A native of the Ukraine, Father Arseniy had fled Communist atheism to lead a congregation of Russian emigrés at a church in the Soviet sector of Vienna. MGB legal residency files, I found, had been doctored to show that he had collaborated with the Nazis during the Great Patriotic War.

I appealed to Kravtsov to drop the case against Father Arseniy. Although he agreed that the charges had no basis in fact, Kravtsov had an MGB quota of successes to fulfill. He went along with Moscow's demands for action.

Between them, the chiefs in Moscow and my boss in Vienna devised a plan to lure Father Arseniy to the Soviet Union for a trial in which, without doubt, he would be convicted of treason. At MGB behest Metropolitan Nikolay Dorofeyevich, the Russian Orthodox Bishop of Moscow and Kolomna, would visit Vienna and try to persuade the local priest to accept an appointment in the USSR. I was the point of contact in the legal residency for Metropolitan Nikolay.[5]

He did meet Father Arseniy as scheduled, but then the MGB plan went awry. Metropolitan Nikolay told me afterward of his decision for the Russian Orthodox Church to keep Father Arseniy where he was, or at least that would be his recommendation to "authorities" in Moscow. He searched his pockets and handed me 600 Austrian schillings. "Here, Comrade," he said, "would you see that Father Arseniy gets this?"

It pleased me to accommodate him, for the priest needed every schilling he could lay hand to. Metropolitan Nikolay evidently won this skirmish with the MGB, for as long as I stayed in Vienna, Father Arseniy ministered to his flock of emigrés. I speculate that he took whatever Metropolitan Nikolay had said as a warning to steer clear of any appointment in the Soviet Union.

MGB trickery with the Shvedovs and Russian Orthodox priests, on top of everything else wrong with the system, put me in the worst frame of mind for the World Peace Council. In November 1953 the International Department of the CPSU Central Committee organized this week-long rally of peacelovers, who were actually or ostensibly neutral in the Cold War. The rally went as planned—an extravaganza of anti-American, pro-Soviet propaganda.

Vienna was the chosen venue for the council partly because of the ease in converting rubles to the schillings that subsidized Communist front groups and sympathizers in Austria. Another reason was that the Vienna newspaper *Osterreichische Volkstimme* could be counted on to give prominent coverage to conference speeches, and Moscow would assure that the propaganda would be replayed by friendly media outlets worldwide. (This newspaper served, for all intents and purposes, as a house organ of the MGB legal residency, which controlled it.) Finally, Vienna was an operational playground for Soviet intelligence, whose officers never were deterred by the Austrian Government from obtaining visas or meeting recruited and potential agents.[6]

Attending several World Peace Council sessions, I listened to Soviet delegates tell lie after lie. The spokesmen for my homeland described living conditions in the USSR that bore no resemblance to realities, such as housing and food shortages. They lauded a Kremlin leadership dedicated to peace, not to the MGB-enforced subservience that I knew and the Leninist goal of world domination through revolution. Their speeches told me that, even with Stalin gone, the chasm between the Communist ideal and the Communist reality was unbridgeable. It was a propaganda forum, pure and simple.

I had bottled up resentment, and now the cork blew out of the bottle. No more would my conscience allow me to be the reluctant worker for this corrupt system. I must change sides.

24

An Urgency to Defect

It might seem a simple matter for someone like me to seek political asylum in Vienna. The border between the Soviet and American sectors was wide open and unguarded. Well, it was not all that simple. By itself, reaching sanctuary in the American sector would not guarantee my safety. In the freewheeling operational styles of 1953–54 Vienna, the MGB would be emboldened to try kidnapping or assassinating an officer who defected from its ranks.

I had to get maximum protection from U.S. intelligence, and I had to get it quickly, before the MGB tracked me down. That was a tall order, given my handicaps. I did not speak English, and my command of German was rudimentary, so it might be impossible to communicate my intentions readily. I did not know one single American, not even by sight, so there was nobody I could approach with trust. And although the legal residency kept files on opposing services, the details were too skimpy to point me toward a particular intelligence installation.

The Liezinger Restaurant and the International Book Store held some promise, since both catered to American and Soviet patrons. Maybe I could find the right American there, someone identifiable by his military insignia, and strike up a conversation in Russian. If that happened, I would show my Soviet credentials and plead to be escorted to U.S.

intelligence. From the end of the World Peace Council sessions until January 1954 I tested that plan about a dozen times. No luck whatsoever.

As my frustration mounted, I became less cautious. Perhaps the MGB double agent I was handling would be an unwitting accomplice in my defection. Once a colonel in the tsar's army, this old man was foreman for the construction of Soviet military barracks outside Vienna. While I was still in Moscow, he reported a recruitment overture by U.S. intelligence. The MGB instructed him to string the Americans along and find out what they wanted. The double agent had the MGB cryptonym "Stroitel" (translation: "Builder").

Arriving in Vienna, I took over as the MGB officer for Stroitel. No thanks to me, the pace of the operation picked up. The Americans levied new intelligence requirements on Stroitel, requirements that gave the MGB solid indications of gaps in the enemy's intelligence on the Red Army.

According to Stroitel, my opponent in this double agent game was a certain Captain Peterson. He told me Peterson spoke Russian, and he provided Peterson's physical description and the address of the safehouse where Peterson met him and that it was located just over the border in the American Sector. I learned, too, that Stroitel had a phone number to call Peterson in an emergency.

I conceived the idea of making Stroitel the intermediary between U.S. intelligence, in the person of Captain Peterson, and me. The double agent, running true to form at our clandestine meetings, would get drunk. In such a state he might be persuaded to introduce me to Peterson at the Americans' safehouse. With that accomplished, I intended to send Stroitel back to the Soviet sector. Then Peterson would become the first to know of my desire to defect.

On a night in January 1954, in a private room of a small bar in the Soviet sector, I bided my time until Stroitel had consumed a large quantity of schnapps.

"Phone your Captain Peterson," I said.

"Why? When?" Stroitel's words were slurred.

"Now. Phone Peterson now. Tell him you have something important to report."

By this time Stroitel's reactions were slow, but eventually he said, "I don't having anything to report. Nothing important. Nothing unimportant."

"Oh, call him anyway and tell him to meet you at the safehouse in 30 minutes."

"Meet me at the safehouse? Captain Peterson?"

"Yes, comrade, Peterson and you and I."

Stroitel started musing out loud why in the world I wanted to go to the safehouse and see Peterson. His remarks reflected suspicion, which raised the ugly possibility of his turning me in to the MGB. Frightened, I tried to make light of the incident.

"Well done, Comrade," I said, laughing. "Exactly as I predicted. My boss insists on checking the reliability of old troopers like you. I told him you'd come through with flying colors, and you have. Let's have more drinks to celebrate."

While Stroitel got glassy-eyed drunk that night, I relaxed in the knowledge that he had already forgotten our conversation. I was, however, no closer to contacting U.S. intelligence.

In early February 1954 developments in one case made it imperative for me to defect to the Americans as soon as possible. Unless I did, unless I alerted U.S. intelligence to the MGB operation, an innocent young woman would die and my conscience would never be clear. The legal residency file can be summarized as follows:

NAME: Maria Avdey.

CRYPTONYM: "Zeppelin." (From the name of the Abwehr unit in which she served.)

HISTORY: Aged 14 when the Germans occupied her native city of Kursk; deported as a slave laborer in the camp of a German Abwehr counterintelligence unit that parachuted men behind Soviet lines; freed by the British Army.

STATUS: Resident in the British Sector of Vienna; employed in menial work at a British military base in Austria.

CHARGE: Treason—failed to return to the USSR after the Great Patriotic War (when the majority of the repatriates were sent directly to prison camps); based on her places of employment, suspected of being an agent of first the Abwehr, then British intelligence.

ORDERS FROM MOSCOW: Get "Zeppelin" out of the British zone, arrest her when she gets to the Soviet zone, and send her to the USSR for trial.

For repatriated prisoners of war such as Maria Avdey, the standard verdict was guilty. They received sentences of death or from 10 to 25 years in prison camps. It was up to me to implement those orders with the help of an agent, a handsome charmer, whose MGB cryptonym was "Numer-1." The first step was for him to buy a car with MGB funds. He did not know about the forthcoming arrest of Maria Avdey, only that he should locate her, strike up an acquaintance, invite her out on a Sunday afternoon drive, and bring her to the Soviet zone. There, we would take Avdey into custody.

I hated the MGB for preying on this innocent woman—it took twisted minds to charge her with treason—and I hated being personally involved in the case.

Through that autumn and winter I dragged my feet in working out the operational details. Kravtsov was angry about the delays and angrier still when I proposed waiting until spring. He rejected my suggestion that Avdey would be more likely to accept Numer-1's invitation for a ride when the weather was better.

Early in February Numer-1 located Avdey's apartment building in the British sector and asked neighbors about her.

"Bad news in the Zeppelin operation," I told Kravtsov.

"Oh, shit! That's all you've given me in this operation, bad news. What's the latest?"

"Zeppelin is bedfast. She has tuberculosis."

"That's not bad news. No, that's good news."

"I don't see it that way, Comrade Colonel."

"I do," Kravtsov said, "because Zeppelin's condition will make the job easier for Numer-1. With all the time you've wasted so far, he won't

have to waste any more courting her. Tell him to gag the bitch. She must
be too weak to put up a fight. Then he carries her out of the building,
throws her in the car, and brings her here, to the Soviet sector."

"That exposes Numer-1 to tuberculosis, Comrade Colonel."

"Who cares? He's expendable."

"Probably Numer-1 cares."

"Just promise him a bonus of a thousand schillings and get going.
The Center wants Zeppelin in our hands."

"Comrade Colonel," I said, "you and I both know that sentencing
the girl to a prison camp is like sentencing her to death. Even with a
minimum sentence, she'd die of tuberculosis."

"You're going soft, Deriabin. Zeppelin is a traitor, and traitors ought
to face the consequences. So she dies in a camp. So what? Now, you've
fooled around with her and Numer-1 too long. I want Zeppelin in our
custody. Not in months, Deriabin. Not in weeks. I want her in days!
Hear me? Days!"

Days to serve Maria Avdey with a death warrant. No one else could
save her, and to save her I had to warn the Americans. I could avert
another post-Stalin atrocity.

I was born on the 13th of February, and on that date in 1954 I
received a strange present. Afterward it seemed an omen, which confirmed my wife's fears while foretelling a new life for me.

Lieutenant Colonel Vladimir Pribytkov of the MGB legal residency
took me to the Moulin Rouge night club for drinks on the evening of
my birthday. He picked up the tab, but, staggering drunk, he refused to
pay it quietly. Pribytkov shouted that the bar bill had been padded, the
hostesses were whores, the manager was a pimp, and Austrians in general did not deserve to be in the same room with us. I quieted him
down, and we left.

Outside, reaching into my overcoat pocket, I touched something that
had not been there when we entered the Moulin Rouge. It was a 6-inch
wooden crucifix.

I showed it to my wife and explained how it had come to me.

"Uh-oh! That's a bad sign," Marina said. "A very, very bad sign for us."

"Why? It's just a crucifix."

"I guess I never mentioned this to you, Petya. In my family we have a superstition that a disaster happens when a crucifix is given away. The only exception is when crucifixes are given on holy days, and the religious calendar doesn't make either your birthday or today a holy day."

"Well, Marina, you're not all that religious. Forget it."

"No, I won't. I'm afraid of what the crucifix will bring."

In the early morning of February 14, around two or three o'clock, Kravtsov called me at the Grand Hotel from his home. Over a line in the Austrian telephone system, he told me that a Soviet civilian had defected and that I should go immediately to our embassy. The chief local representative of the Soviet Ministry of Foreign Trade would meet me there.

That the legal resident would commit so blatant a breach of security—speaking about a defector in a conversation that the "main enemy" might intercept—made me think it a curious case.

I met the Foreign Trade man at the embassy, and he identified the defector as his legal counsel, Anatoliy Skachkov. There wasn't much that either of us could do at that hour, except for me to review the SK file on Skachkov. It gave no clues; he had been leading a normal life in Vienna.

When Kravtsov finally arrived at the legal residency, he said, "Skachkov is a client of yours, I believe. Am I right?"

"Yes, sir." As a Soviet civilian employed in Austria, Skachkov fell within the purview of my SK Section. "I've looked through his file. Nothing remarkable there.

"Skachkov left his apartment night before last," I continued, "and he hasn't shown up at work, according to the guy from the Foreign Trade Ministry. Skachkov's wife claims he said he was going to the Americans. She doesn't seem terribly perturbed about it."

"Then he has defected to the Americans," Kravtsov said. "Now, Deriabin, I want you to look for him here in the Soviet zone. Conduct the normal kind of investigation in such cases."

"Yes, Comrade Colonel, I'll begin right away."

As I turned to leave my boss's office, he said, "One more thing. Don't dig too deeply."

I knew then that the Skachkov case involved special MGB interests. Ordinarily, the SK Section would leave no stone unturned while hunting for absentees from the Soviet colony. The Skachkov case, I thought, could be analogous to a couple of operations that the Austro-German Department had directed. In both, the MGB dispatched agents into West Germany, where they would ask the Americans for political asylum. In both, the objective was to infiltrate and report on the U.S. intelligence channels through which legitimate defectors passed.

Major Litovkin of the legal residency confirmed my suspicions. "I wouldn't break my neck chasing Skachkov if I were you," he advised.

"Oh? What do you know about it, Yura?"

"That fellow who came here last week from the Center, Lieutenant Colonel Smirnov, is a friend of mine. He tipped me off to what's going on."

"I'd like to be in on the big secret, too," I said.

"Well, Smirnov is in counterintelligence, you know."

"No, I didn't know."

"Smirnov came here for one purpose, and one purpose only," Litovkin said. "Guess what it was, Petr Sergeyevich."

"I can make a guess, but I'd rather you told me."

"He came to Vienna to give Skachkov his final instructions. Smirnov dispatched Skachkov[1] on a mission to defect and worm his way into American intelligence. Not American intelligence in Austria. In Germany."

By the time this conversation with Litovkin took place, I assumed that Skachkov had made his way to the Americans. They would be on guard against phony defectors; yet some must be getting through the security net or else the MGB would not keep pushing them into the camp of the "main enemy." Besides, the Skachkov operation must have been an important one to the MGB, considering how Skachkov kept a low profile during the months we were together in Austria and the trip Smirnov made from Moscow.

The Avdey woman had to be protected from an MGB crime, now U.S. intelligence had to be protected from Skachkov. Added to my own longing to be rid of the Soviet system, these cases gave me utmost urgency to defect to the Americans.

25

The Last Day

When I awoke on the morning of February 15, 1954, excitement and sadness overrode the tiredness in my body from too much work and too little sleep. I realized the investigation of Skachkov's disappearance could offer an excuse to break away from my MGB colleagues. Given that opportunity, on this day I would either contact U.S. intelligence or get caught in the attempt.

Whatever the outcome of plunging into the abyss, on this day I would be saying farewells that had a finality. Goodbyes to my wife; to my daughter; and to any likelihood of ever again seeing them, my young sister, my comrades, or my native Altay Kray. I took solace in the knowledge that Marina would escape severe punishment for my defection. According to Soviet law, mothers of children under eight years of age could not be sentenced to death or prison. Larisa was four years old.

Marina poured tea for breakfast in our room at the Grand Hotel. With my hours of work so irregular and working 14 to 18 hours a day—everyday—she asked me every morning, "When will you be back, Petya?"

"I don't know. Maybe never."

We dressed Larisa for kindergarten, but I did not give her my usual goodbye kiss. A kiss would have brought tears impossible for me to explain. Larisa left, and Marina and I followed a few minutes afterward. On the way out I checked my pockets once more. In them were identity papers, keys, about $30 in Austrian schillings, and the wooden crucifix.

Snow was falling and promised to continue. Poor visibility would help my plan to cross by foot into the American Sector.

On the street we walked in silence to the corner. Marina and I separated. She was going to her secretarial job in the forestry section of Soviet civilian administration for Austria. We waved to each other—couples kissing in public, the Party said, was the unsanitary custom of capitalist societies. Turning away, I wept for all I was about to lose.

I had cried one time earlier in my life. Before leaving Moscow, I wanted to take my family on a vacation trip to Altay Kray. Marina, however, refused to go on the long train ride (six days each way), and she objected to staying behind alone with our daughter Larisa. Her reactions cost me a precious last time with my kid sister, Valya.

We had not been together since Valya visited Moscow in 1951. Her visit then for several months revitalized our kinship of a dozen years earlier, before I was conscripted into the Red Army and while she was still a child. We had had no luck enrolling Valya in a Moscow technical arts school, however, and, although she could have stayed with me forever as far as I was concerned, regulations did not permit it. The authorities denied permanent residence in the city to nonstudents and others from the countryside. So Valya had to return to our native Siberia. I saw her off at the Yaroslavskiy Railway Station, and the thought of being separated made me shed a few tears. "Oh, Petya," my sister said, "you've forgotten the proverb. 'If we cry when saying goodbye, we won't ever see each other again.'"

Now the prophecy in the proverb would come true. Either a successful flight to freedom or execution for having tried.

At first the chiefs on duty that morning in the Imperial Hotel offices housing the legal residency disapproved my proposal to search Skachkov's apartment. The Americans might appear on the scene, they warned, and all kinds of problems could arise if this happened. I played upon the MGB's desire to have the Skachkov defection taken at face value, pointing out that a search was part of the normal, routine investigative process.

"Okay, Deriabin, you're the SK section chief. Do it your way, but take somebody with you."

"I'll take Maurin," I said. Not only was Lieutenant Maurin available, and not only did he have a good command of German, but he also was stupid. Maurin was an MGB officer who would follow my instructions without questions or suspicions.

Skachkov's wife had already left for the USSR, but I had the apartment key. Maurin and I conducted a fruitless hunt for clues to the whereabouts of the missing man. By early afternoon both of us were hungry.

"We ought to look around here some more," I told Maurin. "Let's take turns going out for food. I'll leave first. You keep on searching the apartment till I return."

At a street stand I stood under the canopy, gobbled down a wurst, swallowed a lager, and went over what I would say to U.S. intelligence in trying to establish my bona fides rapidly. My name, rank, and position in the legal residency, of course. A quick review of my MGB career. Skachkov the false defector. The operation to kidnap Maria Avdey. The double agent Stroitel and his deceit with U.S. Captain Peterson. Other local MGB cases.

Then what? What else to report that U.S. intelligence could verify overnight, so as to grant me immediately the safety of political asylum? Not the Kremlin power struggles culminating in the defeat of Stalin and the victory of Beria. Not the cause of Stalin's death. Not the full story about how and why Beria was deposed. All too complicated to cover in a short period. All too far away for the Americans in Vienna to analyze against information possibly known from proven sources.

By all accounts, the Americans were impatient. They would want short answers to questions about myself. "Why do you come to us, Major Deriabin? Why didn't you bring your wife and daughter with you? Why, partway up the scale of the elite in the Soviet system, do you want to defect?" There were no short answers if I told the truth. Such answers, I decided, would have to be lies.

I flagged down a passing taxi and directed the driver to go to the Hertzmansky department store on Mariahilferstrasse. Its popularity among Soviet shoppers made it an innocuous enough place for me to visit. Its location along the border between the French and American Sectors suited my objective.

During the brief taxi ride my mind played host to a jumble of thoughts. The doll that I had bought for Larisa a few days before; whether my sister Valya, in her few months left at school, could get by on savings from the money I regularly sent; whether my Volodya, Vladimir Petrochenkov, would damn me for defecting or wish me well; the epithets in the Soviet media about me: "traitor," "turncoat," "enemy of the people;" my reception by the Americans; a poem by Lermontov.

> Farewell, unwashed Russia,
> Land of slaves, land of lords,
> And you blue uniforms,
> And you submissive hordes.
> Perhaps beyond Caucasian peaks,
> I'll find peace from tears,
> From Tsars' all-seeing eyes,
> From their all hearing ears.[1]

On that day Lermontov's "Caucasian peaks" became the Atlantic Ocean and "tsars' all-seeing eyes" the MGB.

The taxi stopped. I paid the driver, entered the department store, and wandered through the ground floor on the watch for Soviet citizens who would recognize me. Seeing none, I edged toward the side entrance closest to the American sector.

I bolted through the door. On the sidewalk a street cleaner was shoveling away the newly fallen snow. Speaking German, I asked him for directions to the nearest American kommandatura. He pointed toward it.

To appear natural, I sauntered as I went past the man and into the street, then over the imaginary line of demarcation for the American sector. Now I walked at a brisker pace. Two sentries in U.S. uniforms stood at the open gates of the kommandatura.

"Where is the chief?" I asked in German.

They waved toward the building beyond the gates and let me pass. I ran as far as the door. For the moment I was safe.

Soon two men arrived to interview me. One called himself "chief." The other addressed me in Russian and said his name was Captain Peterson. In appearance he matched the Peterson description that Stroitel had provided. There was no question but that I had made my vital connection with U.S. intelligence.

After identifying myself and announcing my desire for political asylum, I decided on the spot to lead with an ace. I provided the MGB side of the Stroitel double-agent operation—much to Captain Peterson's obvious surprise and disappointment. While trying to hide his amusement at the reaction of Captain Peterson, "chief" seemed to take a broader view. Playing my ace had been an important first step in establishing my bona fides.

I followed up with the news about Skachkov, then the warning that Avdey should be saved from the MGB and certain death. We took a short break. Shortly after resuming, "chief" began to ask questions through his interpreter, Captain Peterson.

"Why do you ask us for political asylum, Major Deriabin?"

I salted my short, incomplete, misleading answer with flattery. "Because America has more opportunities and a better life than other Western countries."

"Is that your only reason?"

"Oh, not at all. But right now I'll stick to saying I think your government won't cave in when the USSR demands my return."

"You can rest assured on that point. Now, Major Deriabin, you tell us you have a wife and a daughter. Why didn't you bring them with you today?"

"Because," I lied, "Marina has been unfaithful to me."

"Chief" and Captain Peterson accepted my explanation.

After this meeting, U.S. intelligence concentrated on the problem of getting me out of the American sector of Vienna, beyond the reach of the MGB. My new friends hid me inside a container marked for consignment to an American military unit in western Austria. Our train passed through Soviet checkpoints along the route, and I was told that my countrymen were out in force at each checkpoint. I slipped through, into the West, to freedom.

In the United States I corrected the record from that first meeting. Marina had not been unfaithful, I said. She simply was not a woman whom I had loved or could ever love. Regarding my true reasons for defecting, I described the Soviet system and its crimes as I have written about them here.

APPENDIXES

Appendix A: Stalin's Bodyguards (Okhrana) & State Security

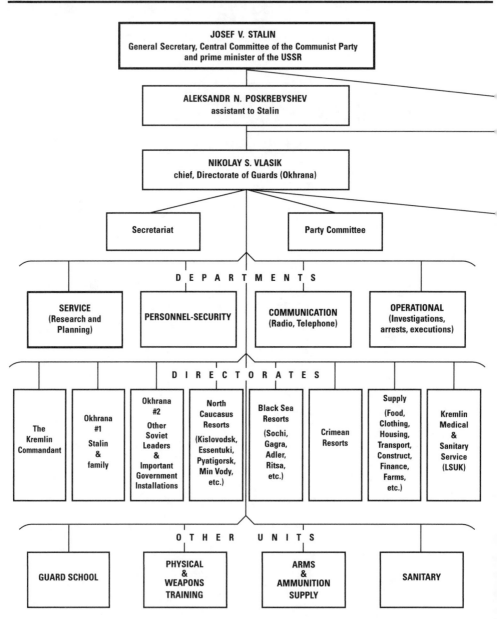

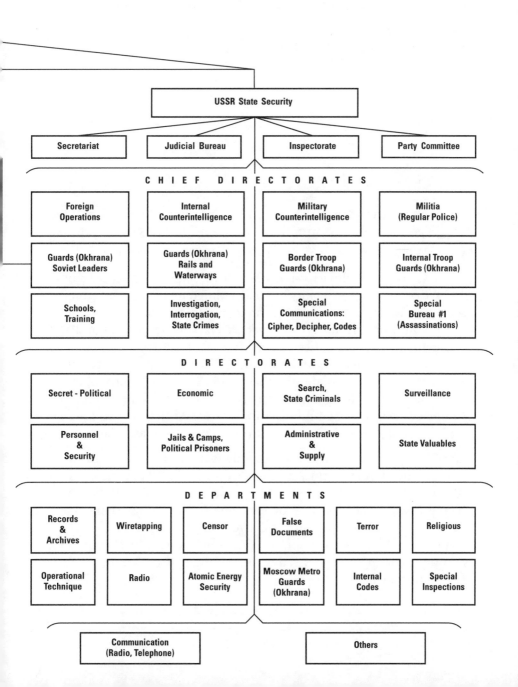

USSR State Security

Secretariat | Judicial Bureau | Inspectorate | Party Committee

CHIEF DIRECTORATES

| Foreign Operations | Internal Counterintelligence | Military Counterintelligence | Militia (Regular Police) |

| Guards (Okhrana) Soviet Leaders | Guards (Okhrana) Rails and Waterways | Border Troop Guards (Okhrana) | Internal Troop Guards (Okhrana) |

| Schools, Training | Investigation, Interrogation, State Crimes | Special Communications: Cipher, Decipher, Codes | Special Bureau #1 (Assassinations) |

DIRECTORATES

| Secret - Political | Economic | Search, State Criminals | Surveillance |

| Personnel & Security | Jails & Camps, Political Prisoners | Administrative & Supply | State Valuables |

DEPARTMENTS

| Records & Archives | Wiretapping | Censor | False Documents | Terror | Religious |

| Operational Technique | Radio | Atomic Energy Security | Moscow Metro Guards (Okhrana) | Internal Codes | Special Inspections |

| Communication (Radio, Telephone) | Others |

Appendix B:

Principal Personalities

Abakumov, Victor Semenovich—b. 1894, executed 12 December 1954; joined State Security in 1917; colonel general; chief of SMERSH during World War II; minister of State Security 1946–51; arrested August 1951.

Beria, Lavrentiy Pavlovich—b. 29 March 1899, executed 23 December 1953; Georgian by nationality but had a Mingrelian father and (rumors said) a Jewish mother; marshal of the Soviet Union since 1945; member of Communist Party since 1917; first secretary of Transcaucasian Party (virtual dictator) and police boss of Transcaucasia 1932–38; people's commissar for Internal Affairs of the USSR 1938–45; deputy prime minister in charge of atomic energy 1945–53; Politburo member 1946–53; after Stalin's death, briefly first deputy chairman of the Council of Ministers and minister for Internal Affairs. He was arrested on June 27, 1953, and executed with six of his closest associates.

Goryshev, Serafim Vasilyevich—b. unknown, d. unknown; born in a poor family; during World War II worked in SMERSH; at the request of Abakumov went to Moscow in 1945; was chief of the First Department in the Central State Security of Personnel (equal to assistant of the deputy minister), assigned to the Guards Directorate in 1947; Colonel; Deputy chief of the Kremlin Guards Directorate; chief Personnel-Security Department; dismissed with Directorate Chief Vlasik in 1952; exiled to Vyatka.

Khrushchev, Nikita Sergeyevich—b. 17 April 1894, d. 11 September 1971; member of Communist Party since 1918; participant in the civil war; party *apparatchik* since 1925; Politburo member 1939–64; first secretary of the CPSU Central Committee 1953–64; chairman of the Council of Ministers of the USSR 1958–64; ousted from all posts and sent into retirement in 1964. (While he was party boss, Khrushchev, who had received no awards whatsoever from Stalin, made himself a Hero of the Soviet Union, the highest Soviet award, four times: the first for his 60th birthday, the second for the development of the "virgin lands" of Siberia, the third for the launching of Sputnik, and the fourth for both his 70th birthday and for "heroism," previously unrecognized during World War II.)[1]

Malenkov, Georgiy Maksimilianovich—b. 1902, d. 1988; member of Communist Party since 1920; graduate of Moscow Technical Institute; Moscow Party *apparatchik* 1921–34; enlisted by Poskrebyshev and Stalin to handle CPSU Central Committee affairs in 1934; Politburo candidate member 1941–46; Politburo full member 1946–57; member of State Defense Committee during World War II; deputy prime minister 1946–53; prime minister under "collective leadership" 1953–55; ousted as prime minister by Khrushchev in 1955; expelled from CPSU Central Committee in 1957 as member of "anti-Party" group; appointed manager of the hydroelectric station in East Kazakhstan in 1957.

Merkulov, Vsevolod Nikolayevich—b. ca. 1900, executed 1953; deputy people's commissar for Internal Affairs of the USSR 1939–43; people's commissar for State Security of the USSR February–June 1941 and 1943–46; minister of State Control 1953; arrested with Beria.

Molotov, Vyacheslav Mikhaylovich—b. 1890, d. 1986; dropped the aristocratic family name of Scriabin; member of Communist Party since 1906; early *Pravda* colleague of Stalin; participant in October Revolution; chairman of Council of People's Commissars of the USSR (prime minister) 1930–40 and deputy chairman 1940–57; deputy chairman of State Defense Committee during World War II; minister of Foreign Affairs 1939–49 and 1953–56; Politburo member 1925–57; ousted by Khrushchev from party and government positions in 1957; ambassador to Mongolia 1957–60; delegate to the International Atomic Energy Commission, Vienna, Austria 1960–61, before being retired.

Poskrebyshev, Aleksandr Nikolayevich—b. 1891, d. 1965 or 1966; Stalin's personal aide; dismissed by Stalin in 1952 for concealing information from Stalin; released from house arrest to aid Stalin in preparations for the 19th Party Congress; last appeared in public during Stalin's funeral.

Vlasik, Nikolay Sidorovich—b. unknown, d. unknown; comrade of Stalin since the 1919 civil war; Stalin's personal photographer; lieutenant general; chief of the Kremlin Guards Directorate; dismissed by Stalin in 1952 for concealing information from Stalin; reassigned to supervisory staff of a labor camp; in an attempt to see Stalin was arrested and taken to Lubyanka Prison, exiled to Krasnoyarsk.

Zhdanov, Andrey Aleksandrovich—b. 14 February 1896, d. 31 August 1948 (murdered?); member of Communist Party since 1915; agitprop worker with Red Army 1919–22; secretary of Gorky Oblast Party Committee 1924–34; first secretary of Leningrad City and Oblast Party Committee 1934–44; a secretary of CPSU Central Committee 1934–48; Politburo member 1939–48; member of Military Council of Leningrad Front during World War II; accused of trying to usurp Stalin's authority; possibly died from poison or a bullet to the head.

Notes

Preface

1. Ponomarenko had been CPSU Central Committee secretary and, for a short time, one of the members of the enlarged Politburo (1952–53). He was a protégé of Politburo member Georgiy Malenkov and longtime associate of S. D. Ignatyev, who figures prominently in the events I describe here. Ponomarenko made his revelations in 1957 while serving as Soviet ambassador in the Netherlands—a fact that leaves no doubt of their official origins.

2. *Khrushchev Remembers*, edited by Strobe Talbott (Boston: Little, Brown and Company, 1970), 316–320.

3. Roy Medvedev, *Let History Judge* (New York: Alfred A. Knopf, 1971), 558–9. In the process, Medvedev made a snide attack on the book written by Stalin's daughter Svetlana—who had become a thorn in the Soviet rulers' sides.

4. Peter Deriabin, *Watchdogs of Terror* (New Rochelle, N.Y.: Arlington House, 1972), 325–327, etc.

5. A. Avtorkhanov, *Zaqadka Smerti Stalina* (Frankfurt: Possev Verlag, 1976), 56–79.

6. I presume that Medvedev here refers to me (although I did not start publishing data until 1959) because I went over to the West less than a year after Stalin died.

7. Both Svetlana and I had reported on Vasiliy Stalin's loud insistence that his father was being, and afterwards had been, killed.

8. Roy Medvedev, *On Stalin and Stalinism* (New York: Oxford University Press, 1979), 153–161.

9. Many other details (and much more deduction) can be found in Avtorkhanov's valuable and serious book—astonishingly, never published in English. It inevitably contains some minor errors. We are dealing here with matters held secret, and deduction based on limited facts can never be perfect. But these do not discredit his important contribution to Western scholarship.

10. After my transfer in May 1952 to another component of the KGB (then called MGB), I continued to live in the bodyguards' apartment building in Moscow. There my friends and neighbors were men, physically close to Stalin and professionally concerned with his well-being, who still considered me one of their own. Also I served as a clandestine bodyguard—covering part of the visitors' gallery—at the 19th Party Congress in October 1952.

11. By Stalin's decision, half of the personal bodyguards were for him. The other half were assigned to members and candidate members of the Politburo, secretaries of the CPSU Central Committee, marshals of the armed forces, and the more important academicians and scientists. (Widows of deceased leaders had no personal bodyguards but did have as many as ten servants.) The security clearances for Stalin's bodyguards were updated every six months, for the Politburo's every year, and for the others every two to three years. The directorate also had sentries standing duty at the Kremlin—they came from the Kremlin Kommandatura—and at many installations in the Moscow area.

Prologue

1. The Russian word for "directorate," *upravleniye*, does not easily translate into English. In Soviet parlance it equates with a major governmental entity subordinate to the next highest authority, here the Council of Ministers. Chiefs of MGB directorates reported to the minister of State Security.

Chapter 1. Back and Forth

1. Bannikov rose to the rank of general and as high in State Security as a deputy chairman of the KGB. In the 1970s he took a seat on the Soviet Supreme Court and became the USSR's second-ranking judge, but was forced by ill health to retire.

2. A sharpshooter in the Red Army, I retained my skill through regular target practice at the MGB range in the catacombs beneath the GUM department store.

3. The two exceptions were Cadillacs, one an American gift to Foreign Minister Vyacheslav Molotov; it was garaged in the Ministry of Foreign Affairs building at Kuznetskiy Most' No. 24, opposite the Guards Directorate Pass Bureau. The other Caddie was in a fleet of about a dozen cars used by MGB Chief Abakumov, and it had been confiscated in Germany.

Chapter 2. Reunion

1. My tenure in the Guards Directorate lasted from 1946 to 1952. The high status of the directorate during that period is reflected in the diagram at Appendix A.

The bodyguards, under various designations over the years, were reorganized in February 1947 as the Main Directorate of Guards (GUO, Glavnoye Upravleniye Okhrany) MGB USSR, which for convenience I here call the Guards Directorate.

In 1990, the directorate was abolished in name and replaced by the USSR KGB Guard Service. This was another reflection of *perestroika* (restructuring), the chief of the Guard Service said in an interview (*Pravda*, March 29, 1990). One duty, according to General Yuriy S. Plekhanov, is to ensure "the security of the Congresses of USSR People's Deputies, the USSR Supreme Soviet sessions, other very important sociopolitical events [like parades on Red Square], and major international forums and . . . it guards installations of statewide significance, leaders of the Soviet state and government, and also heads of state and government of foreign countries who come to the USSR on . . . visits, on vacation, or for treatment. In addition, with regard to the fact that the top legislative and executive organs of power are located in the Kremlin, our service is entrusted with guarding the Moscow Kremlin—the symbol of statehood and culture and an asset of our national history."

2. In the Soviet State Security, especially in the Guards Directorate, the personnel office is responsible not only for hiring, firing, and so forth, but also for security. The personnel office is, in reality, a security office. It is the personnel office that conducts all security investigations and maintains not only personnel files on all officers but also security (special checking) files. No one person, including custodians, would be taken as a candidate to the Guards Directorate without Goryshev's approval. He was also responsible for the investigation and punishment of all officers who committed crimes, engaged in misconduct, or had any shortcomings.

3. As long as Stalin was alive, office hours at MGB headquarters were 11:00 A.M. to midnight Monday through Friday, with a three-hour break late in the afternoon, and 11:00 A.M. to 6:00 P.M. Saturday. In 1953 the new Premier, Georgiy Malenkov, sought to ingratiate himself with us by shortening the State Security workweek.

Since Stalin habitually worked in the Kremlin until four or five o'clock in the morning, the chiefs of departments upwards to the ministers throughout the Government remained at their desks—the Khozyain might need information or issue an order. The all-clear signal came when Stalin left the Kremlin for his dacha in Kuntsevo.

Chapter 3. Two Georgians and Soviet Jewry

1. A different MGB component, Spetsburo Number One, conducted assassinations beyond the borders of the Soviet Union.

2. Leon Trotsky, a Jew who changed his name from Lev Bronstein before the Revolution, was at one time a principal rival of Stalin's. Driven from the Soviet Union, he was murdered in Mexico in 1940 on orders by Stalin.

3. The Soviet historian Roy Medvedev reported that the Jewish wives of Poskrebyshev and others were arrested; he stated that Poskrebyshev's wife was the sister-in-law of the son of Leon Trotsky, whom Stalin had had assassinated in Mexico. (*Let History Judge* [New York: Alfred A. Knopf, 1971]), 309–310.

4. As long as Stalin was in full command, Molotov, Kaganovich, and Defense Minister Kliment Voroshilov did not participate in Party and government decisions. My wife Marina, who was employed in Kaganovich's secretariat, told me that he spent most of the time dictating his memoirs to her.

A half-dozen bags of mail arrived daily in Kaganovich's office. The letters were from Jews, often with requests for advice or assistance, which Kaganovich ignored. Marina was one of the few in Kaganovich's secretariat who were not Jewish and could not translate the many incoming letters written in Hebrew.

5. I also had the confidence of others in the Personnel-Security Department. In particular, I should mention Goryshev's deputy, who had been with the bodyguards since the 1930s, and my colleagues responsible for Stalin's own bodyguards and for uniformed personnel guarding the Kremlin.

Chapter 4. Zhdanov vs. Malenkov

1. After Stalin's death, the assassination order was rescinded. Tito died of natural causes at age 82 in May 1980.

2. Intellectually, Merkulov was high above Abakumov. Merkulov wrote one or two plays, one of which was performed in Moscow's Vakhtangov theater.

3. During the month of February 1949 Stalin also fired Ministers of Foreign Affairs Vyacheslav Molotov, Defense Nikolay Bulganin, and Foreign Trade Anastas Mikoyan, but kept them in the Politburo. His reason was unknown to my friends in the MGB—none of the three ministers had been supporters of Zhdanov or of the proposal to reorganize the RSFSR.

Chapter 5. Vigilance

1. For counterterrorism the MGB had an independent department and a colonel aptly named Khvat', which translates as "Grab."

2. Another participant in managing Okunev's killing was Lieutenant General Rumyantsev, who, despite his rank, held the position of deputy chief under a succession of colonels heading Operod. Rumyantsev had been the wartime chief of Stalin's bodyguards and had been dismissed for having "lost" Stalin while he toured a battlefront. Stalin, however, thought so highly of Rumyantsev that he had Poskrebyshev find him this job in Operod.

3. MGB Spetsburo No. One handled "wet affairs" in foreign countries. Its counterpart for internal operations was under the administration of the Guards Directorate, as described.

4. The Chief Directorate for MGB Special Services supplied technical equipment to the Special Technical Department. This directorate intercepted and decoded foreign radio transmissions and devised the Soviet cipher system. It won literary fame in Solzhenitsyn's *First Circle* as the organization controlling technical research installations (*sharashka* in Russian).

5. One description of prison conditions has been furnished by Stalin's daughter, Svetlana, writing about her aunt. (Stalin jailed the relatives of both of his deceased wives.) "... She had signed all the accusations set before her: spying, poisoning her husband, contacts with foreigners. 'You sign anything there,' she would say, 'just to be left alone and not tortured. At night no one could sleep for the shrieks of agony in the cells. Victims screamed in an unearthly way, begging to be killed, better to be killed....' She spent six years in solitary confinement." (Svetlana Alliluyeva, *Only One Year* [New York: Harper & Row, 1969]), 162.

Chapter 8. A Dread Disease

1. Guards personnel always returned with anecdotes of scandalous behavior, like the one about an automobile accident that killed a Guards colonel following a drinking spree. To save the hides of the Guards officers who survived, Directorate Chief Vlasik told Stalin a cock-and-bull story.

Following another sojourn in the south, bodyguards joked about Stalin literally stumbling onto an extramarital affair. Politburo members, ministers, and lower-level officials shuttled between Moscow and the spas where Stalin stayed, and on this occasion Yakov Chadayev had gone south on Council of Ministers business. As Stalin walked through the garden of his dacha, he tripped over the prostrate bodies of Chadayev and a woman who worked under him. Stalin spit on them. He wheeled around, went to the dacha, and ordered the couple banished from his sight.

2. Under *glasnost,* many Soviet media accounts implicate Beria in teenage rapes but offer sparse details.

3. Svetlana Alliluyeva, *Only One Year* (New York: Harper & Row, 1969), 376.

4. The government operated special stores for our leaders and their families. Coupons were used in the stores to purchase rare domestic items and imported goods that were unavailable to ordinary citizens unless they patronized the black market.

5. Dr. Yefim Smirnov of the Armed Forces Medical Service was minister of health from 1947 to February 1953.

Chapter 9. The Independent Commission

1. As Abakumov was preparing to take over the MGB in late 1946, Stalin doubled the pay of all MGB and MVD personnel.

In 1947 Stalin ordered that all department chiefs and higher receive separate pay envelopes in addition to their regular pay envelopes (cash only, issued at the end of the month). The separate envelopes contained their regular salaries, but this constituted more than a doubling of their wages, since no taxes—16–18 percent—were deducted. The MGB and MVD were excluded. Khrushchev discontinued the practice in 1956.

2. Already Poskrebyshev was in hot water with Stalin over a lost document. Through a microphone hidden by the MGB, Stalin learned of Poskrebyshev's wife having discussed the contents of this document, which led him to conclude that she must be responsible for its loss. His verdict was to arrest her for espionage. According to unsubstantiated rumor, the woman spent several years in jail.

3. "There is evidence (true, now difficult to corroborate with documents) indicating that not long before Stalin's death Beria was hatching plans to usurp power." (Dmitriy Volkogonov, *Triumph and Tragedy: A Political Portrait of I. V. Stalin* [Moscow: *Oktyabr,* 1988]).

Chapter 10. Battleground: The MGB

1. In the end, Beria was not able to put his rehabilitation plans into effect. Khrushchev implemented them several years later and claimed that 7,679 victims

of Stalin's purges had been rehabilitated by March 1956. This was too late for the high percentage who had died in prison camps or in executions.

An underground publication in the USSR reported rehabilitation statistics cited on March 27, 1987, by a student at the Soviet Historical Archival Institute during a Moscow seminar on Stalinism. The student, Dmitriy Yurasov, said that "the exact number" was 612,500 rehabilitated between 1953, the year of Stalin's death, and 1957. He had taken this figure from a secret letter to Khrushchev by the chairman of the USSR Supreme Court. Yurasov went too far with Gorbachev's *glasnost*, for, according to a later underground item, the KGB searched his apartment and seized documents on the rehabilitation of Stalin's victims.

Chapter 11. The 19th Congress of the CPSU

1. The Politburo is the chief policy-making organ of the Communist Party. During the period between 1952 and 1966 the Politburo changed its name to Praesidium.

2. In December 1952 Poskrebyshev wrote an article on "The Great Multinational State" for *Pravda*, and that paper listed him on the new Moscow municipal council as of February 22, 1953. He last appeared in public at Stalin's funeral in March. He is reported to have died in the mid 1960s.

3. The official Soviet Encyclopedic Dictionary, published in 1955, elaborates on the action taken: "After the 11th Party Congress on April 3, 1922, the Central Committee plenum, upon Lenin's suggestion, elected Stalin to the post of general secretary; Stalin remained in this post until October 1952 and then, until his death, was a Central Committee secretary." Thus on October 16, 1952, Stalin was formally dislodged from the Party pinnacle of general secretary to be simply the first among ten equal secretaries.

Chapter 12. "Saboteur-Doctors"

1. It seems possible that these five doctors falsified the cause of Zhdanov's death. If they had been in collusion to murder him by deliberately prescribing the wrong medicines, as Timashuk claimed in her letters to Stalin, their motive remains obscure. On the other hand, if Zhdanov died from a bullet wound, as I was told shortly after he died, attributing the death to natural causes—a heart condition—saved his bodyguards and their chiefs in the Guards Directorate from punishment by Stalin. The former alternative (misprescribing) has been discredited, but as far as I know, the latter alternative (bullet wound) has never been officially investigated.

2. Stalin granted Soviet citizenship to Dimitrov, who took refuge in the USSR following the 1933 Reichstag fire in Berlin. He returned to his native Bulgaria in November 1945. Within a few years Dimitrov incurred Stalin's enmity for considering, with Marshal Tito of Yugoslavia, an alliance that would have moved Balkan countries toward independence from the Soviet Union. After Tito broke with the USSR in 1948, Stalin ordered his assassination.

Another foreign dignitary to die in Moscow while under the care of LSUK was the Mongolian head of state, Marshal Khorlogiyn Choybalsan. *Pravda* announced his death on January 27, 1952.

3. *Khrushchev Remembers,* edited by Strobe Talbott (Boston: Little, Brown and Company, 1970), 601.

4. When interviewed by the Soviet historian Dmitriy Volkogonov, Pitovranov masked the basis for his arrest and gave a misleading explanation for his release. About the latter, he claimed that from prison he wrote Stalin a letter with "some fundamental reasons about improving our counterintelligence"; seeing that Pitovranov was "not a stupid man," Stalin freed him. (Dmitriy Volkogonov, *Triumph and Tragedy: A Political Portrait of I. V. Stalin* [Moscow: *Oktyabr,* 1988]).

5. "Joint" is presumed to mean the Joint Distribution Committee, an American war relief agency. Mikhoels was a stage name; the actor (whom the MGB killed in Minsk in 1948) and the arrested therapeutist M. S. Vovsi were relatives; as its chairman, Mikhoels solicited funds for the Soviets' Anti-Fascist Committee during a wartime tour of the United States. B. B. Kogan of this paragraph was the brother of the M. B. Kogan named elsewhere in the story.

6. The only three Gentiles cited in a *Pravda* article—Vinogradov, Maiorov, and Yegorov—were among the five doctors who signed the death certificates of both Zhdanov and Dimitrov. The fourth signatory, the Gentile Vasilenko, was subsequently identified as having likewise been falsely accused. The fifth Gentile doctor to sign the two death certificates, Fedorov, wasn't mentioned by *Pravda* in 1953.

One of the Jewish physicians arrested, Yakov Rapoport, was quoted by a Soviet magazine in 1988 as saying the doctors were to be tried and executed. Afterward, there were to be pogroms and (as Petrochenkov indicated to me in January 1953) the deportation of all Jews to Siberia. *Druzhba Narodov,* April 1988.

7. Khrushchev glossed over Timashuk's MGB status when he referred to her in the February 1956 Secret Speech.

Chapter 13. Spying on Chairman Mao

1. Sverdlov's brother Yakov was the first president of the Soviet Union. His brother Andrey, of Sled-Chast', was executed after World War II for coauthoring a letter to Stalin that complained about Beria.

2. Doctors at the MGB-run Kremlin Hospital, LSUK, treated Mao for an ailment that prevented him from raising his arms above his shoulders. Stalin accepted Mao's request that two of the doctors return with him to Beijing.

3. In advance of Mao's sojourn in Moscow from December 1949 to February 1950, Liu traveled there for discussions with Stalin and others. His trip stands out in my memory for an incident that puzzled me until Tikhvinskiy explained the purpose.

At the time a lively subject of speculation in the Guards Directorate was the reason for a strange mission which had been carried out by, of all people, our chief assassin from Operod. On this occasion Lieutenant Colonel Okunev departed from his customary practice of killing the target selected by Stalin. Instead, Stalin's orders called for Okunev's staging of an accident in which the passenger of a car, Liu, would be unharmed.

Okunev used a driver and truck from the Transportation Department of the

Guards Directorate, and the operation went as planned. The car-truck collision took place on Dmitrovskoye Highway, chosen for its light traffic and the likelihood of there being no witnesses. Operod officers dressed in militiamen's uniforms arrived to conduct a "police investigation." They fooled around with these proceedings for a couple of hours and detained Liu at the scene throughout.

The collision accomplished the purpose of separating Liu from other Chinese officials for the time Kapitsa of the MGB needed to ask him certain questions. Stalin had wanted additional information from Liu in anticipation of the forthcoming negotiations with Mao.

"Comrade Kapitsa and Liu worked out a tale that the Chinks swallowed," Tikhvinskiy chortled. "Liu told the people in his delegation that he had slept through the whole affair."

4. We were together again when Tikhvinskiy traveled to Vienna in the autumn of 1953 for operational meetings with influential Westerners attending the CPSU-sponsored World Peace Congress. Public records show him stationed later in London and then Tokyo as counsellor of embassy. More recently Tikhvinskiy has been rector of the Higher Diplomatic Academy of the Ministry of Foreign Affairs, deputy chairman of the Society of Soviet Historians, and chairman of the Sino-Soviet Friendship Society.

5. Another China operations officer mentioned by Tikhvinskiy was Major General Vasiliy Zarubin. He headed the MGB Higher Intelligence School after a long operational career in Shanghai and New York City.

Kapitsa later rose to prominence as deputy minister of Foreign Affairs, concentrating on the PRC and leading attempts to settle differences with Beijing.

At the conclusion of his second tour as Soviet ambassador in China, Panyushkin was succeeded by Deputy Foreign Minister Vasiliy Kuznetsov. Panyushkin, said the *Pravda* report of March 10, 1953, was being transferred "to other duties." Panyushkin soon became chief of the Foreign Operations Directorate with the rank of general.

6. The author of *Samoye Pamyatnoye (The Very Memorable)* is V. I. Ivanenko. Purportedly a Soviet diplomat and journalist, Ivanenko wrote *Khorosheye Nachalo (A Good Beginning)* with Kapitsa. Tikhvinskiy edited another of his books, *Tropoyu Pamyati (Down Memory Lane)*.

7. Tikhvinskiy invariably referred to a Chinese person by the disparaging Russian slang word *Khodya*, which I translate into the equally disparaging English slang word "Chink."

8. Nikita Khrushchev, *Khrushchev Remembers, The Last Testament* (Boston: Little, Brown and Company, 1974), 280.

Chapter 14. A Policy Defeat

1. Mekhlis suffered a heart attack in 1950, reportedly after being told that the position he had vacated would be filled by Merkulov. This protégé of Beria, whom Mekhlis despised, took over as chairman of the State Control Commission. That organization audited and investigated the fulfillment of economic plans in the civilian sector.

2. During World War II, Shtemenko, Chief of Operations, joined Stalin at the Kirovskaya Metro Station (two levels below ground), which was two stops

away from the Kremlin. All other members of the General Staff assembled in the Byelorussian Metro Station (one level below ground) to work during the German advance on Moscow.

Only during World War II, and then only in one situation, did Stalin use a double. From time to time Stalin's double made an appearance entering and leaving the Kirovskaya Metro Station.

3. On the day of Kosynkin's death the ambassador of India met with Stalin in the Kremlin, according to accounts that later appeared in the West. Stalin is reported to have doodled pictures of wolves during the interview. Seemingly apropos of nothing, he volunteered that Russian peasants learned how to fight wolves—they killed them.

4. Beria put Spiridonov under house arrest in March 1953. Although Spiridonov was permitted to retire from the MGB that summer for reasons of health, he lived into the 1970s.

5. Stalin had lost the power of support by a Politburo majority. One non-event was the drought of substantive information about the doctors' plot, Stalin's fabrication from false confessions by the accused. The second was the absence of the purge portended in the announcement about the plot. There was no exodus of Jews from Moscow to the prison camps that had been ready to receive them since December or earlier. There was no second wave of arrests, least of all arrests of Beria or any other leaders whom Stalin had earmarked.

6. To quote Khrushchev in his Secret Speech to the 20th Congress of the CPSU in 1956: "Stalin evidently had plans to finish off the old members of the Politburo." The addition of the 16 newcomers, Khrushchev added, was "a design for the future annihilation of the old Politburo members." (*Khrushchev Remembers*, edited by Strobe Talbott [Boston: Little, Brown and Company, 1970], 615).

Chapter 15. The Assault and the Cover-Up

1. Beria's use of blackjacks was rumored in the Guards Directorate years before Stalin died. Also, a confidential letter disseminated by the CPSU Central Committee much later in 1953 regarding Beria contained an allegation about his practice of beating prisoners with blackjacks. The Guards Directorate rumors and the Central Committee allegation provide some substantiation for the eyewitness story I heard from Colonel Nosarev. For many years leading up to the time I left for Vienna in September 1953, Nosarev held the position of chief personnel-security officer for the Kremlin Kommandatura, a component of the Guards Directorate.

2. Each of us in the MGB feared Beria for his unilateral power of life and death over subordinates while he headed the combined MGB-MVD in 1953. As long as he was our minister of Internal Affairs, then, that fear all but eliminated the possibility that MGB officers would talk about known and suspected crimes of Beria. This was the reason why Nosarev, as he indicated to me, and the other Guards officers didn't disclose their information until the threat had been removed. My conversations with them took place during the summer of 1953.

3. Svetlana Alliluyeva, *Twenty Letters to a Friend* (New York: Hutchinson & Company; 1967), 6.

4. Tretyakov succeeded Smirnov as minister in February 1953. Under Beria's auspices, Kuperin replaced the imprisoned Yegorov as head of LSUK prior to March of that year; until then he had been chief of the MGB's own medical office. The names of the "best medical personnel" attending Stalin didn't include those of his personal physician Smirnov nor his predecessor, Vinogradov, who had been jailed with Yegorov.

Incarcerated as of March 1953, former Guards Directorate Chief Vlasik later insisted that Beria "helped" in Stalin's death but attributed this "assistance" to Beria's having switched the personal physicians who attended Stalin. (Dmitriy Volkogonov, *Triumph and Tragedy: A Political Portrait of I. V. Stalin* [Moscow: *Oktyabr*, 1988]).

Chapter 17. "I Am the Politburo"

1. Beria made way for Ryasnoy and revealed his new attitude toward Malenkov by decommissioning Pitovranov from the MGB. Pitovranov and Malenkov were brothers-in-law, married to sisters.

2. The weekly newspaper *Moscow News* on February 7, 1988, labeled as false the rumors of Timashuk's murder in a staged automobile accident during the mid-1950s. She died of "old age," the newspaper said.

3. Demichev progressed through the ranks to become minister of Culture, an official of the CPSU Central Committee, and a Candidate (nonvoting) member of the Politburo. He was reported by the Western press (*Washington Post*, March 12, 1988) to have gone to Azerbaijan to assist in quelling riots. In April 1989 Gorbachev dropped him from the Politburo. Demichev was one of 74 Central Committee members to "resign" at Gorbachev's insistence.

4. Beria released the criminals "to show off his 'liberalism,'" Khrushchev asserted, but the criminals "went right back to their old trades—thieving and murdering." (*Khrushchev Remembers, The Last Testament* [Boston: Little, Brown and Company, 1974], 100).

5. Patolichev's steady climb through the Party apparatus had been sponsored by Stalin, who adopted him in his childhood. From the Khrushchev regime to the Gorbachev regime, Patolichev was minister of Foreign Trade.

6. Coincidentally, the United States on June 19 executed Julius and Ethel Rosenberg, the American spies who contributed to the A-bomb success of Beria's Directorate Number One, under the Council of Ministers.

7. Beria's henchman in the State Control Commission, Merkulov, the one-time head of State Security, wrote a "Dear Lavrentiy" letter appealing for a job in the combined MGB-MVD. I speculate that once Beria became the self-appointed CPSU general secretary, he would have made Merkulov our next minister of Internal Affairs.

8. We were admitted to the Center from mid-March to June if our badges bore the initials "DSB" and afterward if they bore the initials "DSEB." We said in jest that "DSB" stood for *dozhidaysya sokrashcheniye budet* (await reductions in personnel) and "DSEB" for *dozhidaysya sokrashcheniye eshche budet* (await more reductions in personnel).

Chapter 18. A Coup Aborted

1. As soon as Beria became minister of Internal Affairs, he had our directorate move into the main headquarters building.

2. In May 1953 Beria transferred his protégé, Lieutenant General Vasiliy Ryasnoy, from head of the Foreign Operations Directorate to chief of the Moscow City and Oblast MGB-MVD. The new assignment placed him in a position important to the support of Beria's plans for the weekend of June 27–28. On the Sunday following Beria's arrest, Ryasnoy disappeared, presumably taken into custody by the Red Army for trial and execution.

3. *Nedelya*, February 24, 1988, and *Krasnaya Zvezda*, March 18–20, 1988. It may be no coincidence that these two accounts appeared only after the death of another eyewitness, then-Politburo member Malenkov, on February 2, 1988. They make Malenkov out to be one of the heroes that night, whereas the Soviet media generally now ignore him for better or worse.

4. Zhukov resented Beria's provision of information to support the decision by Stalin in 1946 to bar Zhukov from service in Moscow.

5. When Kobulov lost his State Security job and was sent to East Germany in 1946, his home next to the Institute of International Relations near Krimskiy Bridge was converted into a safehouse by Spetsburo No. One of the Foreign Operations Directorate. At that safehouse in the early 1950s Spetsburo No. One trained Nikolay Khokhlov for the mission of assassinating the director of the anti-Soviet Society of National Unity in West Germany. Khokhlov's wife, a good-looking blond, stayed at the safehouse and shopped at a neighborhood dietetic store where I encountered her from time to time while buying milk for my daughter Larisa. In West Germany in 1954 Khokhlov defected to the United States rather than fulfill his assassination assignment.

6. In charge of the investigation was Lieutenant General Nikolay Chistyakov, a State Security graduate who was chairman of the Soviet Military Tribunal. Chistyakov presided at the 1964 trial of Colonel Oleg Penkovskiy, found guilty of espionage for the Americans and British; Penkovskiy was executed.

Chapter 19. After Beria

1. Soviet authorities subsequently and repeatedly have described a Beria-Abakumov relationship that is fictitious. They make Abakumov the tool of Beria. By doing so they implicitly shift from Stalin to Beria much of the blame for Kremlin crimes committed in the years when Abakumov headed the MGB, from 1946 to 1951. Stalin knew, better than any latter-day historians, whether or not Abakumov was "Beria's man." When in late 1945 Stalin rid himself of Georgians from his bodyguard and of Beria's men from State Security—Merkulov, Kobulov, Dekanozov, Goglidze, and others—he not only kept Abakumov, but promoted him to command of State Security.

2. Afterward the government ordered custodians of the encyclopedia to scissor out the pages with the Beria biography, which had been second only to Stalin's in length. The substitute pages furnished a biography of an 18th century leader whose last name began with the letters "Ber" and an article, with a photograph, on the Bering Sea.

3. Before departing, Pitovranov vowed to us in the Austro-German Department that top priority would be placed on the recruitment of Dr. Otto John as a Soviet agent. Dr. John was director of the West German Federal Internal Security Office, and Pitovranov thought that one pressure point in recruiting him would be the report by a secret source that Dr. John had collaborated with the Nazis.

Dr. John disappeared in July 1954 in Communist-controlled East Berlin during the celebration of the tenth anniversary of the plot to assassinate Hitler. While in Soviet/East German custody, he issued propaganda statements against the West. Dr. John returned to West Germany later in 1954, claiming that he had been kidnapped and forced to propagandize. He was tried for treason by a West German court, found guilty, and sentenced to a term of five years (subsequently lowered to two years).

Chapter 20. Trials of State Security Chiefs

1. The names of Beria's codefendants and their positions at the time of the arrests were: Bogdan Kobulov, the deputy minister of Internal Affairs responsible for the MGB; Vsevolod Merkulov, minister of State Control (and former State Security minister); L. E. Vlodzimirskiy, chief of Sled-Chast'; Sergey Goglidze, chief of the MGB Directorate for Counterintelligence and Security in the Armed Forces; Pavel Meshik, chief, Ukrainian MGB-MVD; and Vladimir Dekanozov, chief, Georgian MGB-MVD.

2. Sitting with Konev on the court were the regular first deputy chairman of the Supreme Court, the chairman of the Moscow City Court, a recently named first deputy minister of the MGB-MVD, an army general (one rank below marshal), two trade union officials, and the secretary of a major CPSU committee.

3. Statement by the Procurator General's Office on the pretrial investigation, *Pravda*, December 17, 1953; and statement based on Supreme Court proceedings, *Pravda*, December 24, 1953.

4. *Nedelya*, Issue No. 8, February 22–28, 1988.

5. *Krasnaya Zvezda*, March 20, 1988.

6. *Nedelya*, Issue No. 8, February 1988. Colonel General Pavel Batitskiy, then deputy commander of Moscow Antiaircraft Defense, was the officer who shot Beria.

7. In Russian, "provocation" has the connotation reflected in the English and French term "agent provocateur." Webster's Dictionary defines the term as "one employed to associate himself with suspected persons and by pretending sympathy with their aims to incite them to some incriminating action."

8. Tried with Abakumov were a former chief and two former deputy chiefs of Sled-Chast' and two principal aides to Abakumov, Colonels Ivan Chernov and Yakov Broverman.

9. This entire paragraph flies in the face of facts cited above. Because Stalin appointed Abakumov as minister with a directive to seal Beria off from the MGB, it is doubtful that Beria would have "nominated" him for the job—whatever the forum where such a "nomination" might have been made. Neither Beria nor any of the six protégés convicted with him served in the MGB while

Abakumov was minister. In that official capacity, therefore, Abakumov could not have been guilty as charged; it would also have been impossible to have done so in an unofficial capacity.

Chapter 21. Khrushchev: Accuser and Defender

1. Nikita Khrushchev, *Khrushchev Remembers, The Last Testament* (Boston: Little, Brown and Company, 1974), 7.

2. The second and third volumes add virtually nothing to the litany of Politburo member's crimes.

3. *Khrushchev Remembers,* edited by Strobe Talbott (Boston: Little, Brown and Company, 1970), 351.

4. *The Confession,* a documentary program broadcast by BBC Television in September 1990; and *Berlin Tunnel Intelligence: A Bumbling KGB,* by Joseph C. Evans, *International Journal of Intelligence and Counterintelligence,* Volume 9, No. 1 (Spring 1996).

5. Yossi Melman and Dan Raviv, "The Journalist's Connections: How Israel Got Russia's Biggest Pre-glasnost Secret," *International Journal of Intelligence and Counterintelligence,* Volume 4, No. 2, (Summer 1990).

6. *Washington Post,* July 28, 1988, and April 6, 1989.

7. At least as of 1989.

8. "... I was a contemporary and a close associate of Stalin's. I know a lot about him. I was a witness to Stalin's policies of treachery and banditry." (Nikita Khrushchev, *Khrushchev Remembers, The Last Testament,* p. 7.)

9. Although Beria had a stake in purging the Leningrad Party Organization, he did not play the part that Khrushchev ascribes to him. Using Abakumov as the main partition, Stalin sealed Beria off from the Ministry of State Security in 1946. After the Leningrad Affair and after Abakumov's arrest, Beria insinuated himself into ministry matters.

10. Not surprisingly, Khrushchev spared Malenkov and Kaganovich his harsh words when speaking at the 20th Party Congress. Both remained with him in the Politburo.

11. An anecdote, repeated in *Khrushchev Remembers,* p. 258, involves Bulganin. "We were leaving Stalin's after dinner one night and he said, 'You come to Stalin's table as a friend, but you never know if you'll go home by yourself or if you'll be given a ride—to prison!'"

Chapter 22. Stalin: Family Murderer

1. Colonel Nikolay Strekachev, deputy chief of my department, was one of the two or three officers in the directorate whose service dated to many years before the war. Strekachev started with the bodyguards as a member of the uniformed detachment called the Kremlin Kommandatura. That unit was responsible for physical security of the offices and residences, including Stalin's, within the walled compound. It was Strekachev who advised me soon after my arrival in the Center, "You'll hear a lot that isn't known outside our directorate. Swallow

what you hear, Captain Deriabin. These things shouldn't be known in other MGB outfits or, need I add, elsewhere."

2. The Polish literary figure Ignatiy Shenfeld has written of his country's Communist leaders having been privately informed in 1956 that Stalin murdered Nadezhda. The allegation was made by Nikita Khrushchev, long at Stalin's side in the Party and in 1956 the head of the CPSU. (*Obozreniye*, Issue No. 18; Boston, January 1987) I do not trust testimony by Khrushchev, especially when it arrives via such a roundabout route, but I cite this report because until now it is the only one to attribute the death of Nadezhda to murder by Stalin.

3. Svetlana Alliluyeva, *Twenty Letters to a Friend* (New York: Hutchinson & Co., 1967), 108–110.

4. *Oktyabr*, Issues No. 10–12, 1988, and Issue No. 1, 1989.

Chapter 23. Doubts About the System

1. Besides the MGB, the GRU (*Glavnoe Razvedyvatelnoe Upravleniye*, the Chief Intelligence Directorate of the Soviet General Staff, Ministry of Defense) had about 20 to 25 officers in Vienna. It was the representative of the Ministry of Foreign Trade in our embassy, however, who collected scientific and technical intelligence on Austria, Switzerland, and Italy.

2. Yevgeniy Kravtsov was his true name, but in Vienna he purported to be Yevgeniy Kovalev, an alias supported by official (false) Soviet documentation. He was previously stationed in Turkey, Switzerland, and East Germany.

3. *Mole*, William Hood, New York: Norton and Company, 1982.

4. As victors in the Great Patriotic War, the three Western nations and the Soviet Union each occupied a separate sector in Vienna and a separate zone in the rest of Austria.

5. In one of our private conversations, Metropolitan Nikolay disclosed his role as an official witness in 1944 at a disinterment that the MGB had stage-managed. The bodies exhumed were those of Polish officers whom Soviet State Security had executed in the Katyn Forest. (The toll reached 15,000, according to many reports.) The purpose of the disinterment was to support the Soviet claim that the Nazis were responsible for the mass murders. "How could a clergyman participate in such a thing?" I asked Metropolitan Nikolay. "In our country," he replied, "you cannot serve God unless you serve the MGB."

6. I had an operational role at the council, selecting out-of-the-way restaurants for Colonel Tikhvinskiy, my former office mate at MGB headquarters, who flew in from Moscow. Tikhvinskiy went to the restaurants to meet in private with British and Canadian parliamentarians and with the Reverend Hewlitt Johnson, the "red dean of Canterbury."

Chapter 24. An Urgency to Defect

1. Skachkov later confessed that he was a Soviet intelligence agent after being sent to the West, and he subsequently became a drunkard. The KGB sent him several recall notices. He died on July 22, 1959.

Chapter 25. The Last Day

1. Translation by John Mersereau Jr. in his book *Mikhail Lermontov* (Carbondale: Southern Illinois University Press, 1962), 23.

Appendix B

1. Peter Deriabin, *Watchdogs of Terror* (Frederick, Md: University Publications of America, 1984), 416.

Glossary

Apparatchiki—full-time employees.

CPSU—Communist Party of the Soviet Union

Cominform—short for Communist Information Bureau.

Dacha—country house.

GRU—*Glavnoye Razvedyvatelnoye Upravleniye,* Chief Intelligence Directorate of the General Staff, Ministry of Defense.

Instantsiya—unsigned order from the highest Party or government authority, i.e., Stalin.

KGB—*Komitet Gosudarstvennoy Bezopasnosti,* Committee for State Security.

Khozyain—the Big Chief. (Stalin)

LSUK—*Luchebno-Sanitarnoye Upravleniye Kremlya,* Medical Sanitary Directorate of the Kremlin.

MGB—*Ministerstvo Gosudarstvennoy Bezopasnosti,* Ministry of State Security, predecessor to KGB.

Operod—*Opertivniyy Otdel,* Operations Department

Politburo/Praesidium—the chief policy-making organ of the Communist Party. Between 1952 and 1966 the Politburo was named Praesidium.

Sled-Chast'—Sledstvennaya Chast', the MGB Unit to Investigate Especially Important Cases.

SMERSH—Smert Shpionam, Death to Spies, Military Counterintelligence.

Sovinformburo—Soviet Information Bureau, a propaganda organization of the Party.

Spetsburo Number One—conducted assassinations outside the borders of the Soviet Union.

Special Technical Department—conducted eavesdropping.

Index

About the Authors

The late Peter S. Deriabin was the only known member of the Kremlin Guards Directorate (Stalin's KGB bodyguards) ever to escape the Soviet Union. While living in hiding in the United States, Mr. Deriabin worked for the Central Intelligence Agency, was a consultant to other members of the US intelligence community, and wrote or coauthored five books, including the award-winning *The Spy Who Saved the World*.

Joseph C. Evans is a retired CIA officer who specialized in counterintelligence activities directed against the KGB and other East Bloc services. He is national affairs editor of the *International Journal of Intelligence and Counterintelligence*.